ENGLISH COUNTRY HOUSES AND LANDED ESTATES

CROOM HELM HISTORICAL GEOGRAPHY SERIES
Edited by R.A. Butlin, University of Loughborough

THE DEVELOPMENT OF THE IRISH TOWN
Edited by R.A. Butlin

THE MAKING OF URBAN SCOTLAND
I.H. Adams

THE FUR TRADE OF THE AMERICAN WEST, 1807-1840
David J. Wishart

THE MAKING OF THE SCOTTISH COUNTRYSIDE
Edited by M.L. Parry and T.R. Slater

AGRICULTURE IN FRANCE ON THE EVE OF THE RAILWAY AGE
Hugh Clout

LORD AND PEASANT IN NINETEENTH-CENTURY BRITAIN
Dennis R. Mills

THE ORIGINS OF OPEN FIELD AGRICULTURE
Edited by Trevor Rowley

English Country Houses and Landed Estates

HEATHER A. CLEMENSON

CROOM HELM
London & Sydney

ST. MARTIN'S PRESS
New York

British Library Cataloguing in Publication Data

Clemenson, Heather A.
    English country houses and landed estates. − (Croom Helm
    historical geography series)
    1. Land tenure − England − History
    I. Title
    333.3'0942   HD603
    ISBN 0-85664-987-2

First published in the United States of America in 1982
All rights reserved. For information write:
St. Martin's Press, Inc., 175 Fifth Avenue, New York,
N.Y. 10010

Library of Congress Cataloging in Publication Data

Clemenson, Heather.
    English country houses and landed estates.

    1. Country homes − England. 2. Manors − England.
    3. England − Description and travel − 1971 −
    I. Title.
    DA660.C57   1982   942.081   82-3298
    ISBN 0-312-25414-8   AACR2

To my parents, Menna and Arthur, for their constant support.

CONTENTS

List of Figures

List of Tables

Preface

Abbreviations

Introduction   1

PART ONE: LANDOWNERSHIP AND THE ESTATE IN
THE RURAL LANDSCAPE TO CIRCA 1880

1 The Landowners   7

2 The Study Population and Estate Definitions   33

3 The Country House in the Landscape from the   39
   Middle Ages to the Late Victorian Era

4 Estate Amenity Land   59

5 Power and Prestige Beyond the 'Park Walls'   74

6 The Seeds of Decline in the Nineteenth Century   96

PART TWO: A CENTURY OF CHANGE 1880 to 1980

7 Private Landownership and Estate Decline   109

8 Country-house Losses   133

9 Country-house Survival and Adaptation   151

10 Amenity Land and Other Estate Features   178

11 Conclusions - The Future   212

Appendix One: Great Landowners and Greater Gentry: 229
               Per Cent Land Area Owned and Density
               of Seats Per County c. 1880

Contents

Appendix Two: The Sample Selection   231

Appendix Three: The Sample Population   236

Appendix Four: Non-private Ownership: 238
                  Classification of Public, Semi-public
                  and Institutional Landowners

Index   239

FIGURES

1.1 Per Cent of County Area Owned by Large Landowners c. 1880   23

1.2 Density of Large-landowner Seats per County c.
1880   26

3.1 Investment in Country Houses on the Sample
Estates c. 1500 to 1900   49

4.1 Deer Parks and Paddocks on the Sample Estates
c. 1867-92   61

4.2 Landscape Parks and Gardens on the Sample
Estates Attributed to Bridgeman, Kent, Brown
and Repton   68

8.1 Country-house Demolitions c. 1875 to c. 1980   135

8.2 Sample Estates: Country-house Demolitions since
1880   143

9.1 The Sample Estate Country Houses in Private
Ownership c. 1980   152

9.2 The Sample Estate Country Houses in Public,
Semi-public and Institutional Ownership c. 1980   153

9.3 Country-house Changes of Ownership on the
Sample Estates c. 1880 to c. 1980   155

9.4 Country Houses still in Residential Use: Single
and Multiple Occupancy   159

9.5 Country Houses in Educational Use   163

9.6 Country Houses Open to the Public for Tourism
and Recreation   165

TABLES

1.1 Regional Distribution of Large-landowner Acreage c. 1880   24

2.1 Home-estate Acreage as a Per Cent of Total Acreage   36

3.1 Regional Per Cent Distribution of Country Houses According to Period of Origin   51

5.1 Population Growth of 'Closed' Estate-Village Parishes Compared with 'Open' Parishes, Lindsey, Lincolnshire 1801 to 1861   83

7.1 Number and Extent of Historic Estates, Minimum Area 1,000 Acres, in Original Family Ownership c. 1980   119

7.2 Number and Extent of Historic Estate Land Areas, Minimum 1,000 Acres, in Original Family Ownership c. 1980 from which the Heartland has been detached by Sale or Transfer   121

7.3 Summary: Original Family Ownership c. 1980   122

7.4 Number and Extent of Estate Heartlands in Private Ownership c. 1980   123-4

7.5 Number and Extent of Estate Heartlands in Public, Semi-public and Institutional Ownership c. 1980   125

7.6 Classification of Public, Semi-public and Institutional Bodies Owning Sample Estate Heartlands c. 1980   126

8.1 Date of Country-house Demolition Cross-tabulated with Period of Origin   141

9.1 Original Family Ownership of the Country House, Former House Sites, Replaced and Ruinous Houses, in Relation to the Principal Estate Land Owned c. 1980   154

9.2 Major Present-day Uses of Country Houses   158

10.1 Amenity Acreage Loss c. 1880 to c. 1980 – by Region and c. 1880 Landowner Class   179

10.2 Estate Distribution According to Amenity Acreage c. 1980 as a Per Cent of c. 1880   180

10.3 Major Present-day Uses of Estate Amenity Land   182-3

10.4 Country Parks Associated with Former and Ongoing Landed Estates   194

A2.1 Total Population and Sample Number according to County and Landownership Categories   232

A2.2 The Regional Breakdown   235

PREFACE

In the early 1970s I travelled to a corner of rural England to gather material for a higher degree. The object of my research was an ongoing and privately owned landed estate until that point in time merely a name, a collection of historic facts, a lengthy genealogy of successive owners and a list of parishes that testified to its extensive size. During my time in the locality two facts became impressed on my mind: the distinctive visual impact of the estate in the landscape, in the buildings, surrounding woodlands and other local landmarks, and the continuing sense of an estate community. Whether attending a social event in the village hall with estate workers, farm tenants and their families, or talking to the *après* hunt crowd fresh from the chase behind one of his Lordship's dog packs, the attachment of one sort or another to the landed estate and the family in the 'big house' was still apparent.

My curiosity and interest in the continuity of historic landed estates dates from that time. Though I emigrated to Canada within the year the seeds of future research were planted, but the practicality of a field-study approach, negated by distance, became translated into a systematic study of estate ownership in England, in an attempt to be a modern-day J. Bateman (see Chapter 1), and to identify and trace the continuity of estate property that was in existence in the late nineteenth century.

The aim of the book is to present a comprehensive examination of the privately owned landed estate in the past and in the present day. Too often component parts of historic estates have been the subject of examination in isolation, and few studies have attempted to look at the landed estate as a whole. The task was a daunting one. The balance of the work, past versus present, what to emphasise and what, if anything, could be omitted provided a major methodological problem. Readers well versed in the history of the English landscape will find that much in Part One covers generally well-known material woven around a description of the 500 landed estates that form the sample population throughout the book. This section provides the background for a clearer comprehension of the nature of loss and extent of change in the present century and has been principally drawn from secondary data sources. It is in Part Two that new material is added to the general body of knowledge on the landed estate, based on primary data accumulated over a period of three years from late 1977 to 1980. Since collecting the material further sales of land have taken place, and a number of country houses have assumed new ownership and use. The scene is constantly changing. What is described in this book is the picture to *circa* 1980.

My approach has been from the perspective of an historical geographer though the examination of people and property both in the past and in the present has necessitated the integration of a diverse number of disciplines in few of which can I claim any expertise. It has been stimulating to explore aspects of architecture, landscape architecture, economics, economic history, land law, planning and politics, and I can only trust that my interpretation and description of events and phenomena are accurate and acceptable to those with expertise in fields that I have strayed across.

It is apparent that a study of this nature cannot explore to the intricate depths afforded by research at the local level. Such an overview as presented here, a report on the picture as a whole, nevertheless can provide a framework for more intensive localised research. It is my hope that the book makes a contribution to the study of landownership in England and has value as a broad history of the traditional landed estate.

There are few advantages to a study undertaken thousands of miles from the principal subject. The need for clarity of purpose, the avoidance of too many tangents or temptations to collect material *ad infinitum* were perhaps beneficial aspects of location in Canada. Distance also proved an expensive factor in data collection. Since its inception the work has been a personal hobby with no external financial support and thus has presented the added challenge of research on a shoestring. When, for example, a landowner replied to my questionnaire and made use of the enclosed stamped addressed envelope only to say that I could better use my 'grant money' elsewhere than to pry into the private concerns of such as he, I nearly resorted to defensive correspondence. My hand was stayed only at the thought of yet another wasted stamp!

I have of necessity relied heavily on the word of others as the opportunities for first-hand visits to estate properties have been few and far between. Though constrained by both locational and financial limitations, the invaluable assistance and co-operation that I have received from countless people in England and the general interest shown in the topic brought constant motivation to continue the study and made the entire undertaking a satisfying endeavour throughout.

I have met very few of the landowners and others who responded to the questionnaire and follow-up correspondence, but I am indebted to them for their co-operation and encouragement. I also thank the staff of every County Record Office in England who, in the majority of cases, spent time completing a fairly lengthy statement of the availability of estate records and the present ownership of estate properties in their county. I trust they will forgive me for not listing individual names. To the local Secretaries of the Country Landowners' Association who responded to enquiries concerning landowners and property within their present or former jurisdiction, I also extend my thanks, especially to Major J.R. Hazard for data on Shropshire and Staffordshire and to Brigadier J.R. Fishbourne not only for the valuable information on estates in Essex and Suffolk, but also for his advice and suggestions on the format of the questionnaire subsequently sent to individual landowners. My gratitude for information on a particular county also goes to the following, O.J.P. Bott (Cheshire), D.R. Palmer and P. Shepphard (Cornwall), V. Chapman (County Durham), R. Olney (Lincolnshire), M.J. Sayer (Norfolk), K. Clark, (Northumberland), L.W. Wood (Oxfordshire), D.R.J. Neave (East Riding) and to countless others, land agents, estate agents, local historians, solicitors and county planners who have helped along the way.

At the University of Guelph (Canada) my thanks go to Tony Fuller for his encouragement and advice throughout the entire project and to Peter MacCaskell for technical assistance with the data.

In England I am particularly indebted to the following people for their valuable comments, suggestions and criticisms to specific parts or all of the text; to Marcus Binney (Architectural Editor, *Country Life*), Alan Harrison (University of Reading), Alan Harris and Jay Appleton (University of Hull) and to David Lowenthal and Hugh Prince (University College London).

Finally, I am grateful to Sharon Bruder and Jodi Murray in Canada and to Bea in England for their perseverance and tolerance in typing the manuscript in its various stages of preparation.

Heather A. Clemenson

ABBREVIATIONS

BPP	British Parliamentary Papers
BTA	British Tourist Authority
CLA	Country Landowners' Association
CPRE	Council for the Protection of Rural England
CTT	Capital Transfer Tax
HBC(E)	Historic Buildings Council (for England)
JRASE	Journal of the Royal Agricultural Society of England
LAO	Lincolnshire Archives Office
TIBG	Transactions of the Institute of British Geographers
TRHS	Transactions of the Royal Historical Society
VCH	The Victoria County History

The location of estate property is identified by pre-1974 county boundaries for which standard abbreviations have been used.

Area is stated in acres throughout the text; 1 acre = 2.4 hectares.

INTRODUCTION

The English countryside is predominantly a man-made landscape in which remnants of past occupation have persisted throughout the passage of time, their continuing prominence dependant on the use of the land by succeeding generations. This study examines the principal estates of five hundred landed families, over a third of the largest private landowners in England in the late nineteenth century, and the visual impact of the organisation of their land and buildings in the rural landscape past and present. The book is presented in two sections, pre and post-*circa* 1880, the divide marking a watershed separating the period when large-scale private ownership and landed estates were at their greatest extent from the onset of their decline.

Part One traces the history of large-scale private landownership in England and the evolution of the major physical components that characterised a traditional estate by the late nineteenth century. Who the large landowners were, from which strata of society they came, and how extensive was their property provide the necessary keys to an understanding of the display of wealth and power evident in the landscape of a traditional landed estate. The complexity of the visual history of the estate is well demonstrated by the development of the country house. Changes in tastes and fashions, in the social and economic values of generation after generation of landowners were expressed in the successive modification, adaptation, redesign and rebuilding of country houses. Hence by the late nineteenth century at the core of every traditional estate stood a unique contribution to English architectural heritage. The gardens and parkland, aesthetic and picturesque settings for the country houses, were similarly subjected to the exigencies of changing fashion and, along with the house, reflected the social and economic status and aspirations of the proprietor. In the surrounding rural area evidence of the power and prestige of the landed classes created distinctive estate landscapes which, like the ripples of a stone thrown in water, diminished in visual intensity with increasing distance from the estate heartland.

The heyday of the traditional estate occurred in the eighteenth and nineteenth centuries. By the late nineteenth century the large landed estates in the English countryside whether owned by long established members of landed society or the *nouveau riche* of the industrial revolution reached a peak in territorial extent. Part One concludes with a discussion of the forces of change that began to undermine the power of private landowners from the early

1

nineteenth century. The Great Depression (*c*. 1873-96) marked a turning point in the history of many large estate properties and was evidence for landed society that the balance of economic power, moving inexorably away from the rural and agricultural land base, had finally swung and settled in favour of control by industrial and urban society.

Whether the demise of the privately owned landed estate is reflected upon with nostalgia and regret as the passing of a unique social and economic phenomenon that was once the focal point of English rural society, or is viewed as the necessary extinction of an outmoded form of spatial and social organisation, the fact remains that relatively little is known of the actual extent of loss or degree of survival of historic landed estates in the present day. Their break-up has been likened to the social and economic upheaval consequent upon the dissolution of the monasteries, but the speed and devastation of dissolution has not been matched. The traditional estate has fallen prey to an organic and more gradual, though persistent, process of decline at times interspersed with notable bouts of loss and destruction that have brought alarm not only to private landowners still retaining their ancestral property, but also to others concerned with heritage preservation.

The principal objective of Part Two is to examine the major factors that have contributed to the continuing decline of the privately owned historic estate, to analyse and illustrate changes in ownership, to look at the destruction of the physical components of landed estates, and to describe the means by which estate property, land and buildings, have been adapted for alternative uses.

Changes that have affected landed estates over the past century have taken a variety of forms ranging from transfers of ownership that have left a property operationally intact, to the physical alteration of estate landscapes and, more drastic, the complete break-up of property and the obliteration of former estate features. Ownership changes are examined in Chapter 7. The destruction of country houses is discussed in Chapter 8 while Chapter 9 focuses on country houses still surviving and examines this group with regard to ownership, present use and long-term future. Chapter 10 looks at the remainder of the estate property, the ownership and current use of amenity lands and the more notable changes that have taken place over the wider estate landscape. As an integral part of the English countryside not only heritage preservation but also other conservation concerns affect estate property. The modern dogma of technological efficiency in agriculture with little tolerance of aesthetic values or concerns for environmental conservation has had far reaching effects on traditional estate landscapes.

As an integral part of England's heritage the historic landed estate, more especially the country house and amenity lands, have assumed an important role in the post-war development of tourism and recreation, both for the benefit of the British population and the overseas visitor, and there remains much potential for future development. The loss of notable heritage features has been considerable and the preservation of that which continues in private ownership is in jeopardy under present capital taxation policies. Political policy leading to a reduction in private wealth may well culminate in the further loss of heritage, despite the provision of grants and loans for maintenance and repairs and various piecemeal tax concessions, unless alternative means are devised to protect valued heritage irrespective of ownership.

The final chapter discusses the future of large-scale private landownership and the historic landed estate. The questions remain, what to preserve for future generations as the visual record of the social and cultural history of our forefathers, who should own and manage such resources, and how they may be best protected and utilised given the present rural land use demands of agriculture, forestry, mineral extraction, recreation and tourism. The landed estate as an operational unit is capable of integrating a diverse range of land uses, and much can be said in favour of retaining the traditional estate as a heritage asset and as a unit of land management.

PART ONE:

LANDOWNERSHIP AND THE ESTATE

IN THE RURAL LANDSCAPE TO CIRCA 1880

1 THE LANDOWNERS

There is no other body of men in the country who administer so large a capital on their own account, or whose influence is so widely extended and universally present. J. Caird, *The Landed Interest and the Supply of Food* (Cassell Petter and Galpin, 1878), p. 58.

Throughout the history of England one of the most fought over, sought after and desirable assets has been land. Yet despite its importance the question of who owns land has been and continues to be shrouded in an aura of mystique reflected in the fact that in the last 800 years there have been only two comprehensive surveys of land ownership; the Domesday Survey of 1086 and the *Return of Owners of Land* in 1873, the latter often referred to as the 'New Domesday'.[1] For the centuries between 1086 and 1873 there is a relative lack of precise data concerning the distribution of land although a body of knowledge, based on the assembly and interpretation of piecemeal evidence, has been accumulated through historical research. It is not intended here to add new evidence to the ongoing debate over the relative ascendency of one group of landowners *vis-à-vis* another. Existing research for the period prior to the 1873 *Return* is drawn upon only to establish the changing distribution of land over time. The increasing territorial dominance of large private landowners, the classes of society from which they came, the origins and extent of their landed wealth and the manner by which they chose to display it on the rural landscape over past centuries underlie the present-day heritage of the large landed estates and help to place in greater perspective the changes that have occurred over the past hundred years.

LANDOWNERSHIP DEFINITIONS

A large landowner for the purpose of this study is defined by the possession of 3,000 or more acres of land and a minimum of £3,000 annual rental circa 1880. The study population therefore comprises the members of England's landowning hierarchy as recorded by Bateman in *The Great Landowners of Great Britain and Ireland*,[2] a list based on the New Domesday survey. Within this population two major sub-groups are identified on the basis of landed wealth: the 'great landowners' and the 'greater gentry'. *A great landowner is defined as possessing a minimum of 10,000 acres,* a figure also used by Thompson in his work *English Landed Society in the*

7

Nineteenth Century.[3] 'Landed aristocrat' is also used as being synonymous with a great landowner even though the title implied a certain social status and had connotations beyond that described simply by estate size. At the apex of the great landowner group were the 'land magnates' or 'territorial magnates' each owning a minimum of 30,000 acres.

A member of the 'greater gentry' is defined as possessing an estate of between 3,000 and 9,999 acres with a minimum rental value of £3,000. This size classification is partly based on that adopted by Bateman in that 3,000 acres and £3,000 rental is taken to be the dividing line between the 'greater gentry' and the 'lesser gentry'; the latter classed by Bateman as the 'squirearchy'.[4] As the focus of this work is on landed estates, albeit those in private ownership, the economic criterion of size provides an acceptable base from which to begin. Ownership of land cut across the conventional class boundaries that distinguished between the titled minority of the peerage, baronetage and knightage[5] and the untitled majority, the commoners. Even so, contemporary as well as modern historians have tended to differentiate owners on the basis of legal status, social and political class lines rather than on economic criteria. A problem therefore arises in attempting to extrapolate back in time. Temporal comparison of the relative landed dominance of large private landowners, whether great landowners or greater gentry, is complicated by the lack of consensus among historians as to the precise composition and definition of the large landowner group over time.

The peerage, or landed nobility, generally have been associated with the great-landowner class, even though it has been shown that some were virtually landless[6] while others in terms of acreage owned would fall within the greater gentry category as defined above. Nevertheless, a number of calculations of the proportion of England owned by great landowners in past centuries has been based on an initial assessment of the number of titled landowners.[7] There is also inconsistency in the lower acreage limit used to define a great landowner and a tendency to use the term without precise definition on the assumption that the word 'great' defines a recognisable landed elite. Cooper, for instance, put forward no minimum definition of great landowner acreage for his assessment of the landed wealth of this class in the fifteenth century although he did estimate that the average land holding of a 'great knight' was between 8,000 and 9,000 acres.[8] For the late eighteenth century Mingay identified the minimum acreage for a great landowner as 5,000 acres, but did suggest that a sum of £10,000 provided a comfortable income to support a great landowner family, and if all were to be derived from rent an estate size of 10,000 to 20,000 acres would be necessary.[9]

The diversity in wealth and origin of the gentry has made chronological identification of this group of landowners even more problematical. Generally the term 'gentry' has been used to describe all landowners who derived income from the rent of land, a group often further demarcated on class lines as being comprised only of

untitled landowners, that is, 'landed proprietors, above the
yeomanry, and below the peerage'.[10] However, in a definition
based on estate size both titled and untitled landowners fall within
the group. The inappropriateness of using the broad title of
'landed gentry' to apply to a class whose wealth ranged from a
few hundred to many thousands of acres has led to a number of
attempts to differentiate sub-categories. Trevor-Roper chose to
distinguish between those who received income from offices and
other external sources - 'city gentry' - and those who possessed
only landed wealth - 'mere gentry' or 'country gentry'. No acreage
figure was used to distinguish either category.[11] Mingay used the
terms 'greater' or 'wealthy' gentry and 'lesser' gentry or 'squires'.
They owned estates from 1,000 to 5,000 acres, sometimes reaching
6,000 or 7,000 acres; with income ranges from £3,000 to £5,000 for
the greater gentry and from £1,000 to £3,000 for the lesser gentry.[12]

It is not intended to argue the merits of respective definitions
but merely to indicate the problems faced in attempting a temporal
assessment of large landowners spanning many centuries. It is
possible, nevertheless, with considerable caution and recognising
the problems of inconsistency in definition, to ascertain major
trends in the changing distribution of land and the relative proportions of the land area held by large landowners prior to 1880.

LANDOWNERSHIP BEFORE 1880

Large private landowners formed the backbone of the English land
system from the Commonwealth to the late nineteenth century, but
their landed influence was paralleled in earlier times by that of the
Church and the Crown. From feudal times, however, a relatively
high proportion of land was already in the hands of the Barons,
the upper ranks of the nobility from whom descended many of the
great landed families, who together with the Church and Crown
constituted the territorial magnates of England.

The sixteenth century was a period of profound social and
economic change. The agricultural system underwent adjustment to
the growth of commercialism which brought about the initial decline
in the subsistence economy of the communal open fields and the
rise of farming based on individual occupation and management of
land. Commerce and trade expanded and flourished, and the
economy maintained a sustained period of inflation which saw a
steady rise in prices for almost 150 years. An active land market
was made more buoyant following the Dissolution of the Monasteries
and the need for short-term finance by the Crown which brought
an unprecedented volume of land onto the market and stimulated a
period of speculation.

Estimates for the early fifteenth century have suggested that
20 per cent to 25 per cent of usable land was owned by the Church
and 5 per cent by the Crown.[13] The Church lost its landed power
with the Dissolution of the Monasteries in 1536 at which time the
Crown became the initial recipient of the large-scale transfer of

monastic estates. From 1539 to 1547, however, the Crown alienated
much of its newly acquired land and contemporary estimates calculated that from two-thirds to seven-eights was alienated within
a decade.[14] Relatively few properties were transferred in the form
of grants. The majority were sold. The rapidity of transfer is well
illustrated by the example of Hertfordshire where Munby has
shown that

> of 395 manors or similar estates whose successive owners can be
> traced through county histories, 168 (42.5%) were in the hands
> of the Crown in 1540. By 1550 only 12 of these 168 properties
> remained in the hands of the Crown.[15]

The impact of the dispersal of monastic lands varied from county
to county. In Lincolnshire most of the land purchasers were already prominent in county society and many who had been, 'on
the fringe of county establishment became firmly members of it as
a consequence of their increased wealth'.[16] The bulk of lands dispersed by the Crown in the sixteenth century went to people with
Court connections, but not all had possessed land in the first
instance. There are notable examples of newly founded landed
estates that arose from the upheaval of Dissolution. Thus, in 1540
John Thynne, son of a Shropshire farmer, purchased 60 acres of
land for £53 which included, 'a rabbit warren, orchard, water mill
and tumble-down Wiltshire priory called "Longlete"'.[17] As steward
in the Earl of Hertford's household he was in an opportune position
to acquire further monastic land, manors and church livings, and
through purchase during subsequent years built up a landed
territory of some 6,000 acres around Longleat.[18] Other Church
properties were also to become the heartlands of large private
estates, retaining the name and in many cases the fabric of the
Church buildings if not the buildings themselves. Of note are three
examples in Nottinghamshire; Newstead Priory, Rufford Abbey
and Welbeck Abbey, monastic estates originally carved out of the
Royal Forest of Sherwood. In 1537, George, 4th Earl of Shrewsbury,
obtained a grant in fee of the site of Rufford Abbey and its lands;[19]
in 1539 Richard Walley of Shelford obtained the grant in fee on
payment of £500 for the Abbey of Welbeck,[20] and in 1540 the Priory
of Newstead was purchased with 750 acres of land for £810 by Sir
John Byron of Colwick.[21] The three recipients in this case, however,
were all landowners prior to their acquisition of monastic lands.
For England as a whole research has tended to support the idea
that, 'very few new or appreciably large estates were built up
entirely or even principally out of monastic lands'[22] and that the
bulk of land transfers were important in altering the balance of
property distribution and power among landowners already in
existence.[23] The Crown continued to relinquish its position of
landed wealth throughout the century following Dissolution. In
1603 it was estimated that the revenue obtained from land sales
during the reign of Elizabeth I exceeded £817,000.[24] Sales, occasioned in Elizabeth's time to finance wars with Spain, continued

throughout the reign of James I and Charles I to finance a succession of national crises, so that, immediately prior to the Civil War, Crown land to an estimated value of £2,240,000 had been dispersed. When the remainder was put up for auction in the Civil War the sum realised was under £2,000,000.[25]

The major lay recipients of monastic and Crown lands can be broadly divided into two groups; the first comprised members of the peerage, a number of whom were territorial magnates possessing estates distributed over many counties of England and who individually received the largest grants. The second were landowners more prominent in local county society who made up part of the gentry class and who in aggregate received the largest share.[26] Based on the subsequent history of the land in question it has been suggested that the latter had greater success in retaining the land they acquired and as a group the gentry continued to expand their numbers and wealth over the following century.[27] The gentry were drawn not only from families with strong landed ties but increasingly from city merchants, lawyers, and financiers and other members of the expanding commercial class with capital and vitality to benefit from activities of the land market and to turn price inflation to their advantage. The growth of this heterogeneous group collectively known as 'the gentry' has been the subject of considerable controversy, much debate having focused on the extent to which the rise of this landowning class was at the expense of the other landed nobility, the great estate owners.[28] Certainly among the landed nobility were those who through economic vicissitudes were forced to sell part of their land, especially in the second half of the sixteenth century. It was suggested by both Tawney and Habakkuk that the more conservative of the great landowners neither experimented with modernisation in agriculture nor adapted their estate organisation at a time of inflation when real income was falling, but chose to sell land when faced with financial hardship.[29] In this manner many of the former monastic estates acquired by great landowners were resold to the gentry. Sales of manorial lands by the peerage were particularly notable towards the end of the sixteenth century. Stone provided evidence that real income and property of the peerage fell sharply in the period 1558 to 1601.[30] Examination of the nature of sales revealed that much of the land comprised outlying manors of the great estates. In a period of enclosure and agricultural change the sale of peripheral lands could also have reflected attempts to redefine estate boundaries and to rationalise holdings. Stone argues that this interpretation does not stand up to close examination, but Thompson suggested that such a conclusion cannot be lightly dismissed.[31]

Although land revenues in general had risen from the second quarter of the sixteenth century and in some cases more than doubled between 1560 and 1590, it appears that on many of the great estates major rises of income were delayed until the 1590s.[32] From the 1590s to the 1620s land revenues rose sharply and, combined with an apparent increase in Court favours in the early seventeenth century, led to a recovery of the great landed class.[33] Thompson also concluded that from 1601 to 1641 there was some growth of great estates and some increase in the share of the land held by great landowners.[34]

Members of the nobility and greater gentry who were prominent in the Royal Court during the reign of the Tudor and Stuart monarchs were not only recipients of Court favours but equally ran risks of attainder or forfeiture of their property. It has been observed that some of the oldest territorial families in England owe part of their longevity to a lack of prominence in the Royal Courts of the sixteenth and seventeenth centuries.[35] A number of families emerged from the Interregnum with estates reduced in size or heavily indebted as a consequence of their Royalist support. Some undoubtedly lost their land completely, though research has suggested that the loss of property during the Interregnum was considerably less than that originally believed.[36] The proportional distribution of land among the respective classes in fact remained fairly stable in the first half of the seventeenth century.

For the next two hundred or so years to the early nineteenth century the agricultural sector was the dominant employer and mainstay of the economy and the foundations of society continued to be rooted in the ownership of land. Completion of the transition from medieval to modern agriculture, the enclosure of the common fields and wastes and the consolidation of farm holdings resulted in a further change in the overall distribution of land, with the general trend from around 1680 onwards in favour of the large landowner. New families attained a place in the upper landed ranks and both the number of large landowners and the acreage owned by them increased. Part of the increase was inevitably, though not exclusively, at the expense of the small landowners, the lesser gentry and the yeomen. Johnson concluded that the most critical years for the small landowner were the closing years of the seventeenth century and the first fifty years of the eighteenth.[37] The combination of low agricultural prices, poor harvests and indebtedness forced many yeomen proprietors to quit the land.[38] An increased burden of taxation, particularly the Land Tax instituted in 1692, weighed most heavily on landlords whose income derived exclusively from rents, and has been credited as playing a major role in the decline of many 'lesser-gentry' estates from 1692 to 1720.[39]

It was long held by contemporary commentators and early historians of the period that parliamentary enclosures resulted in the decline of small landowners. Johnson showed, however, that enclosures *per se* were not the primary cause of the decimation of numbers, rather it was the general trends in the development of commercial agriculture that led to the decline. He provided evidence that from 1785 to 1802 'there was an increase rather than a decrease of the yeomen proper'.[40] The years were good for agriculture and the small owner-occupiers were tempted to hold on.

The prime movers in the emerging agricultural system were the large landowners with the capital and technical knowledge to

increase the productivity of land, and alternative non-agricultural
sources of income to withstand fluctuations in the agrarian economy
and heavy taxation. The expansion of productive land area, as
former wastes were brought into cultivation, also tended to benefit the large and wealthy landowners. Estate aggrandisement, consolidation and rationalisation of land holdings became the order
of the day. Outlying lands, whether fortuitously acquired through
inheritance or marriage, were sold to be complemented by purchases
of adjacent property in a policy of aggrandisement and consolidation of a 'home' estate in a single county.[41] Though less land
entered the market from the mid-eighteenth century landowners
continued to extend their property through marriage, inheritance
and piecemeal land purchases. As the nineteenth century progressed the rate of growth of the large estates slowed down though
the territorial position of the large landowners remained firm to
the end of the century.

It is well to emphasise at this point that the broad pattern of an
increasing concentration of land in the hands of a few private
landowners obscures an extremely complex phenomenon at the
regional, county and individual family level. Though differences
existed in the timing and impact of economic vicissitudes and in
the relative composition of the landed hierarchy, detailed studies
to date nevertheless tend to support the general orthodoxy regarding the development of broad patterns of landownership.

PROPORTIONAL ESTIMATES OF LAND AREA OWNED

Landownership is a dynamic and constantly changing phenomenon.
The social and economic mobility of private landowners between
various ownership groups has further complicated attempts to
proportion the distribution of landownership over intervals of time.
Thus, while there has been general agreement on the broader trends
in the changing pattern, there have been relatively few attempts
to quantify, either in proportional or in acreage terms, the respective holdings of each group of landowners during past centuries.
Certainly the task is further complicated, as was recognised earlier,
by the paucity of ownership data and, for comparative purposes,
by the lack of temporal consensus in the definition of each landowner group. However, estimates have been made as to the proportion of land held by great landowners around which there seems
to be some general acceptance.

Cooper put the extent of lands held by great landowners as
being approximately 20 per cent of usable area in 1436, that is,
between 3 million and 4 million acres.[42] Based on Stone's estimates
of peerage income Thompson calculated that by 1641, from 10 to
15 per cent or roughly 3 million acres of land was owned by the
peerage and, in his assessment, as they comprised no more than
two-thirds of the aggregate number of great landowners, he put
forward that a total figure of 4 million to 4½ million acres, or from
15 to 20 per cent of cultivable area, was owned by the great land-

owners.[43] If both figures are plausible it would appear that, even though the individual members that made up the group may have changed, the proportional area occupied by great landowners at the two points in time was more or less the same, fluctuations between the two dates, decline pre-1601 and resurgence 1601 to 1641 resulting in little change in relative proportions. In the four hundred years from the sixteenth to the late nineteenth century, however, the extent of the cultivated land area also grew from an estimated 20 million acres in 1436 to around 29 million acres.[44] It is conceivable, therefore, that the proportional area remained more or less the same from 1436 to 1641 while the total acreage of great-landowner properties actually increased; a supposition, however, that cannot be conclusively substantiated one way or another. The proportion of land held by great landowners appears to have remained around the 15 to 20 per cent mark up to 1688 but rose considerably during the eighteenth century such that estimates for 1790 place the figure around 20 to 25 per cent, a proportion that was sustained and slightly increased throughout the nineteenth century.

The basis for differentiating the gentry makes comparison over time more hazardous than that for the great landowners. Even figures for their total number at one period in time are so diverse as to cast doubt on the validity of temporal comparison. For example, in the eighteenth century estimates ranged from as low as 8,000 to more than 20,000.[45] Nevertheless, Mingay attempted a chronological summary of the proportional land area occupied by the gentry from the fifteenth to the late nineteenth century.[46] For the initial calculation he adopted the £5 to £100 income landowners as identified by Cooper to represent the gentry class in 1436.[47] As a group they held approximately 25 per cent of the land area. By 1690 the proportion was between 45 and 50 per cent, a figure that was more or less maintained for the next two hundred years, rising only slightly from an estimated 50 per cent in 1790 to 55 per cent in 1873. As an example of the range of proportions ascribed to this group, contemporary estimates by Chamberlayne in 1692 would place only a tenth of the land area in gentry ownership although it is maintained by Cooper that such a figure is too low and leaves far too much land in the ownership of small freeholders.[48] It should also be recalled that Mingay's definition of 'greater' and 'lesser' gentry ascribes different acreage and income values to each category from those adopted in this study. Thus, the proportion owned by the gentry, using the study classification, would be around 31 per cent in the late nineteenth century; 19 per cent owned by the 'greater gentry' and 12 per cent by the 'lesser gentry'.[49]

Despite the lack of detailed statistical information it remains clear that the landed power of the gentry was greatly enhanced in the sixteenth century and that along with the great landowners the upper ranks of the gentry slowly but progressively acquired a stronger territorial position in England up to the late nineteenth century.

At the onset of the period commencing in 1880 a more precise evaluation both of actual numbers and acreage is possible through the New Domesday survey and the work of Bateman. However, it is appropriate at this point to pause and briefly consider a further dimension of the landownership picture, namely the means by which the large landed properties assembled and created by one generation were passed to successive generations.

ESTATE PRESERVATION - INHERITANCE AND MARRIAGE

The law and custom of primogeniture, whereby the family property was passed to the eldest son, cannot be over-emphasised as one of the most important factors preserving the large landed properties over time. The essential tenet of the law of primogeniture had been introduced with feudal tenures by Norman lawyers. Initially it was associated with the need of the manorial lord to ensure that tenant obligations were duly fulfilled when their land changed hands. The right of the eldest son to inherit his father's estate was fully recognised in the case of knight service not long after the Norman conquest and by the thirteenth century these rights were extended to include socage tenures.[50] The law was applicable only in cases of intestacy which gave the eldest son rights to all realty, but divided personalty amongst all children in the family.

The custom of primogeniture was by no means common practice throughout England. By the Middle Ages a number of different forms of inheritance were practised including 'gavelkind', the division of land amongst all heirs, and 'borough English' whereby the last born succeeded to the estate. Primogeniture gained popularity among the gentry from the sixteenth century and eventually came to be regarded as 'a fundamental law of nature by the gentry and nobility alike'.[51] It had practical and effective expression in the system of strict family settlements which became accepted as legally binding contracts around the mid-seventeenth century. The use of strict settlements, sometimes referred to as marriage settlements as they were usually fixed at the time of the eldest son's marriage,[52] is well echoed in the sentiments expressed by Edmund Burke that the landed interest is, 'a partnership not only between those who are living, but between those who are living, those who are dead, and those who are to be born.'[53] Whereas under the law of primogeniture an heir to a property, upon succession, would hold it as a tenant in fee simple, under a family settlement the incumbent of a property would hold it as a tenant-for-life and future heirs, sons and grandsons would be named to succeed as tenants-in-tail. Thus, an heir to a settled estate was in essence an hereditary trustee or limited owner, during his lifetime serving as the guardian of the family patrimony in order to pass it on intact to the next generation. The duration of a settlement was limited to three generations such that no entail could be made on the unborn child of an unborn child. As estates passed to successive heirs periodic renewal of entails took place, normally within each generation. Few settlements were permitted to run their full course as to do so would have allowed the final tenant-for-life to become the absolute owner with no legal restrictions on his powers of alienation, sale or bequest. Further limitations were also placed on the ability of the tenant-for-life to dispose of settled property through the device that appointed trustees to preserve 'contingent remainders'. Their purpose was to secure in settlements a provision for the future of children of an intended marriage, that is, to uphold the interests of the unborn. By the early eighteenth century the use of this arrangement was common.

A settlement could be broken only by a private Act of Parliament and few opportunities other than at the time of settlement renegotiation were available for the disposal of land. It was not until the Settled Land Act of 1882 that the tenant-for-life was given the powers of dealing with the land 'by way of sale, exchange, lease and otherwise'.[54] Thus, from the seventeenth century the combined effects of the general adoption of the rule of primogeniture by the large landowners and the legal framework of strict settlements effectively prevented the disintegration of the large landed properties, whether the estates of the older nobility or those of more recent creation. Property, once assembled, was closely preserved and by the mid-eighteenth century evidence suggested that as much as half of England's land was held under strict settlement.[55]

Relatively few large estates entered the land market in the eighteenth and nineteenth centuries. Financial necessity sometimes forced the sale of sizeable portions of a great estate but, 'families who incurred debts of such a size that they were forced to sell their main estates were . . . the exception'.[56] Some upgrading within the landed ranks was possible by piecemeal land purchases and was particularly enhanced by the sale of lesser gentry and yeomen estates in the early eighteenth century. But the status conferred by landownership, the social, economic and political power that was seen to emanate from its acquisition, ensured that once acquired properties were jealously protected and preserved. Consequently there were progressively fewer opportunities for large-scale purchase either by new families aspiring to enter landed society or for smaller landowners intent on moving up the landed ladder.

The door to landed society was effectively locked to those with only purchasing power as the key, but was opened for some, as indeed it had been throughout history, by the institution of marriage. It was aptly described by Sir J.B. Burke when he wrote in 1873 that, 'one cannot help perceiving that the chief houses still existing have been built on the foundations laid by feudalism, largely increased at the dissolution of the monasteries, and constantly enriched by the heritages of lady ancestors'.[57] Marriage was the means by which new families with wealth from commerce and trade became interwoven with families of ancient lineage in the fabric of landed society. For established landowners marriage was one of the most important means of estate aggrandisement to further strengthen their position in society. A wealthy family could enhance its social status through the arrangement of marriage between a daughter and the heir apparent, if not the owner, of a landed estate. Family connections once made ensured the proverbial foot was in the door to gain further access to the wider social circle of landed society. Generous dowries were therefore bestowed on daughters to attract appropriate matches. During the eighteenth century there was an observed tendency for dowry portions to increase as daughters of wealthy merchants, industrialists, bankers and other professional men entered the marriage market alongside daughters of the landed classes.[58] Dowried daughters, particularly from the commercial or professional classes, brought valuable capital to indebted estates, capital not only to bolster the declining estate fortunes but also to facilitate the purchase of more land or to refurbish estate property.

Indebtedness on many estates was often incurred as a result of financial provisions made for wives, younger sons and daughters in family settlements. With the emergence of the mortgage as an instrument of long-term debt from the late seventeenth century, families invariably raised capital to provide for dowries, portions, jointures and other financial arrangements involved in the complex negotiation of settlements, by mortgaging part of the estate, an act which invariably led to an increased burden of debt for future generations. It appears, however, that few cases of estate loss or extensive land sales were occasioned by the overbearing financial burdens of settlement provisions.[59] A notable exception resulted from the bequests of the 3rd Earl of Salisbury, who at his death in 1683, left a gross income of £12,000 yet made provision for his three daughters and four younger sons to the sum of £78,000, a settlement that necessitated considerable land sales. The marriage of his heir to Frances Bennet, co-heiress to the estates of Simon Bennet of Beechampton (Bucks.) brought valuable capital to the impoverished estate.[60]

The important contribution to estate capital from the marriage portions of the daughters of the wealthy has been overshadowed in significance by marriages to landed heiresses. Such marriages though in comparison few and far between played a major role in founding new landed families and in enlarging existing estate properties. Succession by daughters was provided for in some family settlements although the general bias, particularly among the great landowners, was towards male heirs.[61] Some landowners were reluctant to pass property in the female line and made provision for collateral relatives to inherit, conditional upon adopting the family name so as to continue the historic association of family and estate.[62]

There were far more landed heiresses among the gentry and it is particularly through alliances with this class that commercial families, government officials, lawyers, and other professionals were integrated into landed society. Thus William Blathwayt, Secretary of State and Secretary at War to William III, established his family name in landed society in 1686 when he married Mary Wynter, heiress of the Dyrham estate in Gloucestershire.

The aggrandisement of the great estates of the Duke of Buckingham and Chandos, the Duke of Leeds, the Duke of Sutherland
(Leveson-Gowers) and the Earl Cooper as well as of other members
of the landed nobility rested in large part on a history of fortuitous
alliances of landed property through marriage.[63] The most noted
rise was that of the Leveson-Gowers, a brief account of which
bears repeating to emphasise the importance of inheritance and
marriage in estate accumulation. Disraeli, it is said, remarked of
this family that it 'had made good by its talent for absorbing
heiresses'.[64] In 1689 the properties of the Levesons centred on
Trentham (Staffs.) and that of the Gowers based at Stittenham
(Yorks.) were legally joined, Thomas Gower having married the
co-heiress of Sir John Leveson. Sir John Leveson-Gower (1675-
1709) married the daughter of the Duke of Rutland who brought
with her a substantial marriage portion of £15,000. Granville
Leveson-Gower (2nd Earl Gower and 1st Marquis of Stafford, 1721-
1803) was connected by marriage to the Dukes of Bedford and
Bridgwater and the Earls of Galloway and Carlisle. He was
married three times. His second marriage, to Lady Louisa Egerton,
was of immense importance for the future wealth of the family.
She was the favourite sister of the heirless Duke of Bridgwater,
who on his death in 1803 left the profits of the Bridgwater canal
to Stafford's first son, George Granville Leveson-Gower (1758-
1833). The latter 'outdid' all previous family alliances by marriage
in 1785 to the only surviving child and heiress of William Gordon,
the 17th Earl of Sutherland. The union joined the already substantial English estates to the extensive property of the Suther-
lands in Scotland. By the time of Bateman's listing of great landowners *circa* 1880 the Sutherland's not only ranked among the
territorial magnates of England, but the combined total of their
English and Scottish lands, over 1.3 million acres, made the
family the wealthiest of all British landowners in terms of acreage.

THE LANDED ARISTOCRACY, THE LAND QUESTION
AND THE NEW DOMESDAY

The identification of the elite of British society drew increasingly more attention as the nineteenth century progressed as is
evidenced by the quantity of literature produced on the heraldic
and genealogical origins and general family histories of the landed
and governing heirarchy. Of particular note were the many volumes
published by the Burke family.[65] The first volume of 'Burke's
Landed Gentry' was first printed in 1833-5.[66] Shirley's, *The Noble
and Gentle Men of England* was published in 1859. A notable feature
of this work was the identification of county families who had held
land in unbroken male line since the time of Henry VII.[67] It was
closely followed by Walford's first volume of *The County Families
of the United Kingdom* (1860), a publication that attempted a complete survey of all major landowners in mid-Victorian landed society
whether of old or recent origin.[68] Sanford and Townsend's two

volumes of *The Great Governing Families of England* contained a
map that showed the location of the principal seats of over 200 of
the greater owners of land, but the primary focus of the work was
to trace the ascendency of 31 major landed families.[69]

Such discourses, whether on the historic rise of aristocratic
families or on the whereabouts of their county seats, provided
little evidence as to the actual extent of the great estates, yet
conceivably strengthened the view of 'the practical monopoly of
land' expressed by the middle-class radicals. The land question
was a recurring issue throughout the century and one that
brought discussion of the landed elite periodically to the fore in
parliamentary debates.[70] Essentially directed towards the abate-
ment of aristocratic power, the agitators for land reform sought
to abolish the law of primogeniture and introduce some form of
compulsory division of the landed estates. Both sides of the controversy grasped at notional figures to support their case. John
Bright, zealous spokesman of middle-class radicalism, alleged that
fewer than 150 men owned half of England[71] and drew on the 1861
census total of 30,000 landowners to further support reformist
views that land was becoming concentrated in fewer hands. Lord
Derby conversely maintained that the census figure was not merely
deficient but grossly inaccurate, having enumerated only those
who had chosen to call themselves landowners, and suggested that
a multiple of ten times 30,000 would be more realistic. In the belief
that monopolistic allegations would not be substantiated Lord Derby
supported the idea of a comprehensive survey of landownership
and introduced the proposal to the House of Lords in 1872, a proposal duly implemented in 1873 as the *Return of Owners of Land*.

In the method of enumeration and in the final published form the
Return contained many errors and inaccuracies, shortcomings
that were acknowledged and described by contemporaries.[72] Nevertheless, the collated statistics provided political fodder for the
defenders of the *status quo* and land reformers alike. The fact
that more than 900,000 individuals, over a quarter of the population of England, owned property, whether a fraction of an acre
or many thousands of acres, was held up to disprove reformist
accusations that Englishmen had been divorced from the soil.
Numerically the largest group were the cottagers (owners with
less than one acre) who accounted for over 800,000 of the total,
yet in terms of land area occupied less than 13 per cent.[73]

Contemporary aggregations initially suggested that around
43,000 owners possessed one hundred or more acres in England
and Wales, a figure probably more representative of the landowning classes and thus far below Lord Derby's mythical 300,000.[74]
Later calculations gave a total for England of a little under 33,500,
yet of this group nearly 32,000 were yeomen and lesser gentry,
the former defined as possessing estates of from 100 to less than
1,000 acres, while the latter owned from 1,000 to around 3,000
acres.[75] In total the yeomen and lesser gentry held nearly 40 per
cent of the land area of England.

For the remainder, while the ratio of 150 owners to half of

England's land proved fallacious, it was immediately apparent that
a small proportion of the total population held considerable territorial power. The number of large landowners possessing a minimum
of 3,000 acres totalled less than 1,500, yet this group owned around
43 per cent[76] of the land area of England and it was revealed with
italicised emphasis in the *Spectator* of 1876 that, 'Seven hundred
and ten individuals own more than one quarter of the soil of
England and Wales'; a calculation based on the total land holdings
of owners with a minimum of 5,000 acres in any one county.[77]
Although little attention was paid to public and institutional landowners in ensuing discussions, it is as well to note that they owned
only 5 per cent of the total land area, a mere 1.4 million acres;
the overwhelming majority of England's land lay in private hands
and within this sector much lay in the hands of a minority.

THE LARGE LANDOWNERS CIRCA 1880

Data Source
As a primary source of data for the study of the large landowners
of the late nineteenth century the original New Domesday is sur-
passed by the work of Bateman. From the mid-1870s, using the
1873 *Return* as a base, Bateman abstracted from the county returns
all British and Irish landowners possessing a minimum of 3,000
acres,[78] whether located in a single county or scattered throughout many counties. His work was first published in 1876 as *The
Acre-Ocracy of England* a title that received much criticism and
on reflection more befits the jargon of the late twentieth century
than the late nineteenth. He subsequently expanded, corrected
and updated the entries for three further editions all of which
appeared under the title *The Great Landowners of Great Britain
and Ireland*. The fourth edition published in 1883[79] provides the
most accurate listing of the titled and untitled upper ranks of
English landed society at the close of the nineteenth century, an
invaluable picture in the history of landownership. It was fortuitous, although only in hindsight, that the 1873 *Return* and Bateman's work coincided with the watershed in the territorial expansion of large private estates, thus providing a camera image of
the phenomenon at its zenith, the peak before the onset of decline.

The Distribution of Large Landowner Property circa 1880[80]
In 1880 there was a total of 1,363 large landowners in England,[81]
comprising 331 great landowners, including 43 territorial magnates,
and 1,032 greater gentry. It can be argued that precise demarcation into great landowner and greater gentry according to purely
acreage criteria is an oversimplification of a complex social phenomenon. Clearly differentiation on acreage lines, and acreage in
England only, excluded a few from the great-landowner class who
on the basis of land owned elsewhere in Britain undoubtedly belonged to the landed aristocracy. For example, the Marquis of
Conyngham, the Marquis of Downshire, the Earl of Haddington,

the Earl of Rosebery, Viscount Dillon, William Meyrick Bankes and
Charles Morrison, by virtue of their relatively small English acreage, fell into the greater-gentry classification, but all possessed
land elsewhere in the British Isles which amounted to considerably
more than 10,000 acres and which would in fact rank them as
territorial magnates if added to their English acreage. Apart from
these exceptions relatively few landowners held property outside
England that would in total have placed them in a different size
group, although other titled landowners who fell short of the
10,000 acre mark would have classed themselves, using criteria
of political and social status, as members of the aristocracy rather
than as gentry. Undoubtedly, also on class association, there
were commoners who in acreage terms ranked as great landowners,
hence part of the landed aristocracy, but who would perhaps on
social lines have defined themselves as gentry.

County and Regional Land Distribution. Large-landowner property
totalled over 12.5 million acres and occupied 43 per cent of the
land area of England; the great landowners possessed over 7
million acres, slightly over 24 per cent, of which 2 million acres
(8 per cent) were owned by land magnates, while greater-gentry
lands extended over 5.5 million acres, approximately 19 per cent
of the total land area (Table 1.1). The distribution of property
owned by each group varied throughout England and while broad
patterns can be established from county figures it is evident that
sharp contrasts were found from county to county.
    The five counties with the highest proportion of land area
occupied by great-landowner properties were Northumberland
(54 per cent), Rutland (52 per cent), Nottinghamshire (38 per
cent), Dorset (37 per cent) and Wiltshire (36 per cent), all well
above the national average of 24 per cent. At the bottom of the
scale were Middlesex (5 per cent), Essex (9 per cent), Herefordshire (10 per cent), Kent (11 per cent) and Cambridgeshire (12
per cent). The proportional range for great-landowner properties
was therefore considerable from 5 to 54 per cent (Appendix 1).
On the whole a greater area of land lay in the northern counties
while counties around London generally possessed considerably
less than the national average, in all probability related to the
influence of London on the local land market. It may be supposed
that there would be a high demand for land within reasonable
proximity to the city and resultant higher land prices would
militate against both the accumulation and long-term retention of
large properties. Contrary reasons may well have accounted in
part for the prevalence of large landholdings in other counties.
There was, for example, a tendency for extensive estates to be
owned in those counties endowed with large tracts of poor-quality
land such as Northumberland, Yorkshire and Lincolnshire. It is
not inconceivable that large blocks of land may have been acquired
relatively cheaply during different phases of estate expansion.
Vast stretches of open countryside were also bought for the pursuit of the fashionable leisure activities of hunting and shooting,

although some areas of poor land, following the introduction of new farming methods, were converted to arable use. For example, a great expanse of the North Lincolnshire wolds remained uncultivated until the early nineteenth century. Indeed, 'when Will Smith took the Brocklesby horn from his father in 1816 there were only two fences between Horncastle and Brigg'.[82] Transformation when it came was swift. Where Arthur Young in 1813 reported miles of gorse and thousands of rabbits, Phillip Pusey in 1843 recorded over 30,000 acres of good turnip land.[83] Similarly, across the Humber, the Yorkshire wolds comprised a tract of bare uplands in the eighteenth century, but in 1812 a contemporary observer estimated that two-thirds lay under tillage.[84]

Though the apparent correlation of poor quality land with extensive great-landowner acreage holds true for many counties, Westmorland, Devon and Cumberland are notable exceptions as in all cases the proportional figures fell below the national average.

The county ranking of per cent distribution of gentry lands was headed by Shropshire with 29 per cent followed by Hampshire (26 per cent), Oxfordshire (25 per cent), Herefordshire (24 per cent) and Norfolk (23 per cent), while at the bottom of the list were Cambridgeshire and Cumberland each with 10 per cent, Durham and Middlesex with 11 per cent and Devon with 14 per cent; a less extreme proportional range of from 10 to 29 per cent (Appendix 1). In eleven counties of central and southern England – Shropshire, Hampshire, Oxfordshire, Herefordshire, Norfolk, Huntingdonshire, Berkshire, Kent, Worcestershire, Leicestershire – greater-gentry estates occupied a higher proportion of total county acreage than great-landowner properties although elsewhere the opposite prevailed. Certainly in the northern counties of Cumberland, Durham, Northumberland and Westmorland proportionally more land was owned by great landowners, the four counties being among the lowest ranked in terms of gentry acreage. But while Northumberland and Durham were two of the more important great-landowner counties, Westmorland and more clearly Cumberland were also in the lowest ranks in terms of great-landowner acreage.

While it is evident that certain counties were more endowed with great-landowner estates and others with greater-gentry, there were those in which the presence of large-landowner property as a whole was negligible. Such counties are clearly identified when acreages are combined to present a picture of the distribution of large-landowner properties as a whole (Figure 1.1). Rutland proved to be the most 'landed' of English Counties with nearly 70 per cent of the county area in the hands of large landowners. A further six counties had values of over 50 per cent; Northumberland (68 per cent), Nottinghamshire (57 per cent), Dorset (57 per cent), Wiltshire (55 per cent), Shropshire (54 per cent) and Cheshire (52 per cent). Less than one-third of the land of each of the counties of Middlesex, Cambridgeshire, Essex, Surrey, Cumberland and Kent was owned by large landowners. For the most part in these counties smaller landowners predominated, the squirearchy or 'lesser gentry' formed a substantial group in the case of Surrey, while Middlesex, Cambridgeshire and Cumberland each had a high proportion of yeoman farmers and small proprietors. In addition, Middlesex and Cambridgeshire were the highest-ranking counties in terms of area occupied by public and institutional land with proportions of 15 per cent and 12 per cent respectively.

Figure 1.1: Per Cent of County Area Owned by Large Landowners c. 1880

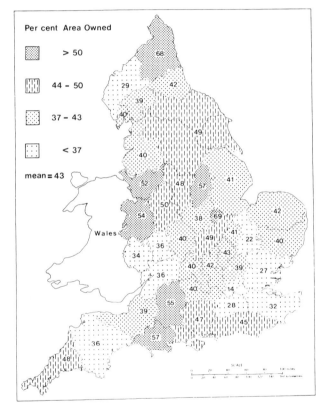

Source: J. Bateman, *The Great Landowners of Great Britain and Ireland*, 4th edn (1883).

Finally, in summary, six regions have been identified based on a broad association with recognised administrative regions and major agricultural areas, demarcated according to pre-1974 county boundaries.[85] A clear picture emerges of the relative dominance of the respective landowner groups and the broad distribution of

Table 1.1: Regional Distribution of Large-landowner Acreage
c. 1880

Region	Total acreage	Great landowners (%)		Greater gentry (%)		Large landowners (%)	
North	3,808	1,389	36	630	17	2,019	53
North West	4,210	1,127	27	838	20	1,964	47
East	5,208	1,136	22	890	17	2,026	39
Midlands	4,124	921	22	930	23	1,851	45
South East	6,205	1,041	17	1,280	21	2,321	37
South West	5,352	1,392	26	935	17	2,327	43
England	28,907	7,006	24	5,503	19	12,508	43

000s Acres

Source: J. Bateman, *The Great Landowners of Great Britain and Ireland,* 4th edn (1883).

large landowner property in England (Table 1.1). The highest
proportional acreage for great landowners was found in the North.
The North West and South West also recorded higher-than-average
figures while the Midlands and East fell slightly below the national
average. South East England had the lowest per cent of great-
landowner property. In the distribution of greater-gentry land,
the North, East and South West were less well endowed while the
Midlands was the most favoured region. As a whole, however, at
the aggregate regional level greater-gentry property appeared
fairly evenly distributed. The South East and Midlands had a
higher proportion of greater-gentry than great-landowner properties, the former no doubt reflecting the general attraction of owning land in close proximity to London. Overall, however, the South
East had the lowest per cent of large-landowner property while
the North had the highest.

The distribution of large landed properties by 1880 was the
product of centuries of evolution. Periods of dramatic national
change, as at the dissolution of the monasteries, periods of
aggrandisement and estate accretion or land loss by a particular
class of landowner, underpinned by the ups and downs of individual family histories, of fortuitous marriages, untimely deaths,
lack of heirs or financial crises all affected the ownership of
land. Thus, the pattern that emerged by the late nineteenth
century has no simple explanation, although one or two factors
such as the pull of London or the availability of inexpensive,
poor land may have played a modifying role in the complex set of
circumstances over time.

Quantity of land provides a good yardstick as to the potential
influence of large landowners in each county, but the ownership
of land did not necessarily imply residency. From the perspective
of landscape impact a more significant factor is the location of the

principal estate heartland, the focal point of which was the country house. It was not uncommon for members of the landed classes, more especially the great landowners, to own more than one large country house. However, only the principal family seat will be used as a point of reference to indicate which counties were more favoured as residential locations. The principal seat for 1,336 landowners was identified and assigned to the appropriate county and, for purposes of comparison, the density of seats per 1,000 acres was calculated for each county (Appendix 1).

For great landowners the counties that ranked highest in terms of acreage, for the most part, also ranked highest in terms of the density of seats. A notable exception, however, was Derbyshire where the proportional acreage was high but the density low due to the territorial dominance of the Duke of Devonshire's estate at Chatsworth and the relative lack of other great-landowner properties in the county. A group of counties, predominantly in the south, with lower-than-average great-landowner acreage had a higher-than-average density of seats namely, Hertfordshire, Surrey, Hampshire, Buckinghamshire, Suffolk, Norfolk, Sussex and Gloucestershire.

The ranked density of greater-gentry seats was more in line with the ranking of acreages although the majority of counties in the South East ranked perceptably higher in terms of density values in comparison to acreage values, Oxfordshire, Berkshire, Hampshire, Kent, Buckinghamshire and Sussex were all within the top ten in terms of density of seats. All also had above the national average of acreage while Essex, Hertfordshire, Gloucestershire and Rutland were the only counties with lower-than-average acreage but above-average density of seats.

Putting both landowner groups together, of the 14 counties with a higher-than-national-average acreage owned by large landowners, ten also had a higher-than-average density of seats, the four exceptions being, Cornwall, Derbyshire, Dorset and Northumberland, whereas of the 25 counties with below-average acreage, eleven had above-average density values and all eleven were located in the south of England.[86] It is apparent that factors other than size of property were, therefore, important in the choice of residential location. The pattern of density values revealed a greater concentration of seats in the South East and Midlands while the extreme North, parts of the East region and extreme South West were less favoured areas (Figure 1.2). A more pronounced density in counties of the South East confirms the magnetism of London and other research also supports this idea. Stone, for example, wrote of Hertfordshire that, 'through all periods it has been a favourite area for the purchase of a landed estate by successful London merchants.'[87] During the eighteenth and nineteenth centuries the development of national transport networks provided almost all areas of rural England with relatively good access to London, or at least an important urban centre, but the heartlands of many landed properties had been established in earlier centuries when the attraction of London was strong whether

Figure 1.2: Density of Large-landowner Seats per County c. 1880

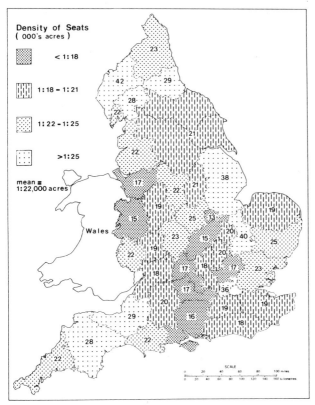

Source: J. Bateman, *The Great Landowners of Great Britain and Ireland*, 4th edn (1883).

for commercial purposes or for attendance at the Royal Courts. Even though much rebuilding of country houses took place during the eighteenth and nineteenth centuries, geographical inertia led to the majority being built on or near the site of former houses, while London as a centre of trade and commerce continued to exert a notable influence on the location of new greater-gentry seats. Though the South was in density terms more preferable generally than the North, no county was without its complement of large-landowner residences. In the total number of seats many northern counties in fact exceeded their southern counterparts and preference for a southern location rests purely on a density comparison.

The Titled and Untitled Large Landowners
Finally, any discussion of the distribution of landed property in
the late nineteenth century would perhaps be incomplete without
reference to the social status of the landowners. By 1880 the large
landowners of England comprised a diverse group of families from
a wide range of social, economic and political backgrounds whose
wealth originated from innumerable sources in addition to land,
and whose association with landed society could date back in years,
decades or centuries. Although it could be said that landowners
with a minimum of 3,000 acres economically were of the same class
in that all belonged to the sector of society which derived part, if
not in some cases all, of its income from the exploitation of proprietory rights in land, there was a notable division within the
group, a fundamental line that demarcated titled from untitled
landowners, the peerage or landed nobility from the commoners.

By the late nineteenth century the peerage derived from a wide
variety of backgrounds. Still prominent were the chief territorial
magnates, descendants of the feudal barons, while among the class
were descendants of more recently created peers and a group of
new peers whose elevation in status had stemmed from their position in society as eminent lawyers, diplomats, naval and military
commanders, merchants and industrialists.[88] Sir Bernard Burke,
writing in 1873, nevertheless maintained that although new elements were introduced the creations of later times were still
generally made from county gentlemen of landed importance.[89] Not
all peers, however, were large landowners, and it was estimated
by Bateman that some 60 or more appeared to have been virtually
landless.[90]

Association with large landed property and the tradition of
landownership were not the prerogative of the nobility. A substantial group of untitled owners could trace their landed ancestry
back in time further than many of the peerage. A small number,
including the Dymokes of Scrivelsby, the Berkeleys of Berkeley
Castle and the Giffords of Chillington possessed lands granted to
them in the eleventh and twelfth centuries.

Confusion sometimes arises, in discussing the landed hierarchy,
when the peerage are equated with the great landowners and hence
the greater gentry are implicitly comprised of the untitled remainder. A division along such lines undoubtedly contained a substantial element of truth, as generally the more extensive landed
properties belonged to the titled aristocracy, but only at the
territorial-magnate level of landownership were titled families
overwhelmingly dominant; less than 8 per cent in this size group
possessed no title. Out of the total of 331 great landowners 69
per cent were titled (54 per cent peerage, 15 per cent baronetage
and knightage) but nearly one-third of the owners possessing
estates of 10,000 acres could not lay claim to a title. The converse
was the case for the greater-gentry group where 68 per cent were
commoners, 17 per cent were from the baronetage and knightage
while as many as 155 members of the peerage (15 per cent) held
below 10,000 acres of land in England. Lands owned by titled and

untitled landowners displayed no overwhelming regional differentiation other than a slightly greater association of titled owners,
whether great landowners or gentry, with the Midlands and South
East region, and untitled with counties of the North and East. A
similar pattern was apparent in the location of seats with a marginally greater emphasis of titled landowners in the Midlands and
South of England, excluding a number of counties in the South
West.

In their control over a large section of the land area of England
the large landowners were in a position to affect the course and
nature of landscape change. It was apparent that their influence
was not uniform throughout the countryside. By 1880 the distribution of large-landowner property presented a diverse pattern
whereby some counties were more characterised by great-landowner
estates and others by those of the greater gentry, while certain
counties appeared comparatively more favoured for residential
location. Adjacent counties often displayed considerable disparities
of landownership characteristics, nevertheless the lack of uni-
formity did not translate into a clearly defined picture of any
region being overwhelmingly dominated or totally devoid of large
landed property and as an element in the late-nineteenth-century
landscape the estates owned by large landowners were found
throughout the length and breadth of England. Whether their
survival into the late twentieth century has been in any way related to the location of the principal estate heartland, or the total
area of land owned are questions that remain to be examined.

NOTES

1   'Return of Owners of Land 1872-3' (BPP, 1874, LXXII).
2   J. Bateman, 'The Great Landowners of Great Britain and
    Ireland', 4th edn (1883, reprinted Leicester Univ. Press,
    1971).
3   F.M.L. Thompson, 'English Landed Society in the Nineteenth
    Century' (Routledge and Kegan Paul, London, 1963), pp. 27-32.
4   Bateman, 'Great Landowners', p. 501.
5   The Baronetage is linked with the nobility by virtue of an
    hereditary claim to a title but only Peers can sit in the House
    of Lords. A knightage is not hereditary but is a titled honour
    bestowed on an individual by the sovereign.
6   Bateman, 'Great Landowners', pp. 499-500.
7   J.P. Cooper, The Social Distribution of Land and Men in
    England, 1436-1700, 'Econ. Hist. Rev.', 2nd ser., vol. 20,
    no. 3 (1967), p. 420, used the income tax assessments for a
    group of 234 landowners, 51 Barons and 183 Great Knights,
    to estimate the extent of great landowner acreage for 1436;
    L. Stone, 'The Crisis of the Aristocracy 1558-1641' (Clarendon,
    Oxford, 1965), calculated that the peerage formed about two-
    thirds of the entire group of great landowners. This figure
    was also used by F.M.L. Thompson for estimating the propor-

tion of land owned by great landlords in 1641 and 1688; F.M.L. Thompson, The Social Distribution of Landed Property in England since the Sixteenth Century, 'Econ. Hist. Rev.', 2nd ser., vol. 29, no. 3 (1966), pp. 509-10.

8   Cooper, The Social Distribution, p. 420.
9   G.E. Mingay, 'English Landed Society in the Eighteenth Century' (Routledge and Kegan Paul, London, 1963), p. 19.
10 R.H. Tawney, The Rise of the Gentry, 1558-1640, 'Econ. Hist. Rev.', vol. 11 (1941), p. 4.
11 H.R. Trevor-Roper, The Gentry, 1540-1640, 'Econ. Hist. Rev.', Supplement no. 1 (1953), p. 17.
12 Mingay, 'English Landed Society', pp. 22-3.
13 Cooper, The Social Distribution, p. 420.
14 R.B. Pugh, 'The Crown Estate' (HMSO, London, 1960), p. 10.
15 L.M. Munby, 'The Hertfordshire Landscape' (Hodder and Stoughton, London, 1977), p. 139.
16 G.A.J. Hodgett, 'Tudor Lincolnshire (History of Lincolnshire, vol. 6, Lincoln, 1975), p. 49.
17 D. Burnett, 'Longleat' (Collins, London, 1978), p. 15.
18 Ibid., p. 20.
19 W. Page (ed.) 'VCH of Nottingham' (1910, reprinted Dawsons, London, 1970), vol. 2, p. 104.
20 Ibid., p. 137.
21 Ibid., p. 117.
22 J. Youings, 'The Dissolution of the Monasteries' (Allen and Unwin, London, 1971), p. 130.
23 H.J. Habakkuk, The Market for Monastic Property, 1539-1703 'Econ. Hist. Rev.', 2nd ser., vol. 10, no. 3 (1958), p. 30.
24 S.J. Madge, 'The Domesday of Crown Lands', (Frank Cass, London, 1938), pp. 41-2.
25 Ibid., p. 256.
26 Tawney, The Rise of the Gentry, p. 26.
27 Ibid., p. 26.
28 Debate over the rise of the gentry was reviewed by Tawney, ibid. pp. 1-38, whose thesis was criticised by Trevor-Roper, The Gentry, pp. 1-55. J.H. Hexter, Storm Over the Gentry, 'Encounter', May (1958), pp. 22-35, entered the discussion followed subsequently by contributions from Cooper, The Social Distribution, pp. 419-37, and Stone, 'Crisis of the Aristocracy'. A concise review of the main arguments in the debate is presented in G.E. Mingay, 'The Gentry' (Longmans, London, 1976), pp. 50-7.
29 Tawney, The Rise of the Gentry, pp. 9-10; H.J. Habakkuk, English Landownership, 1680-1740, 'Econ. Hist. Rev.', vol. 10, no. 1 (1940), p. 2.
30 Stone, 'Crisis of the Aristocracy', pp. 152-64.
31 Ibid., p. 158; Thompson, The Social Distribution of Landed Property, p. 511.
32 Mingay, 'The Gentry', p. 56.
33 Stone, 'Crisis of the Aristocracy', pp. 152-64.
34 Thompson, The Social Distribution of Landed Property, p. 510.

35   E.P. Shirley in 1859 described the lineage of 330 nobles and
      landed gentry who could trace their descent back to a period
      before the dissolution of the monasteries, E.P. Shirley, 'The
      Noble and Gentle Men of England' (John Bowyer Nichols,
      Westminster, 1859).
36   P. Roebuck, 'Yorkshire Baronets 1640-1760' (Univ. of Hull,
      1980), p. 3.
37   A.H. Johnson, 'The Disappearance of the Small Landowner'
      (1909, reprinted Merlin Press, 1963).
38   G.E. Mingay, The Size of Farms in the Eighteenth Century,
      'Econ. Hist. Rev.', 2nd ser., vol. 14, no. 3 (1962), pp. 469-
      88.
39   Habakkuk, English Landownership, p. 9.
40   Johnson, 'Small Landowner', p. 144.
41   J.V. Beckett, English Landownership in the Later Seventeeth
      and Eighteenth Centuries: The Debate and Problems, 'Econ.
      Hist. Rev.', 2nd ser., vol. 30 (1977), p. 581.
42   Cooper, The Social Distribution, p. 421.
43   Thompson, The Social Distribution, p. 509.
44   Cooper, The Social Distribution, p. 420; Bateman, 'Great
      Landowners', pp. 501-11.
45   Mingay, 'English Landed Society', p. 6.
46   Mingay, 'The Gentry', p. 59.
47   Cooper, The Social Distribution, p. 421.
48   Ibid., p. 432.
49   Calculated from Bateman, 'Great Landowners'.
50   Knight service and socage were types of land tenure involving
      payment of rent or service, in the former case military service,
      to a feudal lord.
51   G.C. Brodrick, 'English Land and English Landlords' (1881,
      reprinted David and Charles, Newton Abbot, 1968), p. 99.
      See also J.R. Goody, J. Thirsk and E.P. Thompson (eds),
      'Family and Inheritance: Rural Society in Western Europe,
      1200-1800' (Cambridge Univ. Press, 1976), ch. 7.
52   There is controversy among economic historians over the
      differentiation between strict settlements and marriage settle-
      ments and the extent to which they contributed to the accumu-
      lation and preservation of great estates. See, H.J. Habakkuk,
      Marriage Settlements in the Eighteenth Century, 'TRHS', 4th
      ser., vol. 32 (1950), pp. 15-30; L. Bonfield, Marriage Settle-
      ments and the "Rise of Great Estates": The Demographic
      Aspect, 'Econ. Hist. Rev.', 2nd ser., vol. 32 (1979), pp. 483-
      93; B. English and J. Saville, Family Settlement and the "Rise
      of Great Estates", 'Econ. Hist. Rev.', 2nd ser., vol. 33
      (1980), pp. 556-8; L. Bonfield, Marriage Settlements and the
      "Rise of Great Estates": A Rejoinder, 'Econ. Hist. Rev.',
      2nd ser., vol. 33 (1980), pp. 559-63.
53   The quotation does not refer to landownership *per se* but is
      an apt description of the binding commitment of the strict
      settlement. E. Burke, 'Reflections on the Revolution in France',
      C.C. O'Brien (ed.) (Penguin, Harmondsworth, 1968), pp. 194-5.

54 G.C. Cheshire, 'The Modern Law of Real Property', 9th edn
    (Butterworths, London, 1962), p. 77.
55 Habakkuk, Marriage Settlements, p. 18.
56 H.J. Habakkuk, The Rise and Fall of English Landed Families
    1600-1800, 'TRHS', 5th ser., vol. 29 (1978), p. 206.
57 J.B. Burke, 'The Rise of Great Families', 2nd edn (Longmans
    Green, London, 1873), p. 41.
58 Habakkuk, Marriage Settlements, p. 23.
59 Ibid., p. 30.
60 Stone, 'Crisis of the Aristocracy', pp. 175-6.
61 Habakkuk, The Rise and Fall, pp. 190-1.
62 C. Clay, Marriage, Inheritance and the Rise of Large Estates
    in England, 1660-1815, 'Econ. Hist. Rev.', 2nd ser., vol. 21
    (1968), pp. 503-18.
63 Burke, 'The Rise of Great Families', pp. 19-22.
64 E. Richards, 'The Leviathan of Wealth' (Routledge and Kegan
    Paul, London, 1973), p. 5. The book describes the Sutherland
    family fortune in the Industrial Revolution and contains a
    detailed account of the rise of the Leveson-Gowers, pp. 5-13.
65 The complete bibliography of publications put out by Burke's
    Peerage is contained in 'Burke's Family Index' (Burke's
    Peerage, London, 1976), pp. xiii-xxx.
66 The first printing of the Landed Gentry appeared in 3 volumes
    under the title, 'A Genealogical and Heraldic History of the
    Commoners of Great Britain and Ireland, enjoying territorial
    possessions of High Official Rank, but invested with Heritable
    Honours' (Burke's, London, 1833-5).
67 See note 35.
68 E. Walford, 'The County Families of the United Kingdom' (R.
    Hardwicke and Boque, London, 1860).
69 J.L. Sanford and M. Townsend, 'The Great Governing
    Families of England' (2 vols., William Blackwood, London,
    1865).
70 For a discussion of the land question see, F.M.L. Thompson,
    Land and Politics in England in the Nineteenth Century,
    'TRHS', 5th ser., vol. 15 (1965), pp. 23-44.
71 G. Barnett Smith, 'Life and Speeches of John Bright' (2 vols.,
    Hodder and Stoughton, London, 1881), vol. 1, p. 227.
72 Brodrick, 'English Land', pp. 157-66; Bateman, 'Great Land-
    owners', pp. v-xxvi.
73 Bateman, 'Great Landowners', pp. 501-11.
74 'Spectator', 12 Feb. 1876, p. 201.
75 Bateman, 'Great Landowners', pp. 501-11.
76 Ibid., pp. 501-11.
77 'Spectator', 4 March 1876, p. 306.
78 For later editions Bateman also included landowners with over
    2,000 acres of land.
79 The 2nd and 3rd editions of Bateman, 'Great Landowners',
    were published in 1878 and 1879.
80 Bateman's 4th edn, 'Great Landowners', was printed in 1883
    but the data base is 1873 and though it contained some updated

entries the material essentially spans the decade 1873 to 1883, hence the adoption here of the date *circa* 1880.

81   Calculated from Bateman, 'Great Landowners', pp. 1-494.
Individual entries for each landowner record both the acreage
and rental value of the total property and their breakdown
by county. It was possible therefore to identify those landowners with a minimum of 3,000 acres in England. The number
of owners is a misnomer for the number of families as with few
exceptions Bateman added the son's acres to the father, the
Dowager's property in every case where it would go back to
the main estate, to her eldest son and the wife's property to
the husband.
82   G.E. Collins, 'History of the Brocklesby Hounds 1700-1901'
(Sampson, Low Maston, London, 1902), p. 9.
83   P. Pusey, On the Agricultural Improvements of Lincolnshire,
'JRASE', vol. 4 (1843), p. 299.
84   H.E. Strickland, 'General View of the Agriculture of the East
Riding of Yorkshire' (London, 1812), p. 107.
85   The county grouping tends to correspond with generally recognised administrative regions before the re-organisation of
county boundaries under the 'Local Authority Act, 1972'
(effective 1974). Some adjustments have been made in the
Midlands, East and North West to provide a regional definition
more aligned with major agricultural areas. Pre-1974 counties
have been adhered to in order to more accurately use the
data from Bateman, 'Great Landowners'. For purposes of comparison pre-1974 boundaries have been retained throughout
the book.
86   For county calculations the three Ridings of Yorkshire were
amalgamated, giving a total of 39 counties. Monmouth is
excluded.
87   L. Stone and J.C.F. Stone, Country Houses and their Owners
in Hertfordshire 1540-1879 in W.O. Aydelotte, A.C. Boque and
R.W. Fogel (eds), 'The Dimensions of Quantitative Research
in History' (Princeton Univ. Press, New Jersey, 1972), p. 58.
88   Burke, 'The Rise of Great Families', p. 37.
89   Ibid., p. 41.
90   Bateman, 'Great Landowners', pp. 499-500.

2 THE STUDY POPULATION AND ESTATE DEFINITIONS

THE SAMPLE

It was beyond the limitations of present work to attempt to assemble information on the history of all large landowners and their family property prior to 1800 and to trace each through to 1980. By means of a sample the total population of 1,363 has been reduced to a more manageable number of 500, and it is information pertaining to this group which forms the basis of quantitative evaluation and descriptive analysis in the remainder of the book. The procedure adopted in the sample survey and the selection problems encountered are given in Appendices 2 and 3. An attempt was made to obtain a proportional representation of principal estates from each county in England such that the balance of great-landowner and greater-gentry estates per county and for England as a whole represented a microcosm of the 1880 picture. The 500 sample estates constitute over a third of the total large-landowner group and comprised 124 great landowners (25 per cent) and 376 greater gentry (75 per cent).

ESTATE DEFINITIONS

To the layman an estate is a tangible entity of physical parts. More popularly, the mental image of an English estate is rural rather than urban and certainly the term 'landed estate' appears to have both rural and historic connotations. Usually implicit in the association is the presence of a country house and park forming the core of the property and an area of farm land in part or entirely operated under the landlord-tenant system. Such a meaning is precisely that implied here by the terms 'landed estate', 'historic estate' and 'traditional estate'. In the present context it is the major physical characteristics and generally recognised visual elements of a 'traditional estate' that are of major concern.

To this point the discussion of large-landowner property has been based on the total extent of each landowner's acreage in England, a figure used to define the size category for landed status, that is, whether great-landowner or greater-gentry. While land distribution has been described on a county and regional basis, the land belonging to each owner has been treated as an amorphous area. It is next appropriate to examine the physical characteristics of land in relation to the above definition of a 'landed estate', and to define more precisely the land area that forms the focus of this study.

Estate growth seldom was and seldom is a neat process of land accretion around a central core. Through time properties may have been consolidated by piecemeal purchase and exchange of adjacent lands and sales of outlying portions, but in the late nineteenth century many estates appear to have comprised a number of separate land parcels of varying sizes within the boundaries of one county or widely scattered over a number of counties. Thus, the respective properties of two owners may be equal in size but vastly different in shape. Take, for example, the nearly 57,000-acre property of the 4th Earl of Yarborough held in a fairly compact block in North Lincolnshire in the 1880s as compared with nearly 58,000 acres owned by the 3rd Earl Brownlow spread over seven English counties with little contiguity. Does the first situation constitute an estate while the second represent many estates? In his study *Estate Capital*, Denman introduced the notion of managerial control as the deciding factor of definition so that a property, whether compact or scattered, administered centrally was taken to be one estate.[1] This idea is accepted in principle, but in reality is only applicable in a situation where knowledge of estate management can be readily obtained. In an historical study such information is not always available. As a result a more qualified spatial division of landed property has been adopted here based on the location of the major residential and administrative nucleus. The distinction has been made between the 'home' or 'principal' estate, 'secondary' estates and 'peripheral' land. The 'home' estate is defined as *that land area, for the most part located within the confines of a single county, which included within its boundaries the estate 'nucleus', 'core' or 'heartland', that is, the principal country house, related buildings and amenity lands owned by the family.*

As the primary data base for all property in 1880 was the county it was considered appropriate to work at the scale for which data were available. As a general rule, therefore, the extent of a home estate was equated with the total acreage in the county containing the principal country house. Although the majority of home estates were in fact located within a single county, a number of objections can be raised at such a definitional straitjacket. It was apparent, for example, from sales catalogues, estate maps and other records that a landed estate, whether ring fenced or scattered in a number of blocks, sometimes occupied land in two or more adjacent counties. In a few cases in the sample a county boundary cut across the amenity land of a home estate, as at Rushmore Park where the country house and part of the park woodlands lay in Wiltshire, while the majority of the estate lay in Dorset. The extensive land area of the Burghley Estate straddled the county boundaries of Northamptonshire, Huntingdonshire (the Soke of Peterborough) and Lincolnshire where they converged near Stamford. The Greenlands Estate was cut in two by the River Thames which formed part of the Buckinghamshire/Berkshire boundary, while part of

the Wytham Abbey home estate occupied the panhandle in north
Berkshire and the remainder lay in the surrounding countryside
of Oxfordshire. In a number of cases it was apparent from the
location of the estate heartland in close proximity to a county
boundary that an acreage listed in the adjacent county probably
formed part of the home estate. Where confirmation was available
the acreage was added to the home estate figure but without precise knowledge of the location of each property it could not be
presupposed that land owned in an adjacent county was aligned
with the home estate or with a secondary estate. It is not inconceivable, therefore, that in a number of cases the acreage recorded
as the home estate underestimated the actual extent of the home
property. However, as a corollary, a family sometimes held more
than one estate heartland within a county, that is, owned more
than one large country house and associated amenity land. The
two, or more, estates even though combined under the same total
county acreage would remain distinct in name and may well have
been administered separately. For example, the acreage of the
Duke of Devonshire's land in Derbyshire as recorded by Bateman
included not only the home estate at Chatsworth but also the
Hardwick Hall Estate, a family property held by the Duke's son
Lord Hartington.[2] Thus the adoption of the total county acreage
in some instances embraced more than the home estate and may
have included one or even more secondary estates, though only
the principal country house and amenity lands were followed
through to the present day. Clearly the larger the county the
more likely that the entire home estate would be within its bounds,
but also possibly there could be another detached secondary
estate in the same county and in such cases the extent of the home
estate would be exaggerated.

Given the constraints and recognised limitations the county
figures were nevertheless used for the majority of sample properties to denote the size of the home estate. In most cases the county
acreage represented a significant proportion of a landowner's total
acreage (Table 2.1). In over 75 per cent of the sample, 382 cases,
the home estate comprised over 70 per cent of the total land area
while as high as 90 per cent of the sample group held over half of
their land in one county. Looked at in a slightly different manner
for 450 of the 500 landowners, the home estate was over 3,000
acres in extent, for 47 it was between 1,000 and 3,000 acres and
in only three cases was it less than 1,000 acres.

The property of great landowners was generally more dispersed
than that of the greater gentry, but extensive size, as already
shown (p. 34), did not necessarily imply that estate land was
scattered over a number of counties. Over half of the great landowners had 90 per cent or more of their land contained within a
single county and this included five of the twenty-one territorial
magnates; the Earl of Feversham (Yorks.), the Earl of Leicester
(Norfolk), the Earl of Pembroke (Wilts.), Sir Tatton Sykes (Yorks.)
and the Earl of Yarborough (Lincs.).

Even though the home estate may have been a large proportion

Table 2.1: Home-estate Acreage as a Per Cent of Total Acreage[a]

Percentage	100%		70-99%		50-69%		<50%		Total
Category	No.	%	No.	%	No.	%	No.	%	No.
Great landowners	39	31	43	35	19	15	23	19	124
Greater gentry	185	49	115	31	51	14	25	7	376
Total of large landowners	224	45	158	32	70	14	48	10	500

Note: a. English acreage only.
Source: Bateman, *Great Landowners*.

of total acreage, the remaining land could be scattered over many counties. The Duke of Cleveland, the Earl Cooper, the Duke of Devonshire, the Earl Howe and Lord Overstone each held land in ten or more counties and it was not uncommon for great landowners or greater gentry to hold property whether a few acres, a few hundred or a few thousand, in four or more counties.

Land not considered to be part of the home estate can be defined under two categories either as peripheral land or as a secondary estate. *Peripheral land implies a block of land or scattered land parcels seemingly detached from any estate nucleus and outside the home estate county. A secondary estate is another landed estate complete with country house and amenity land but given secondary status in relation to the dominant home estate.* Often secondary estates had been acquired in marriage or through inheritance and were occupied by the Dowager, a landowner's married sons and daughters, or were used as a seasonal residence by the landed family. It was not always clear, however, which country house was the principal family residence in 1880, and therefore which property was to be defined and studied as the home estate. For the most part the estate name listed by Bateman was taken to be the major residence, but some families undoubtedly maintained a number of large country houses which had more or less equal claim to fly the family flag. Country houses belonging to the 3rd Earl Brownlow in 1880 well illustrate the point. The ancestral property of the family was located at Belton in Lincolnshire, but in 1849, under the terms of John William Egerton's will, among other extensive properties the Ashridge Estate in Hertfordshire passed to the eldest son of the 1st Earl Brownlow. Evidence for the late nineteenth century, at the time of the 3rd Earl, would seem to suggest that both estate houses were maintained on a more or less equal footing; Belton was favoured by the Earl but Ashridge was convenient to London.[3] In the sample selection the balance was weighted towards Belton in that it was the original family seat and also listed by Bateman. The home-estate property was thus identified with Lincolnshire and not Hertfordshire; and the latter was defined as a secondary estate.

The total extent of a landowner's property thus consisted of either a home estate, or any combination of a home estate with

peripheral lands and/or secondary estates. The home estate was
a typically defined landed estate. It contained an estate nucleus
comprising the principal country house, gardens and parkland
and surrounding this core, whether as a ring fence or scattered
property, but predominantly within the confines of the same
county would be the remaining rural land whether in part farmed,
wooded, quarried, or mined, occupied by rural settlement, let or
in-hand.

In terms of the physical changes and landscape impact of landed
estates it is the home estate that is the primary focus of attention
throughout this work. However, it will be seen that sales of
peripheral land and secondary estates have been instrumental in
prolonging the life of many home estates and in some cases secondary estates later assumed principal status. Consequently, land
external to the home estate cannot be entirely disregarded in this
analysis.

Finally, it should be recognised that an estate is a complex
entity having abstract as well as physical dimensions. The abstract
qualities of temporal continuity or duration and legal ownership
and control are not so apparent as physical attributes but are
equally as important in that they have played, and continue to
play, a role in determining the character and survival of landed
estates.[4]

The temporal aspect of estate continuity relates both to the
land area and to ownership. Over time most properties fluctuate
in size and shape as land is bought, sold, exchanged or inherited.
The question is raised as to whether these physical changes alter
an estate so that successive generations in effect inherit a new
property, or whether an 'estate' endures through the line of inheritance no matter how changed its physical form might be.[5] The
latter appears the generally accepted understanding. The distinction made between an estate heartland and the remaining land
area permits a more tangible definition of this somewhat abstract
notion. Just as an amoebic organism may constantly change its
shape and size, but ceases to exist without a nucleus, so also the
loss of an estate heartland, whether through physical destruction
or legal separation from all other land, can be said to destroy the
temporal and historic continuity of a traditional landed estate.

The temporal dimension of ownership refers to the length of time
a landed estate has been owned by the same family. Thus, with
reference to the 500 sample properties, by 1880 some were of fairly
recent origin having been acquired in the eighteenth and nineteenth
centuries compared with others that had remained in the same
family since the twelfth or thirteenth centuries.

A family association with an estate also has definition in legal
terms. In land law an 'estate' is an abstract entity which implies
an interest in land, a condition which permits the exercise of
proprietary rights for a prescribed period of time. The duration
of an 'estate' in this sense is limited according to the method by
which it is held. A freehold estate may be held in fee simple, in
fee tail or for life. In all cases the 'tenant' is considered to be the

owner of the land, but in each situation the freedom to exercise proprietory rights differs. Curtailment of rights imposed on inheritors of settled estates, prior to the Settled Land Act of 1882, effectively prevented the break-up of estate property. Thus, the legal dimensions of ownership have been and continue to be relevant to the long-term preservation of landed estates. But the duration of a family association with a landed estate is not strictly bound by the legal root of ownership. Denman, coining the term 'ownership personality', has clearly described the complex relationship between estate, duration, legal and temporal ownership.[6] The creation of new forms of ownership in the twentieth century have led to changes in 'ownership personality', legal ownership in some instances being transferred from a private individual to an estate company or trust but leaving the family control over the estate virtually unaffected. Thus, the association between family and estate continues even though the legal ownership may change, a notion that has played a key role in the present day survival of a number of landed estates.

Equipped with a sample population and definitional entity known as the home estate it remains to examine some of the major physical characteristics of the 500 properties in order to compose a picture of the variety, distinctiveness and scale of features that comprised the landscape of English landed estates in the late nineteenth century.

NOTES

1   D.R. Denman, 'Estate Capital' (Allen and Unwin, London, 1957), p. 22.
2   J. Bateman, 'Great Landowners of Great Britain and Ireland' 4th edn (1883, reprinted Leicester Univ. Press, 1971), p. 130.
3   D. Colt, 'A Prospect of Ashridge' (Phillimore, London, 1980), p. 207.
4   Denman, 'Estate Capital', p. 19.
5   Ibid., p. 27.
6   Ibid., p. 27.

3 THE COUNTRY HOUSE IN THE LANDSCAPE FROM THE MIDDLE AGES TO THE LATE VICTORIAN ERA

It may be large, it may be small; it may be palatial, it may be manorial; it may be of stone, brick, or stucco, or even of beams and plaster; it may be the seat of the aristocracy or the home of the gentry - what it is, it possesses one outstanding character-istic: it is the English country house. V. Sackville-West, 'English Country Houses' in W.J. Turner (ed.), *The Englishman's Country* (Collins, London, 1945), p. 53.

The country house[1] is the focal point and principal physical struc-ture of a traditional landed estate and more than any other feature a visual symbol of the wealth and status of the landowner. But country houses are more than this. Their collective history presents a cultural index of upper-class English society, a spectrum of changing values, fashions and tastes mirrored in the architectural styles and decorations selected by each generation of landowners. It has been frequently said that the country house is the greatest contribution made by England to the visual arts. Sheer volume of documentation alone does much to underline this statement and undoubtedly more attention has been paid to the country house than to any other estate landscape feature. Innumerable works have described the internal and external detail of country houses, collections contained within them, and their association with famous people, both the architects who designed them and the families who occupied them.[2] What has happened to England's country houses over the past hundred years is a major concern of this book, but in order to appreciate the significance of changes that have occurred, it is necessary first to understand something of the origin and development of the country house. This chapter thus paints the picture to the end of the nineteenth century to that period described as the 'zenith of country-house culture' when the landed estates and their country houses were most per-vasive in the English landscape. The immense and rich variety of country houses evident by 1880 is well illustrated by houses in the sample group which contained examples that ranged from those originating in the Middle Ages to those newly built in the Victorian era. The principal focus is the houses themselves rather than their contents or the history enacted within their walls, even though it is fully recognised that their heritage value is assessed in more than 'bricks and mortar'.

CHANGING ARCHITECTURAL STYLES TO c. 1880

Many sample estate heartlands were in all probability the site of
early manors that existed even before the Domesday Survey of
1086, but by 1880 relatively few possessed a house that could be
dated prior to 1500, not necessarily as a complete unit but preserving within its physical structure a portion, small or large, of
such early origin. Among the more notable survivals of the Middle
Ages were the castles[3], although the majority that were constructed
prior to the sixteenth century in most cases had been incorporated
into subsequent extensions, alterations and rebuildings by 1880.
Dunster Castle (Somerset), Leeds Castle (Kent), Raby Castle
(Durham) and Warwick Castle, for example, were all extended over
many generations and retained much of their early fabric and
character; Ford Castle (Northld.) suffered several times at the
hands of the Scots but some of its early towers remained among a
range of new buildings constructed from the seventeenth century
onwards. Rowton Castle (Salop), Kimbolton Castle (Hunts.) and
Streatlam Castle (Durham) were replaced by new country houses
such that by the late nineteenth century their early origins had
been obscured. At Ripley (West Riding) only the gatehouse survived from the medieval castle; the remainder, with the exception
of the Tower built in 1555, was rebuilt in 1780. Part of the early
fabric of Rockingham Castle (Northants.), Norman masonry and
thirteenth-century work, survived the remodelling of the sixteenth
and seventeenth centuries which transformed the appearance of
the building from a castle to a house, although its defensive hill-
top position and outer bailey were reminders of its previous history.
While the original site was retained for subsequent rebuilding at
Rockingham, such was not the case at Scotney (Kent) where the
fourteenth-century moated castle shared the grounds in 1880 with
a late-Georgian country house which replaced the castle as the
principal estate residence.
    In Cumberland, Westmorland and Northumberland a number of
country houses in the sample originated as fortified Keeps or Pele
towers built for defensive purposes at a time when the north of
England was in danger of Scottish invasion, a threat not removed
until the Act of Union in 1604. Callaly Castle, Dovenby Hall,
Hutton-in-the-Forest, Levens Hall and Netherby Hall each incorporated a Pele tower into later house extensions. The tower at
Dovenby probably dated from the twelfth century[4] while the others
originated in the fourteenth century.
    In other regions of England fortified manor houses or manor
houses enclosed within fortifications also survived from the Middle
Ages to the late nineteenth century. Powderham Castle (Devon),
the name belying its origins as a fourteenth-century defensive
manor, was damaged in the Civil War but reconstructed and remodelled in the eighteenth and nineteenth centuries. Penshurst
Place (Kent) was built around 1340 as a medieval manor house and
was enclosed within a curtain of fortified walls later in the century.
After further additions in the sixteenth and early seventeenth

centuries it remained essentially unaltered until some repairs were undertaken in 1820; one of the few houses to retain much of its medieval character and to escape drastic alteration in the seventeenth and eighteenth centuries. Broughton Castle (Oxford.) had a somewhat parallel history. It also originated as an early-fourteenth-century fortified manor and was subsequently enclosed by a defensive wall of which little remained by the late nineteenth century. Broughton was later transformed into an Elizabethan mansion but much of its early fabric was retained and little external alterations took place in the following years. Oxburgh Hall (Norfolk) was a moated brick mansion built in 1482, a house more famed for its essentially ornamental gatehouse than any other feature. The external façade of this house was much altered in the nineteenth century. Hampton Court in Herefordshire, said to have been built on the proceeds of ransom money from French prisoners captured at Agincourt, dated from 1434. It was remodelled in 1700 and reconstructed in the 1830s but retained its external Tudor character. Country houses at Hunstanton (Norfolk) and Cornbury (Oxford.) also had their origin rooted in medieval times as did other sample houses, but many underwent drastic alteration and rebuilding which obliterated their early history and relatively few houses of note survived virtually intact from the pre-1500 era. The majority that occupied estate heartlands by the late nineteenth century dated from after 1500. Thus, Petworth (Sussex) was completely rebuilt in the late seventeenth century obscuring its origin as a thirteenth-century manor house,[5] and a new house was erected on a virgin site at Harlaxton (Lincs.) in the 1830s prior to the demolition of the medieval manor that had served as the principal estate residence to that time.

In the early Middle Ages houses in the countryside served as temporary dwellings for feudal lords who moved successively from one to another covering their extensive manorial domains. The lord's house came to serve as the social, legal and administrative hub of the local manor, or group of manors, but the transition from house in the country, as a transitory dwelling, to country house, a permanent focal point of a landed estate, was a gradual process that evolved from the late Middle Ages when manor houses became the residences and homes of lesser lords and knights who began to establish closer ties with their landed property.

Fortified castles and moated manors were characteristic of this early period and requirements of defence found expression in architectural style and in the choice of site. Styles, for the most part, were irregular and asymmetrical and houses were sited for strategic reasons on hilltops or surrounded by water with less apparent regard for the aesthetic qualities of landscape setting compared with the centuries that followed.

The dissolution of the monasteries and the dispersal of monastic lands in the mid-sixteenth century provided opportunities for the creation of a number of country houses adapted from ecclesiastical buildings as exemplified in the sample by Chicksands Priory (Beds.), Milton Abbey (Dorset), Hitchin Priory (Herts.),

Walsingham Abbey (Norfolk), Delapre Abbey (Northants.),
Mottisfont Abbey and Palace House, Beaulieu (Hants). In the
century following Dissolution other houses were built on the site
of former monastic properties. Rufford Abbey (Notts.) was built
in the period 1580 to 1610 from the stones of the former abbey,
and Wroxton Abbey (Oxford.) was erected in the early seventeenth
century on the site of a former priory, both estates and houses
retaining their ecclesiastic name. Garendon Hall (Leics.),
Lanhydrock (Cornwall) and Wilton House (Wilts.), all built in the
seventeenth century, also occupied sites of former monastic
buildings.

As the country house became established as a permanent residence and focal point of a landed property there also emerged an
appreciation of more aesthetic ideals in building which hinged on
a romantic sense of antiquity and led to a move away from the
traditions of gothic design that had dominated medieval ecclesiastical
architecture, towards the gradual adoption of classical decoration
and ideals for secular buildings, particularly country houses.

Though, as noted by Summerson, the Renaissance proper was
over in Italy by 1520, the spirit of the Renaissance spread
throughout Europe in the sixteenth century and classical design
also became manifest in a variety of forms in English architecture.[6]
Italian artists were present at the Royal Courts from the time of
Henry VIII, but ties with Italy were partially severed following
the break with the Church of Rome in 1533 and much of the early
classical influence to affect English architecture, principally the
use of ornamental detail and symmetry in design, was indirectly
imported via the Low Countries. With regard to the adoption of
classical concepts it has been said of this period that 'the Eliza-
bethans approached the classical treasury in the spirit of pirates
rather than as disciples'.[7] House-building traditions of earlier
centuries died hard and the domestic architecture of the late
Tudor, Elizabethan and Jacobean eras exhibited a synthesis of
medieval and classical features which produced a stimulating and
rich variety of individual country houses.[8]

One of the most important 'prodigy-houses'[9] erected in the
Elizabethan era was John Thynne's new house at Longleat. The
priory that occupied the site in 1541 had been rebuilt as the
principal estate residence but it was destroyed by fire in 1567.
In 1568 work began on a new house that provided a fine example
of the hybrid style which brought together medieval and classical
details. Adherence to classical symmetry in the external design
was thrown out of balance at the skyline where the irregular
arrangement of eight pepperpot domes and other ornamentation
reflected a refusal to break the ties with traditional decoration.
Robert Smythson, (master mason to Elizabeth I) who was involved
in the building of Longleat also built three other houses in the
sample group; Burton Agnes (East Riding[10]), Doddington Hall
(Lincs.) and Lulworth Castle (Dorset).[11] The house at Burton
Agnes, constructed from 1601 to 1610, similarly embraced the
Renaissance in its symmetrical façade, yet also retained a medieval

spirit in its high gables and vertical proportions. Defensive
structures, throwbacks to bygone centuries were also retained
in house design, but turrets became decorative features and gate-
houses, similar in purpose to that designed at Oxburgh (Norfolk)
a century earlier, served only to set off the house at both Burton
Agnes and Doddington Hall.

Among the other great houses of this era in the sample, each
portraying a synthesis of Renaissance and traditional detail were
Burghley House begun in the mid-1550s and Castle Ashby in 1574
both in Northamptonshire and Audley End (Essex) the most
classical of the three, constructed in the Jacobean period from
1603 to 1616.

The prodigy-houses were built for ostentation and display, some
occupied prominent and assertive sites and made no compromise
with nature. Little attempt was made to harmonise with landscape
setting. Much of the incentive for their construction derived from
the influence of the Royal Court. Elizabeth I, more than her successors James I and Charles I, made annual pilgrimages into the
English countryside to the large country houses of the nobility
which were purposefully designed or adapted for the reception,
entertainment and lodging of the entire Court. Hospitality to the
monarchy could bring rewards of favour, perhaps a title, a grant
of land, an office or a pension.

The immense scale of prodigy-houses was by no means reflected
in all country houses of the period. They were monumental edifices
in comparison to those designed to serve as the family seat and
ancestral home of the less ambitious, or less wealthy, nobility
and gentry. In Sussex, Glynde Place, an Elizabethan courtyard
house was built about 1568, and at Parham Park the foundation
stone for a new house was laid in 1577. Sherborne Castle in
Dorset provided a fine example of Elizabethan romanticism, built
by Sir Walter Raleigh in 1594 and later extended with the addition
of four wings in 1625. Over sixty houses in the sample had their
origin in the sixteenth century of which only a handful were
prodigy-houses.

Compared with the Elizabethan and Jacobean eras the Caroline
period from 1625 to 1685 was one of relative inactivity and few
great houses were constructed in the decades preceeding and
following the Civil War, though there were exceptions. Of outstanding note was Wilton House (Wilts.) which was rebuilt for the
Earl of Pembroke in the 1630s. Raynham (Norfolk) was begun in
1622 and Rousham (Oxford.) around 1635; both were later remodelled in the eighteenth century by William Kent. Chevening,
Godinton, Somerhill and Less Court, all in Kent, were also
creations of this period. Two other houses in the sample are notable
examples of the prevailing Dutch and Flemish influence in house
building. Broome Park (Kent) built in the 1630s has been described as Jacobean in spirit, its design was wholly symmetrical in
an H-plan, typical of the period, and the external façade was
enriched with Dutch gables and cut and moulded brickwork laid
in Flemish style.[12] Swakeleys (Middlesex) was built from 1629

to 1638, also in an H-plan. It too was brick built and was rich in external detail including Dutch gabling. Towards the end of the Caroline era, in the more stable years following the Commonwealth, French influence was notable in the design of a number of larger homes as at Euston Hall (Suffolk) built from 1666 to 1670 and at Ragley Hall (Warwicks.) built in 1677.

As the seventeenth century progressed, classical philosophy became the most authoritative force in English architecture and the eccentricities of medieval traditionalism were gradually submerged by the rules of classical ideology. Aspiring artists and architects in their search for classical inspiration were patronised in their travels by wealthy landowners, and the early disciples of the Grand Tour spread the popularity of imported design ideas and concepts from continental Europe. Italian buildings designed by Palladio (1518–80) were a strong influence on English classical tastes, and the ideals of design in the work of Inigo Jones (1573–1652), the most renowned apostle of Palladianism, marked a turning point in the history of English architecture.[13] Although Jones returned from his last visit to Italy as early as 1613 and had completed the Banqueting House by 1622, a model of Renaissance idealism, his style of architecture did not immediately influence contemporary English tastes either amongst the court aristocracy or the emerging landed gentry and it took a full fifty years or more before his classical ideals were absorbed into the English tradition.

The Renaissance was evident in most country-house building during the seventeenth century in the regard for symmetry and the use of classical decorations, but it was in the late seventeenth and eighteenth century that a mania for building in the classical style took hold on England. As with earlier periods some houses were grandiose while others were of a lesser scale, but the adoption of classical style and detail was pervasive both in the monumental Baroque edifices created in the period 1690 to 1730 and associated with the names of Wren, Vanbrugh and Hawksmoor, and in the fashionable villas of the greater gentry built in the eighteenth century. Of the former, which included Blenheim Palace, Castle Howard and Chatsworth, only Chatsworth is in the sample survey, an Elizabethan house completely rebuilt by William Talman for the 1st Duke of Devonshire from 1687 to 1707.

Even though country houses of the early Georgian period from 1715 to 1760 betrayed a superficial homogeneity of style, the classical hold was constantly challenged by the individualism and variety of English taste. Notable houses in the sample that were built in this period in predominantly Palladian style included Sutton Scarsdale (Derby.), begun in the 1720s, Bretton Park and Nostell Priory (Yorks.), products of the 1720s and 1730s, and Clandon Park (Surrey) built for the Onslow family by Giacomo Leoni in 1729, a house that was renowned as much for its Palladian interior as its classical exterior. One of the largest was Holkham Hall in Norfolk, described as a complete Anglo-Palladian synthesis on a monumental scale, begun in 1734 for Thomas Coke.[14] Holkham was designed in collaboration with William Kent and Lord Burlington, the latter renowned as one of the most important patrons of Palladian architecture in England.

Houses already in existence were modified to incorporate classical features, well exemplified by Lyme Park in Cheshire built in the Elizabethan era but remodelled and given a classical Palladian exterior by Giacomo Leoni from 1725 to 1735.

In the mid-Georgian period from 1760 to 1800, neo-classicism and the pure lines of the neo-Grecian style became fashionable in country house architecture, but aligned with this development were the emerging forces of romanticism, a philosophy that pursued the aesthetic ideal of natural beauty. The idea of movement in architecture and the blending of country house and surrounding landscape were present in the work of Vanbrugh at the turn of the century and the concept was fundamentally explored in the late eighteenth century through the classical building style. This was the era of the great landscape gardeners when house and setting were viewed as an integral whole, and when the heartlands of the landed estates became artistic masterpieces.

The undercurrent of romanticism was manifest in a variety of forms not least among which was the revival of gothic design. The reconstruction of Strawberry Hill by Horace Walpole from 1747 to 1776 and the building of Downton Castle (Hereford.) by Richard Payne Knight in 1778 were among the first major attempts to break away from the classical ideals in country-house building. The contrived castellated appearance and asymmetrical composition of Downton Castle said to have been inspired by the semi-fortified mansions in the background of paintings by Claude Lorrain and Gaspard Poussin, epitomised the principles of the Picturesque, a cult which emerged first in landscape gardening and later in country-house building towards the turn of the century. There followed attempts to reassert the purity of gothic design as 'the style' by Loudon in 1896, by A.W.N. Pugin in 1836 and later by Ruskin.[15] However, throughout the late Georgian era, from 1800 to 1840, country houses embraced a synthesis of classical regularity and gothic design and it was not until the Victorian period that classicism was effectively submerged as a force in English architecture.

A significant group of houses in the sample built from the mid-Georgian to the end of the late Georgian period were predominantly classical in style, a mode that found expression throughout the English countryside. Neo-classicism of the late eighteenth century was well expressed by the work of Robert Adam and more than any other house that he remodelled or designed, the south front of Kedleston Hall in Derbyshire begun about 1761 embodied the synthesis of neo-classicism and movement in architecture. In collaboration with John Carr of York he also designed Harewood House for Edwin Lascelles, one of the largest country houses in Yorkshire. Other Renaissance houses in the sample group include Berrington Hall (Hereford.), newly constructed in the late 1770s, and Attingham (Salop), a modest Queen Anne house that was transformed into a classical mansion for the 1st Lord Berwick in 1785. The turn of the century witnessed the building of Dodington Park (Glos.), a classical work undertaken by James Wyatt for Christopher Bethell Codrington, begun in 1796 and completed around 1813 and Southill Park (Beds.) described as one of the most sophisticated neo-classical houses in England.[16] The latter was remodelled for Samuel Whitbread II whose father, founder of the Whitbread Brewery, had purchased the estate at Southill in 1795 for £85,000.[17] The Grange (Hants) was remodelled in 1804; Castletown House (Cumberland) built in 1811; Willey Park (Salop) 1813 to 1815; Leigh Court, 1814 and Cothelstone Court in Somerset, 1817 to 1818; Cresswell Hall (Northld.) 1821 to 1824 and Trellisick in 1825, a house referred to as the severest neo-Grecian mansion in Cornwall;[18] many but by no means all of the sample houses that were built, rebuilt and remodelled in the classical mode pre-1840.

Re-emergence of gothic tastes and the syntheses of gothic and picturesque were evident in a number of houses in the sample built in the late Georgian period. Sheffield Park and West Dean Park in Sussex, both influenced by the hand of James Wyatt, were among the earliest country houses to re-embrace the gothic style. Pentillie Castle (Cornwall) was extended around 1815 in Tudor-Gothic style. Snelston Hall (Derby.) was an elaborate gothic construction designed in 1828, Beckett House (Berks.) was another Tudor-Gothic house of the 1830s as was Harlaxton Manor (Lincs.) and Scotney Castle (Kent), the latter not completed until 1843. Scarisbrick Hall (Lancs.) was a picturesque gothic fantasy begun for Charles Scarisbrick by A.W.N. Pugin around 1840 and completed with the addition of a spired gothic tower by Pugin's son in the 1860s. In Suffolk Somerleyton Hall, an eclectic building of predominantly Jacobean style, was remodelled between 1844 and 1851 by the sculptor John Thomas for Sir Morton Peto, a self-made man of the nineteenth century who rose to fortune as a building contractor. In the 1850s, however, Peto's firm ran into financial difficulties and the entire Somerleyton Estate was bought in 1863 by Sir Frank Crossley, the carpet millionaire, whose wealth was already manifest in buildings throughout his native town of Halifax. Preston Hall (Kent), built in 1850 for E.L. Betts, partner to Sir Morton Peto, was also sold for the same reasons, to H.A. Brassey, in 1855.

One of the more acknowledged houses of the late Georgian period built by an amateur architect was Toddington Manor (Glos.), a house rebuilt from 1819 to 1840 by Lord Sudeley. He attempted to adapt gothic architecture to domestic purposes and the result has been described as an historic monument at the meeting point of Georgian and Victorian tastes.[19]

The majority of landed estates that existed in 1880 were already formed by the beginning of the nineteenth century but more than at any other time the years from 1800 to 1880 witnessed a spate of remodelling, rebuilding and extension of country houses at their core. Late Georgian and Victorian England was a period of unprecedented wealth amongst the upper classes. Increased income from agriculture, particularly during the high farming period from the 1840s to the 1870s, from industry and commerce enhanced the wealth of landowners and industrialists. The established landed families were joined in the countryside by the *nouveau riche* of the industrial revolution, and both new and old invested in country-house building as a means of displaying their additional wealth and status. Entertainment on a lavish scale at the ancestral home, more accessible after the 1840s with the development of the railways, was the fashionable pursuit of the times. This was the zenith of the country-house culture. The country house became the centrepiece of the opulent and extravagant life-style of late Georgian and Victorian society. The rationale for the large new houses, for extensive remodelling and for the additional appendages of service wings added to many existing homes, was that such structures would serve many future generations. Landed society did not feel itself threatened even though the undercurrents of change were gathering momentum throughout the century.

It has been said that architecture mirrors the values of society. Late Georgian and Victorian architecture was one of a mixture of styles in an age of extreme extravagance and constant change in a society permeated with confusing and paradoxical values, between profit maximisation on the one hand and the concern for social reform on the other. A general adherence to picturesque principles and a growing anti-classical philosophy emerged in the Victorian period rooted in an impassioned revival of medievalism. Resultant house designs presented an eclectic variety of creations and fashions which carried through to the end of the century. The architecture of this period was also defined in scale. Throughout history house size had been more or less an indicator of status. Even though there was no measurable relationship between the two factors the Elizabethan prodigy-houses and the stately homes of the late seventeenth century undoubtedly demarcated the upper ranks of the titled nobility and wealthy aspirants to titled status, from the remainder of landed society. In the nineteenth century, more especially in the Victorian period, there was an attempt by landed families, old and new, titled and untitled, to stamp their mark of accumulated wealth and status on the landscape; a mark defined as much in scale of building as in any other manner.

Only a few Victorian creations of note in the sample group will be described in an endless list of remodellings, alterations and extensions undertaken throughout England.[20]

In 1865 Robert Kerr was commissioned to design a new country house for John Walter who, as chief proprietor of *The Times*, was a Victorian gentleman of considerable wealth. The Walter family had acquired the estate of Bearwood in Berkshire at the turn of the century and the house was first built as a classical villa in keeping with the prevailing fashion of the day. The new house at Bearwood took nearly a decade to complete at a cost of £120,000 and emerged as a colossal asymmetrical edifice of late Tudor style.

In the nearby county of Bedfordshire, Henry Clutton designed
Old Warden Park, a house of Jacobean style, for John Shuttleworth,
a cotton magnate from Lancashire while further north in the West
Riding, Carlton Hall emerged as Carlton Towers, re-cast in
elaborate gothic detail and considerable quantities of cement by
Edward Pugin from 1874 for Lord Beaumont.

Two of the later Victorian houses to be built on the sample
estates were Stoodleigh Court (Devon) built in Tudor style in
1882 by Sir Ernest George in partnership with H.G. Peto for
Daniel Thomas Carew, and Bryanston (Dorset) built by Norman
Shaw in 1890, a house of more classical design that imitated
ground plans of the early eighteenth century with a central block
and two symmetrical wings. The latter represented one of the
largest English country houses built at the end of the century and
it replaced an earlier house, designed for Viscount Portman by
James Wyatt in 1778. In 1880 Viscount Portman ranked among the
territorial magnates of England, each of whom possessed at least
one country house of considerable, if not colossal proportions.
No doubt motives of visual grandeur appropriate to perceived
status underlay the rebuilding of Bryanston, which was financed
from London ground rents.

DATES OF COUNTRY-HOUSE CONSTRUCTION

From century to century relatively few country houses remained
as testimonials to the dictates of the needs, fashions and tastes
of their period of origin, which poses considerable problems in
attempting to classify the country house that occupied each sample
estate heartland around 1880. Certainly in many cases little insight
as to the age of an estate was provided by the house that stood
at its centre in 1880 as many by that date had been rebuilt several
times. For example, the country house at Kedleston (Derby.) was
the fifth that the Curzon family had built on the same site since
they acquired the estate in the twelfth century. Nor did the
external features of the house c. 1880 necessarily visually reflect
its original period of construction. A high number could be described as houses of many periods. Each major change in style had
brought not only a spate of activity in the form of new houses,
but existing buildings were also remodelled and adapted in the
fashionable mode. It would appear from the sample estates that
modifications to existing houses and complete rebuilding often
occurred with changes of ownership, whether through purchase
or inheritance, which would seem to suggest the need for each
successive owner to stamp a personal mark on the landscape,
the house after all being a tangible monument to the achievements
of the builder. Thus, by the 1880s the majority of older houses
incorporated structural features and decorative details internally
and externally from a number of different periods; changes either
of relatively minor proportion or entirely obscuring the character
of an earlier building.

It is possible, nevertheless, to identify the principal periods and dates of construction for the majority of sample houses and collectively to recognise cycles of investment activity;[21] the term construction denoting not only new houses but also investment in adaptations, alterations and extensions. Clearly an element of caution needs to be introduced in the interpretation of available data since there is generally less material on country-house construction with greater distance back in time, while there are abundant data on what may have been only minor modifications undertaken by prominent architects in more recent times.

Figure 3.1 records both newly built houses as well as instances of investment in alterations. No attempt was made to evaluate the extent of investment, graph 'B' being a total of the occurrences of construction activity details of which were available for nearly four hundred of the sample houses. It was often difficult to distinguish completely rebuilt houses from those only partially remodelled or adapted, but graph 'A' represents the summation, possibly an underestimation, of newly built and completely remodelled or rebuilt houses.

Figure 3.1: Investment in Country Houses on the Sample Estates c. 1500 to 1900

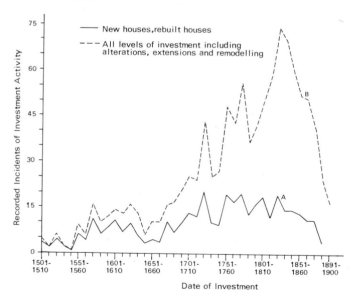

Source: See Note 2.

Four periods of apparent increased activity are evident dating from the beginning of the sixteenth century. The first followed the redistribution of monastic and Crown lands from the mid-sixteenth

century to the early decades of the seventeenth century.[22] It was
a time of economic prosperity in which the acquisition of land by
secular owners, particularly the greater gentry, was reflected in
an increase in the building of new houses and a remodelling of
existing property, including the conversion of ecclesiastical
buildings to country houses. The actual number of residences
built and adapted at this time on the sample estates would in fact
have been greater than that indicated on the graph. Many Tudor,
Elizabethan and Jacobean manor houses were demolished in the
following centuries or superseded by another country house in a
new parkland location on the estate. Only the fate of the principal
country house that occupied the estate heartland in 1880 has been
recorded.

From the mid-seventeenth century investment in house construction appreciably declined in the turbulent and unstable climate
before and after the Civil War. The cycle revived in the 1680s
and 1690s and continued to increase in the early decades of the
eighteenth century. Flinn also tentatively concluded that from the
1690s to the 1730s was one of the major periods of stately-home
investment.[23] Heightened building activity generally took place at
times of internal stability. The wars in the reign of Queen Anne
hardly disrupted investment in house building at the commence-
ment of a period of two centuries of relative peace and economic
expansion, the turn of the century heralding the dawn of a new
era of agricultural and industrial prosperity.

Investment appears to have fallen in the middle decades of the
eighteenth century, but coincident with the general rise in agricultural income and the increase in economic prosperity, at least
among the upper classes, building activity once more accelerated
to new heights. It has been stated that in the nineteenth century
almost as many country houses were built as in the previous three
hundred years.[24] While this may well have been the case within
the entire ranks of landed society it does not hold true for the
properties of the sample group which represented only the highest
of the landed echelon. Indeed, this is not to deny that many new
houses were built, the number per decade being consistently
high from around the mid-eighteenth century, but it was investment in alterations, adaptations, and extensions that rose to
unprecedented heights from the late 1790s reaching a peak around
the 1830s. Stone observed in his work on country houses in Hertfordshire that from 1830 to 1860 there was a lull in new construction, an occurrence that has been noted by architectural historians
who attribute it to the fact that major architects were involved
more with designing public buildings than country houses.[25] Although the number of new-built sample houses began to decline
after 1830 other building investment was sustained at a high level
until later decades of the century. In his analysis Girouard has
clearly shown that investment in Victorian country houses steadily
increased during the course of the nineteenth century until the
mid-1870s, taking an abrupt downswing with the agricultural depression 1879 to 1894,[26] a picture also reflected in the construction

pattern recorded for the sample group.

REGIONAL DIFFERENCES AND PATTERNS

There was differentiation in the cycle of country-house building
and the period of adoption of new styles from region to region and
county to county. On a regional basis, calculation of period of
origin (Table 3.1), within the broad span of each century from

Table 3.1: Regional Per Cent Distribution of Country Houses
According to Period of Origin[a]

Region	Pre-1500 %	1500 to 1600 %	1600 to 1700 %	1700 to 1800 %	1800 to 1900 %
North	15	2	13	33	37
North West	3	19	23	36	19
East	6	10	24	31	28
Midlands	6	18	24	26	26
South East	7	12	24	34	22
South West	6	16	18	29	31

Note: a. Data were obtained for 467 of the 500 country houses in
the sample.
Source: See note 2, Notes.

1500 to 1900 reveals a common superficial pattern of increased
building activity in the eighteenth and nineteenth centuries, although in the North West and South East investment in new houses
appears to have been more concentrated in the eighteenth century
while for the remainder of the country activity was virtually on a
par during the two periods. It should be reiterated, however,
that new houses sometimes replaced those of earlier times and
Table 3.1 reflects only the residences in existence on estate
heartlands in 1880. The North, nevertheless, stands out from the
rest of England. It has the highest proportion of pre-1500 buildings, mostly stone-built, substantial structures, fortified and
defensive houses, each being retained to form the nucleus of a
larger country house by 1880, in part a reflection of its role as a
strategic outpost of England and in part of the durability of the
local building materials used from early times. During the Tudor
and Elizabethan period and even into the seventeenth century
less country-house building was evident in the North compared
with other regions due to the relative isolation and insecurity of
the border counties until after the Act of Union. Here the greatest
building era undoubtedly coincided with advances in mining and
industrial activity and the associated wealth of the industrial re-

volution. On the east and west coasts the exploitation of coal and the development of shipping in particular brought increased wealth to the region. Established landed families who prospered from mineral royalties remodelled or rebuilt existing houses, while the *nouveau riche* of the industrial era bought property in the countryside and built new mansions commensurate with their recently acquired wealth and status. In Northumberland no less than eleven of the nineteen country houses on the sample estates were built, remodelled or enlarged in the period from 1790 to 1830. The work of the architect John Dobson in particular stands out in this county and in neighbouring Durham.[27] He designed or remodelled seven of the sample houses in Northumberland around the 1820s including Nunnykirk, 1825, Mitford, 1828 and Harbottle Castle, 1829, predominantly in neo-classical style. A contemporary, George Webster of Kendal, had a considerable practice on the west coast of northern England and was responsible for building three of the five sample houses in Westmorland in the 1820s; Rigmaden, 1825, Underley, 1825-8, and Dallam Tower remodelled in 1826. Much of Webster's work was classical, but he was also a pioneer of the revived Jacobean style, Underley Hall being one of the earliest examples in England.

It is generally held that diffusion of new building styles, fashion and tastes from the early Tudor period to the late seventeenth century disseminated from London, notably from the Royal Courts and particularly from the artists, master masons and designers employed by the Office of Works.[28] Standards of taste were cultivated and maintained through the Court. New fashions in country-house building tended, therefore, to be evident at an earlier date in counties more accessible to London, though it has been observed that not all changes in fashion had notable impact in adjacent counties. For example, in the period 1580 to 1760 there was relatively little building in Hertfordshire by members of the county elite. Here activity of earlier Tudor decades had provided a plethora of buildings which were not greatly added to until after the mid-eighteenth century.[29]

Fashions set by the monarchy, especially in the construction of palaces, from the Tudor period, were copied by members of the court nobility on their estates and in this manner were spread throughout the countryside; houses of the nobility in turn providing models that were mirrored, on a reduced scale, by other members of landed society, gentry and yeomen alike.

The adoption of new styles appears to have been a variable process. Some areas embraced a fashion long after it had been entrenched for many years elsewhere. Dissemination was not entirely associated with distance as with the quality of comunications in relation to London, parts of southern England being in this sense as remote as counties in the North.

By the eighteenth century architecture came to depend for encouragement and development on the Whig aristocracy, whose patronage of the arts led to the adoption of classical rules of taste as a dominant force throughout most of England. It was only from this time that architecture emerged as a recognised profession. The key architects of the day, those most patronised by the nobility and greater gentry, became disseminators of fashion. It would appear by the nineteenth century that dominant style in a particular region or county at any time could depend as much on the training and background of its more popular local architects as on a general trend of fashion that was prevalent in the country.

PRIMARY BUILDING MATERIALS

Conformity to a particular house style was modified externally by individuality in the use of decoration, in scale, and in the nature of building materials which reflected a wide range of colours and texture throughout the English countryside. Building materials added a further dimension of local and regional variation. For the most part, prior to the development of national transport networks, canals and railways, it was availability rather than choice that governed the primary materials used for the construction of country houses. The immense quantity and weight of stone or brick required meant that, in the majority of cases, local stone quarries and brick earths were used. When it is considered that the country house built at Bearwood from 1865 to 1874 took over $4\frac{1}{2}$ million bricks, one can imagine the problems and expense of assembling such a vast quantity of materials if local resources had not been to hand. For country-house builders their choice of material prior to the industrial revolution was to a large degree determined by local geology. In most instances, therefore, the creations that arose were in harmony in colour and tone with their surrounding environment.

In the North of England country houses were predominantly of stone; carboniferous limestone was widely used but outcrops of sandstone and granite provided additional variations. Red and grey sandstone and millstone grit were widely used in parts of the North West and Midlands, in Lancashire, Cheshire, Shropshire, Derbyshire and Nottinghamshire, although in the more southern counties, large timber-built houses in association with both brick and stone were also found, particularly in Tudor and Elizabethan times. In Cheshire, Tabley Old Hall was a medieval timber-framed house superseded as the principal estate residence in the 1760s by Tabley House, a building of red brick and Runcorn stone. The black and white half-timbered section of Adlington Hall dated from 1581, while Plowden Hall in Shropshire was another timber-framed building of the Elizabethan era.

Stone-built houses characterised a belt of counties that stretched diagonally from the North Riding of Yorkshire through to Dorset. In these counties lay one of the more prestigious of building materials, oolitic limestone, a medium that was used for the construction of important public buildings from medieval times.[30] Further into the South West red sandstone and granite provided the principal materials for many of the country houses in Devon, Cornwall and Somerset.

Generally, the eastern counties from Norfolk and Suffolk, through to Essex and South East England were devoid of good building stone and from the fifteenth century the majority of the large country houses were brick built.

Flint was used as a building stone in chalk areas. In Sussex both Glynde Place, dating from 1568, and West Dean Park, dating from 1804, were constructed of flint, the former was also partly constructed of Caen stone, a material imported into England from Normandy even before the Conquest.[31] Also in the South East, especially in Kent and Sussex, timber-framed manor houses were characteristic during the medieval period.

Brick was an accepted medium throughout the medieval period and became the generally used substitute for wood in those areas devoid of stone.[32] Many houses of the late seventeenth and early eighteenth centuries were brick built; 'Queen Anne'-period houses have a particular association with red brick. A number of notable country houses built in Shropshire around the turn of the century were constructed of brick; Hardwicke Hall built for J. Kynaston in 1693 being a prime example.

Despite the local and regional limitations of materials, from the sixteenth century stone generally came to be preferred for the construction of large country houses for the nobility and gentry. It was more easily carved and moulded for ornamentation and infinitely more suited to the interpretation of the classical style of architecture.

> It is no accident that most of the finest of the Elizabethan country houses are to be found in districts where good building stone was available without too much difficulty, and that, in consequence, stone became associated with wealth and power.[33]

If stone was not available the choice of brick colour was often critical with a range from fiery red to a yellowish-brown hue. The latter, sometimes referred to as yellow or 'white' brick, could be most effectively used to resemble stone. The use of 'white' brick at Holkham (Norfolk) in 1735, though a deliberate choice to imitate Roman brick,[34] could also be construed as being expedient in a county devoid of stone.

The use of stucco to affect the appearance of stone developed as a generally accepted substitute after the mid-eighteenth century when current architectural opinion objected to the use of brick, especially red brick, for country houses.[35] Thonock Hall (Lincs.) was recased and stuccoed early in the nineteenth century as was Wistow Hall (Leics.) in 1811 and Clarendon Park (Wilts.) in 1828. Victorians, however, came to regard stucco as sham and were more accepting in the use of exposed brick as suitable for all sizes of country house.

Only the excessively wealthy could afford to transport materials from any great distance overland prior to the developments of the canal and railway networks. Nevertheless, some landowners did manage to assemble materials from outside their area by means of coastal transport. Houghton Hall in Norfolk, built in 1722 to 1735 for Robert Walpole, Prime Minister of England, was faced with Aislaby sandstone brought by boat from Whitby in Yorkshire. Portland stone was shipped from Dorset via the coast and up the Thames for the construction of many public buildings in London following the Great Fire, but appears to have been mainly used as dressing for country houses built outside the region.

With the development of canals and railways, bulk loads could be carried relatively cheaply over great distances. Improvement of the Avon navigation, completed in 1727, and the Kennet and Avon Canal in the early nineteenth century opened the market for Bath stone which could be shipped to virtually anywhere in Britain.

Canals and railways facilitated a greater choice of materials but the impact was more apparent in the use of slate, tiles and other appurtenances than in the spread of basic raw materials which for the most part, even through to the late nineteenth century, were obtained from within relatively short distances. For the construction of the larger houses, stone was often quarried within the estate boundary. An increasing number of landowners, however, did take advantage of the new transport whether to acquire materials for decorative purposes or for the entire fabric of a new house. Bath stone, for example, was used at Croome Court, Worcestershire in the mid-eighteenth century, at Spetchley Park in the same county in 1811, for the building of Mamhead House in Devon in 1828 and Shelswell Park in Oxfordshire in 1877, and Shephalbury in Hertfordshire was faced with Bath stone in 1865.

By 1880 the proliferation of large country houses in England was reaching its highest number though rebuilding and building, albeit at a reduced rate, continued to the end of the Edwardian era. In style, scale, materials and setting, as a reflection of the tastes of a landed family, whether the work of an individual or the compound expression of many generations of landowners, each country house, to paraphrase the words of Noel Coward, was historically speaking more or less unique.[36] Some merged into the surrounding landscape while others stood out in bold defiance as man-made creations. Some have been described as, 'excrescences which should never have defaced the countryside . . . too often built all of a piece, to gratify the ostentation of some rich man in an age when display meant more than beauty'.[37] But no matter what emotions country houses invoke they nevertheless represent a visual history of English architecture and culture, and their importance in England's heritage goes beyond the fabric of the building to include the families who lived in them and the events in history with which they were associated. However, all shared common ground as the centrepiece and showpiece of a large landed estate, each dependent to a greater or lesser extent on the surrounding countryside for its maintenance and support.

NOTES

1   Country house is a generic term that can be applied to all rural residences of large landowners whether the building be an abbey, a castle, a manor or a hall.

2   Among the many sources consulted for the present chapter the following is a list of some of the more general references for England as a whole. O. Cook and A.F. Kersting, 'The English Country House' (Thames and Hudson, London, 1974); H. Colvin, 'A Biographical Dictionary of British Architects 1600-1840', 2nd edn (John Murray, London, 1978); H.M. Colvin and J. Harris 'The Country Seat' (Allen Lane, London, 1970); M. Girouard, 'The Victorian Country House' (Clarendon, Oxford, 1971); M. Girouard, 'Life in the English Country House' (Yale Univ. Press, New Haven, 1978); C. Hill and J. Cornforth, 'English Country Houses: Caroline 1625-1685' (Country Life, London, 1966); C. Hussey, 'English Country Houses: Early Georgian 1715-1760' (Country Life, London, 1955); C. Hussey, 'English Country Houses: Mid Georgian 1760-1800' (Country Life, London, 1956); C. Hussey, 'English Country Houses: Late Georgian 1800-1840' (Country Life, London, 1958); N. Lloyd, 'A History of the English House' (1931, reprinted Architectural Press, London, 1978); J.N. Summerson, 'Architecture in Britain 1530-1830', 4th edn (Penguin, Harmondsworth, 1953); All volumes in 'The Buildings of England' series, by N. Pevsner *et al.* (Penguin, Harmondsworth).

3   Not all castles were built for military purposes; the tradition of castle building continued for years after the need for defensive castles had ceased; V. Sackville-West, English Country Houses in W.J. Turner (ed.), 'The Englishman's Country' (Collins, London, 1945), p. 60.

4   N. Pevsner, 'The Buildings of England: Cumberland and Westmorland', 2nd edn (Penguin, Harmondsworth, 1973), p.22.

5   Petworth became a castle in the fourteenth century following the granting of a licence to crenellate in 1309.

6   Summerson, 'Architecture in Britain', p. 11, note 5.

7   M. Girouard, 'Robert Smythson and the Architecture of the Elizabethan Era' (Country Life, London, 1966), p. 32.

8   The period c. 1500 to 1620, from the reign of Henry VIII to that of James I has been referred to as the 'Early Renaissance' in English architecture.

9   'Prodigy-house' is a term coined by Sir John Summerson to describe the palatial and individualistic houses of the late sixteenth and early seventeenth century.

10   Now Humberside.

11   Lulworth Castle was built primarily as a grand hunting-lodge. For the most complete account of the work of Robert Smythson see, M. Girouard, 'Robert Smythson'.

12   J. Newman, 'The Buildings of England: North East and East Kent', 2nd edn (Penguin, Harmondsworth, 1976), p. 165;

C. Hill and J. Cornforth, 'English Country Houses: Caroline', p. 22.

13 The period c. 1620 to 1800 has been referred to as the 'Late Renaissance'.

14 Hussey, 'English Country Houses: Early Georgian', p. 25; Thomas Coke received the title of Lord Leicester in 1744.

15 Pugin published a pamphlet in 1836 that praised Gothic design and decried classical forms as being associated with paganism; 'Contrasts; or, A Parallel Between the Noble Edifices of the Fourteenth and Fifteenth Centuries, and Similar Buildings of the Present Day; shewing the Present Decay of Taste: Accompanied by an Appropriate Text'.

16 Hussey, 'English Country Houses: Mid Georgian', p. 22.

17 D. Stroud, 'Henry Holland' (Country Life, London, 1966), p. 127.

18 N. Pevsner and E. Radcliffe, 'The Buildings of England: Cornwall', 2nd edn (Penguin, Harmondsworth, 1970), p. 225.

19 Hussey, 'English Country Houses: Late Georgian', pp. 160-1.

20 M. Girouard, 'The Victorian Country House', is a detailed examination of a number of large country houses newly built, remodelled or adapted during the Victorian period.

21 Most country houses were capable of being classified under a broad period of origin category, but recorded dates of construction were obtained for only 390 of the 500 sample properties.

22 Architectural historians have not found the decades around 1560 to be associated with a marked increase in building activity. Only a slight decrease in activity in the 1560s was evident in the sample group.

23 M.W. Flinn, 'The Origins of the Industrial Revolution' (Longmans, London, 1966), p. 48.

24 Cook and Kersting, 'The English Country House', p. 215.

25 L. Stone and J.C.F. Stone, Country Houses and their Owners in Hertfordshire, 1540-1879 in W.O. Aydelotte, A.C. Boque and R.W. Fogel (eds.), 'The Dimensions of Quantitative Research in History' (Princeton Univ. Press, New Jersey, 1972), p. 109.

26 Girouard, 'The Victorian Country House', p. 6.

27 L. Wilkes, 'John Dobson: Architect and Landscape Gardener' (Oriel Press, Stocksfield, 1980).

28 Also known as the 'King's Works' this department of State recruited expertise from all trades.

29 Stone, Country Houses and their Owners in Hertfordshire, p. 108.

30 Many of the early Oxford colleges were constructed of oolitic limestone.

31 K. Hudson, 'The Fashionable Stone' (Adams and Dart, Bath, 1971), p. 23.

32 For the use of brick from the Middle Ages to 1550, see, J.A. Wight, 'Brick Building in England' (John Baker, London, 1972).

33 Hudson, 'The Fashionable Stone', p. 3.
34 I am grateful to Marcus Binney (Architectural Editor, 'Country Life') for drawing my attention to this point.
35 Hussey, 'English Country Houses: Mid Georgian', p. 27.
36 The well-known verse of a Noel Coward operetta runs as follows: 'The Stately Homes of England although a trifle bleak, historically speaking are more or less unique'.
37 Sackville-West, English Country Houses, p. 54.

4 ESTATE AMENITY LAND

. . . who in a country Seat, From
Storms of Business finds a calm Retreat,
Where all around delightful Landskips lie,
And pleasing Prospects entertain the Eye.
Réne Rapin, *Of Gardens, c.* 1718.

All their imagination all their national and
personal invention have been expended upon their parks.
Hippolyte Taine, *Notes on England,* 1872.

The purpose of this chapter is to illustrate some of the more
important stages in the history of estate parks and gardens and
to review the nature and extent of amenity lands, as reflected by
the sample properties by the late nineteenth century.

As the country house was a symbol of its creator's wealth and
status so also the setting in which the house was viewed, the
surrounding parkland and gardens, emphasised the power and
prestige of the landowner. The evolution of park and garden
design complemented developments in country house architecture,
and the extremes of fashion from rigid formality to contrived
imitations of nature provided a chronological series of contrasting
settings. Most notable in the historic panorama, however, was the
advent of the landscape garden in the eighteenth century which
brought into being a unique expression of English art acclaimed
as one of the highest achievements of man in his relationship with
land.

In their respective histories the park and garden had different
origins yet their development became intertwined and synonymous
during the main period of landscape gardening. Demarcation
between the two is a question of scale, principal land-use and
location. Both can be defined as ornamental enclosed spaces
fundamentally created for motives of pleasure, but while the
garden was, and is, more associated with the cultivation of flowers
and shrubs, the park was, and is, basically comprised of woodland
and pasture. Gardens were laid out in grounds closest to the
house while parkland, generally of larger dimension, lay beyond
the gardens.

PARKLAND - EARLY ORIGINS

The first parks in the English landscape originated as medieval game enclosures, areas of woodland and woodland pasture, often of some hundreds of acres, ringed by an oak palisade or dike to keep in deer and other wild animals. They were the property of the Crown, ecclesiastical and secular nobility, used for the aristocratic pastime of hunting, and usually lay at a distance from the lord's residence occupying the poorest and wildest lands of the manor.

Licences for imparking were introduced in the thirteenth century and provide a record of the early origin of a number of landed estate parklands. Knowsley (Lancs.), which was to become one of the largest parks in northern England, is first mentioned as a park in 1292, and at Thorndon (Essex) a 300-acre park was licensed in 1414. Clandon Park (Surrey) was first imparked by licence of Henry VIII in 1531. It was later disparked and sold in 1642 to Sir Richard Onslow who enclosed it again and whose grandson made it his principal seat.[1]

Evidence of the distribution of medieval deer parks in lowland England would seem to suggest that in the early fourteenth century they were more pervasive in the landscape than at any other period; a figure as high as one park to every four parishes has been put forward by Rackham.[2] Their widespread distribution is recorded on the large-scale maps and county surveys of the sixteenth century. It has been observed that 'upwards of seven hundred are marked on Saxton's maps engraved between the years 1575 and 1580'.[3] The number of deer parks began to decline during the reign of Elizabeth I but were still prominent enough in the landscape as to incite Fynes Moryson to write in his *Itinerary* of 1617 that, 'The English are so naturally inclined to pleasure, as there is no Countrie, wherein the Gentlemen and Lords have so many and large Parkes only reserved for the pleasure of hunting'.[4]

By the mid-seventeenth century parks and woodlands throughout England lay devastated from the ravages of Civil War and from the accumulated years of excessive felling of timber and over-grazing of animals. Restocking of parkland timber began in the 1660s and considerable credit for the increase in tree planting activity has been attributed to John Evelyn who, in his book *Sylva* published in 1664, appealed to landowners 'to adorn . . . their Groves, Parks and Woods with Trees of the most venerable Shade, and profitable timber'.[5]

Following the construction of a new country house at Euston (Suffolk) from 1666 to 1670, the Earl of Arlington in 1671 received a royal licence to impark 2,000 acres in Euston and neighbouring parishes, an addition to an existing park on the estate. Evelyn was consulted in the ordering of trees for the new park and plantations. The latter recorded in his memoirs that he persuaded the Earl 'to bring his parke so neere as to comprehend his house within it, which he resolv'd upon, it being now near a mile to it'.[6]

It is from the Restoration that the meaning of 'park' began to

change and progressively greater emphasis was placed on landscape rather than hunting. Indeed, Evelyn wrote in 1664 in
reference to the value of tree planting, that such undertakings:

> will best of all become the Inspection and care of the noble
> Owners . . . when they delight themselves as much in the good-
> liness of their Trees, as other men generally do in their Dogs
> and Horses, for Races, and Hunting; neither of which Rec-
> reation is comparable to that of Planting, either for Virtue or
> Pleasure . . .[7]

Figure 4.1: Deer Parks and Paddocks on the Sample Estates
c. 1867-92

Source: E.P. Shirley, *Some Account of English Deer Parks* (John
Murray, London, 1867); J. Whitaker, *Descriptive List of the Deer
Parks and Paddocks of England* (Ballantine, London, 1892).

Shirley noted that, 'from the period of the Restoration parks

decreased not only in size but in number, or at least never attained
to the importance which they had occupied in former ages'.[8] Presumably from the title of his book he was referring exclusively to
deer parks which gradually became fewer during succeeding
centuries as the sport of deer-hunting gave way to fox-hunting
and as many medieval parks were transformed into ornamental
parks in the landscaping era of the eighteenth century. In some
the deer remained, as much for aesthetic appeal as for their economic value, but in many they were replaced by cattle and sheep.
By 1867 Shirley recorded only 334 parks stocked with deer in
England.[9] There were around 400 in Whitaker's study of 1892, but
the discrepancy does not necessarily imply an increase between
the two dates but probably confirms Shirley's own doubts as to
the completeness of his survey.[10] In the period 1867 to 1892 at
least 129 (26 per cent) of the 500 sample estates had parks stocked
with deer, but it cannot be assumed, and indeed it was not the
case, that all such parks had medieval origins (Figure 4.1). A
number undoubtedly date from the early eighteenth century when
it became fashionable to introduce a small park or paddock for
deer close to the country house.

GARDENS - EARLY ORIGINS

The English for many centuries have been active and enthusiastic
gardeners which has meant that few gardens remained for long in
the form and fashion of earlier periods.

In the secular world gardens began to adorn the grounds around
the manor house from the Tudor period, but herb gardens,
orchards and vineyards had been cultivated in the walled confines
of the monasteries from an earlier time. Formality was the principal
theme that dominated garden design until the eighteenth century.

The layout of early Tudor gardens embodied geometric concepts
in unnatural stylised forms described variously as knots, labyrinths
and mazes.[11] Gardens were walled and rectangular and, apart from
the use of a mount which permitted a viewer to look out beyond the
wall, they closed out the surrounding and, as yet, untamed rural
landscape. In the Jacobean period a basic division was made between the pleasure garden and the kitchen garden, the latter
henceforth, as a practical necessity, was generally confined within
a walled or hedged enclosure in close proximity to the country
house. Wild gardens were in evidence in the Tudor period as recorded in a sixteenth century account of Nonsuch Palace (Surrey)[12],
but it was the pleasure garden upon which attention was lavished
and which grew in importance especially following the Restoration.

While the exponents of classical architecture looked principally
to Italy for their inspiration, the most influential ideas in garden
design at the time of Charles II originated from France. The work
of Le Nôtre at Versailles provided a model for the elaborate and
extensive formal gardens that embellished the estates of the
nobility and large landowners in the Restoration period. The

parterre[13] and the use of ornamental bodies of water and avenues of trees were the predominant features of French gardening. Ideal beauty was interpreted through the use of the vista which merged the garden with the park. Avenues of trees linked elaborately designed parterres, terraces and fountains in the foreground of the house, to the park-woodlands beyond. No longer wild wooded areas, the newly planted park-woodlands were arranged in geometrically shaped straight-sided stands that were dissected by axial lines to present a series of vistas often focusing on a distant landmark. Thus, at Cirencester Park in the early eighteenth century, ten avenues radiating from Oakley Wood each had a village church as a visual focal point, the main avenue being centred on the parish church in the town of Cirencester.

By the late nineteenth century few formal gardens remained in the English landscape, although detailed evidence of their layout was recorded in contemporary maps, paintings and engravings. Most notable was the collection of bird's-eye view engravings by Johannes Kip from drawings by Leonard Knyff, titled *Britannia Illustrata*, the first volume of which was published in 1707.[14] Within the sample group at least 29 estates had extensive formal gardens that were the subject of illustration in the seventeenth and early eighteenth centuries, of which the gardens at Longleat (Wilts.) provide a typical example. It is apparent, however, that these represented the most famous showpieces and no doubt formal gardens of a lesser scale were to be found on other landed estates in existence at that time. The comparatively small formal garden at Levens Hall (Westmorland), not the subject of Kip's published engravings, was one of the few to survive the landscaping era of the eighteenth century. It was designed in 1690 by Monsieur G. Beaumont, a pupil of Le Nôtre, who it is believed came under Dutch influence while working for King William at Hampton Court,[15] which accounted for the copious topiary work at Levens. Monsieur Beaumont also designed a 'ha-ha'[16] to open up a prospect from the garden to the park, an early example of the use of a device which became popularised in the eighteenth century.

ENGLISH LANDSCAPE GARDENING

The move away from formality of design became evident in the early decades of the eighteenth century when the idealisation of nature became the key concept in art, literature, philosophy and gardening alike. Although there was debate to define what precisely described 'nature' and the 'natural' there was an apparent consensus of opinion in garden design that, in the words of William Kent, 'nature abhors a straight line'. In consequence the reaction against the clipped symmetry of previous centuries led throughout the Georgian era to the destruction of the majority of earlier formal gardens and to the redesigning of park-woodlands.

The landscape gardens that were laid out in the eighteenth century were a unique expression of English design that had no counterpart on the continent. Some were created from existing gardens and park-woodlands, while on other estates the desire for privacy motivated landowners to build new country houses and to set them in landscaped parks on newly enclosed land, or in former and often expanded medieval deer parks.

The new landscape parks, as much graphic art as gardens, were attempts to create in three-dimensional form the scenic portrayal of nature as depicted by such Italian artists as Claude Lorrain (1600-82) and Gaspard Poussin (1613-75). The entire movement beginning with Alexander Pope, and comprising the work of Charles Bridgeman, William Kent, Lancelot 'Capability' Brown and Humphry Repton has been so well documented[17] that detailed description would be pointless, though it is worth briefly emphasising a few of the features that were the 'stock-in-trade' of the well-known gardeners of the 'picture-landscape' period.

Bridgeman, for example, is accredited with popularising the use of the 'ha-ha' which permitted an unrestricted view from the garden to the parkland and facilitated a continuity of landscape from the country house to the surrounding countryside; a key concept throughout the landscape gardening era.

Bodies of water were an essential component of eighteenth century landscape gardens, as indeed they had been in the seventeenth century, but straight-sided geometric shapes were replaced by a variety of 'natural' forms. Landscapes designed by Kent were embellished with serpentine rivers, while 'Capability' Brown more typically dammed rivers and streams to form broad expanses of water. More than any of his contemporaries Brown transformed vast areas of the English countryside into park landscape and it was said of his work that, 'such, however, was the effect of his genius that . . . , he will be least remembered; so closely did he copy nature that his work will be mistaken'.[18] Notable hallmarks were his use of an encircling belt of woodland around a park, well exemplified in his proposals for improvements to Lord Yarborough's estate at Brocklesby and the placing of 'clumps' of trees in a prospect pictorially to balance a scene and to frame a view. However, Brown not only created but also destroyed and was instrumental in the removal of numerous formal gardens which he swept away so as to bring a lawn landscape to the very walls of a country house. Even the kitchen garden was sometimes relocated in order that the view from the house should be totally unobstructed. Few owners stayed his hand but at least one exception has been noted. At Charlecote Park (Warwick.) where he was commissioned in the 1760s by George Lucy, 'to alter the slopes of the park and give the whole a natural easy corresponding level with the house' he was expressly forbidden to remove the avenues of trees.[19]

His successor, Humphry Repton, followed the style of Brown in many aspects but particularly differed in his approach to the landscaping of grounds around the house. While in Brown's compositions the country house stood in a sea of grass and the first incidents in the landscape were some distance away, Repton united the house and the surrounding landscape in a more subtle manner by the use of terraces and parterres. In fact it can be said of Repton that he reintroduced the flower garden and relaxed the rules of landscaping as defined by Brown. In so doing he emerged as one of the early exponents of the picturesque, although he did not fully embrace the ideas as advocated by the Reverend William Gilpin, Sir Richard Payne Knight and Uvedale Price, the major arbiters of the movement.[20]

The Picturesque, which came to the fore at the end of the eighteenth century, challenged the tame and contrived landscapes of manicured lawns, 'clumps' of trees and large expanses of water and endeavoured to capture wilder and more 'natural' elements in landscape design. Picturesque ideals sought visual interpretation of the emotive feelings of nature and were much associated with the philosophical concepts of the beautiful, the sublime and the melancholy. Inspiration in landscape came from upland and mountainous areas, locally from the English Lake District, and on the continent from the Alps of Northern Italy depicted on the canvasses of Salvator Rosa (1615-73) and seen by many travellers on the Grand Tour. The movement did much to influence the direction of nineteenth-century garden design although relatively few gardens were laid out in true Picturesque style. The landscape garden at Hawkstone (Salop), designed in 1806, captured the wild and rugged view of nature espoused by the Picturesque school, but here the natural site, with its complex arrangement of hills and valleys, of ravines and clifftops and quantities of exposed rock, was ideally suited. Later in the century, in the 1840s, William Sawrey Gilpin, nephew of Reverend William Gilpin, advised Edward Hussey on the siting of a new house at Scotney (Kent) and the creation of a Picturesque garden. Stone for the new house was quarried from the garden and the worked-out site was landscaped with shrubs and trees to form the foreground of an idyllic vista from the house that focused on the medieval moated castle in the garden.

BUILDINGS IN LANDSCAPE PARKS AND GARDENS

Not all landscape incidents were created of earth, water or natural vegetation. Prospects and vistas were enhanced and interesting diversions created with ornamental buildings, 'eyecatchers', follies and grottoes, both within the park boundary and in the surrounding countryside. The use of temples constructed in classical style further strengthened the visual conception of creating Italian rather than English landscapes and it is apparent that inspiration for many came directly from Italy. At Garendon Park (Leics.) Ambrose Phillips designed the Temple of Venus and the Triumphal Arch in the 1730s on his return from the Grand Tour; the former was modelled on the Temple of Vesta in Rome and the latter on the Arch of Titus.[21]

The summerhouses, lodges, towers, grottoes and bridges, some functional most ornamental, that adorned landscape gardens and parks were the creations of professionals and amateurs alike. Among the more famous gardens well endowed with ornamental buildings was Stourhead (Wilts.) described by Horace Walpole as, 'one of the most picturesque scenes in the world'. Stourhead was the personal expression of Henry Hoare, a professional city banker but amateur gardener, who designed the 'closed circuit' garden from 1740 to 1760 and adorned it with numerous buildings set in a variety of pictorial cross-views. Its popularity in the eighteenth century was so great that Hoare built a hostel in the nearby village to accommodate visitors.

The deliberate creation of ruins was undertaken to embellish a local scene or to provide an 'eyecatcher' on a distant horizon. In 1747 Sanderson Miller began the construction of a sham castle on the estate at Hagley Hall (Worcester.), one of the first gothic artificial ruins. Another sham ruin, referred to as Yorke's Folly, was built on the Bewerley Estate (West Riding) in the late eighteenth century by John Yorke. It was undertaken in the spirit of philanthropy to give work to the unemployed at a time of economic depression in the district and the men were paid fourpence a day for their labour.[22]

On other estates authentic ruins were incorporated into designs as at Hawkstone (Salop) where the red-sandstone ruin of a medieval castle formed part of the landscape park. The remnants of Roche Abbey augmented the landscape at Sandbeck (West Riding), a park designed by 'Capability' Brown for the 4th Earl of Scarbrough in 1766, and the ruins of Rievaulx Abbey, near Helmsley, are said to have inspired the creation of the Rievaulx Terrace at Duncombe Park, seat of the Earl of Feversham, part of 'one of the boldest and most extensive landscaping enterprises of England'.[23]

Towers and obelisks, commemorative and decorative, were placed on distant horizons to bring all the intervening land under the influence of the landscaper's hand and to demonstrate the great extent of an owner's property. Conygar Hill Tower, for example, on an adjacent hill near Dunster Castle (Somerset), was built as a prospect tower for H.F. Luttrell in 1775.[24]

THE GARDENESQUE AND LATER NINETEENTH-CENTURY DEVELOPMENTS

The idea that a house should be set in a beautiful garden leading to a picturesque park describes much of the development that took place during the nineteenth century. Park landscapes began to assume a less composed and smooth appearance under the designs of Repton, and the ornamental garden and pleasure grounds were revived as a fashionable decoration in the vicinity of the house. In the 1820s John Claudius Loudon developed what he termed the 'gardenesque' style, the scenic display of the individual beauty of trees, shrubs and flowers, that brought together garden design and the botanical appreciation of plant material. Although working on a smaller scale than his predecessors, his principal focus being suburban and villa gardens of the newly emerging middle class, he is nevertheless considered as the father of the 'English garden' as the expression is understood in the present day. His work, which tended towards formal design concepts, was the forerunner of the great display gardens of the Victorian era.

From as early as the Tudor period the importation of exotic flowers, shrubs and trees had increasingly added variety to the plant materials, colours and shapes available to garden designers. In the nineteenth century a mania for collecting and exhibiting exotic plants became evident among the nobility and gentry. Conservatories were built onto country houses and shrubberies, ferneries, sunken gardens, terraces and parterres were set out combining all manner of exotic and native plants. Towards the late nineteenth century William Robinson was advocating a wilder garden style that merged exotic and native plants in a naturalistic setting.

In the Victorian period garden design developed as a mixture of styles in like manner to the contemporary trends in architecture. Formal gardens, re-creations of past eras returned to complement the romantic revival of Tudor buildings. At Penshurst Place (Kent) formal gardens laid out to the south east of the house by George Devey in the 1850s followed the design shown in Kip's engraving of Penshurst in 1720; restoring the association of an authentic Elizabethan house and garden. Italianate and formal styles and wilder gardens adorned the grounds of Victorian country houses, their extent and design matching the ostentation and extravagance characteristic of the architecture of the period. The dimension and complexity of the High Victorian display garden appear to have necessitated nearly as many staff for their upkeep as were required inside the country house. At Eaton Hall (Cheshire) the Duke of Westminster employed 50 indoor servants and no less than 40 gardeners.[25]

SAMPLE ESTATE AMENITY LANDS c. 1880

By no means all landed estates possessed landscape parks or extensive gardens nor did the most acclaimed eighteenth-century landscapers, as far as evidence suggests, advise on the creation of the majority. Many were planned by their owners and other gifted amateurs and a number of individual creations achieved considerable fame as exemplified by the work of Henry Hoare at Stourhead and that of Sir Francis Dashwood at West Wycombe (Bucks.).

In the sample group exactly 100 amenity areas were attributed to either Bridgeman, Kent, Brown or Repton and in at least 14 recorded cases one or more of the four remodelled, added to, or advised modifications to the work of a predecessor (Figure 4.2). Chronologically as the last of the group, the task of redesigning an existing landscape more often befell Humphry Repton. For example, he was commissioned to make alterations to the grounds of Harewood House (West Riding), Holkham (Norfolk), Longleat (Wilts.), Newton Park (Somerset), Panshanger (Herts.) and Sheffield Park (Sussex), all of which had been landscaped by Brown thirty or so years earlier; although Repton's plans for Brocklesby Park (Lincs.), also Brown's work, were not executed and no Red Book[26] survives to indicate the nature of his proposed changes.

Figure 4.2: Landscape Parks and Gardens on the Sample Estates Attributed to Bridgeman, Kent, Brown and Repton

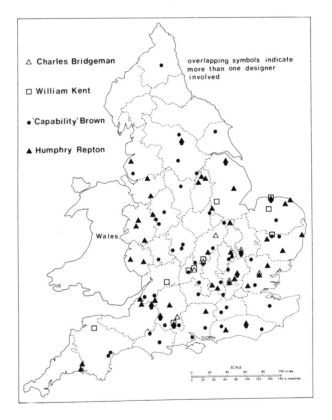

Source: H. Prince, *Parks in England* (Pinhorns, Isle of Wight, 1967).

While Bridgeman and Kent worked only in central and southern England the influence of Brown and Repton was more widespread; even so their clients were predominantly located in the South East, in parts of the Midlands and certain counties of the South West, notably Dorset, Wiltshire and Gloucestershire. Brown travelled furthest afield and executed a number of designs in his native Northumberland, including work for Sir Walter Calverley Blackett both at Wallington and on his nearby estate at Rothley.[27] But neither Brown nor Repton worked in the upland and mountainous counties of Cumberland and Westmorland. Repton's home base was East Anglia and, as would be expected, he was particularly active in this region. His commissions generally tended to be clustered within particular areas, his biographer Dorothy Stroud refers to the more discernible groupings in the counties of Herefordshire, Hertfordshire, South Cornwall, Lancashire, the West Riding and the Bath-Bristol neighbourhood,[28] examples of which are evident in the sample.

In terms of patronage almost an equal number of landowners from the great-landowner and greater-gentry classes employed the services of one or more of the famous four, but whereas this implies that nearly 40 per cent of the great landowners had outstanding professional advice for the design of their amenity lands only 14 per cent of the greater gentry commissioned the well-known designers. It is apparent that their services were not inexpensive. Contracts for landscaping a park could amount to upwards of £3,000 but some were considerably more. At Harewood (West Riding) a contract between Mr. Lascelles and Brown is reported to have amounted to £5,500,[29] while for work at Blenheim Brown was paid over £21,500.[30]

Brown and Repton in particular were coveted within the circle of aristocratic patronage, the recognised font of eighteenth-century taste. A park landscaped by either one, or both, was not only aesthetically pleasing but also the height of fashion. But only the more wealthy members of landed society could afford the most famous designers. The principles of landscaping as laid down by the most popular exponents, however, were closely emulated by other less well-known designers and by this means the landscape park became ubiquitous in the English countryside. William Eames, imitating the style of 'Capability' Brown was responsible for much of the eighteenth-century landscaping at Belton (Lincs.). Improvements to the grounds at Saltram (Devon) undertaken by a man called Richmond, about whom little is known, were in Brown's style as were the designs of Richard Woods in the East Anglian countryside, of which the layout of Wivenhoe Park (Essex) was a notable example.

As the nineteenth century progressed fewer landowners appear to have been concerned with landscaping parkland although trees were planted according to the plans and designs of both Brown and Repton for years after their death. It should be emphasised, however, that few parklands, no matter when their origin, were entirely ornamental. Though the visual importance of the park assumed greater priority from the sixteenth century, the land usually served a variety of uses. Parks were productive land areas providing grazing for deer, cattle and sheep. Trees were

planted for commercial as well as ornamental purposes. The piecemeal addition of park-woodlands and plantations was notable on
many estates during the nineteenth century and the sale of parkland timber was a valuable source of revenue.[31] Neither was all
land within a park enclosure uncultivated. It has been observed
in Nottinghamshire, for example, that the arable use of many parks
increased in the nineteenth century as land was enclosed for
cultivation[32] and on a number of the great estates throughout
England, well exemplified by Holkham (Norfolk), the home farm
was located within the park walls.

Notable changes to the sample estate amenity lands in the nineteenth century were associated with the layout of grounds in the
vicinity of the house. For example, another dimension was added
to the history of the Chatsworth Estate (Derby.) during the
thirty years when Paxton was head gardener. The grounds at
Chatsworth had passed through the successive movements of the
seventeenth-century formality, recorded in an engraving by Kip,
to the open park landscape of 'Capability' Brown. From 1826 the
garden art and horticultural engineering of Paxton became indelibly
associated with Chatsworth, one of the most famous of England's
gardens.[33]

W.A. Nesfield stands out among the nineteenth-century exponents of the formal garden concept. He collaborated with the
architect Sir Charles Barry over the design of garden terraces
at Shrublands Park (Suffolk) and at Harewood House (West Riding)
as well as creating the formal, Italianised gardens at Duncombe
Park (North Riding), Holkham (Norfolk) and Witley Court
(Worcester).

ESTATE AMENITY LAND AREA c. 1880

In terms of acreage no comprehensive assessment exists of the
individual or total extent of estate amenity lands by the late
nineteenth century. Published sources of the period dealing
specifically with parks and gardens are few. Shirley's *Some
Account of English Deer Parks,* 1867, and Whitaker's *Descriptive
List of the Deer Parks and Paddocks of England,* 1892 contain
some useful acreage figures. Directories and topographies note
the presence of parkland at least for the more important county
seats often with an accompanying, although not wholly reliable
acreage figure. The second edition of the one-inch Ordnance
Survey indicates 'park or ornamental ground', however, the six-
inch coverage provides the better basemap for acreage assessment.
Accurate acreages, itemising and differentiating parks and gardens
are found in estate records, notably surveys and valuations, but
such detail for the late nineteenth century is available for only a
small proportion of estates and more often for great-landowner
than for greater-gentry property. Sales catalogues provide yet
another detailed source, but one of even more sporadic coverage.

From available sources it was possible to verify the existence of

amenity land for the majority of sample properties and to deduce
a reasonably accurate acreage c. 1880. The average extent in
England was just over 280 acres but there was a notable regional
variation. Estates in the North and South West generally possessed
smaller areas of amenity land, an average of 163 and 219 acres
respectively, in comparison with the regional average for the
remainder of England which exceeded 300 acres. By far the
largest landscape parks were located in the Midland counties
although the largest two in the entire sample were the 2,500-
acre park at Knowsley in Lancashire and the 3,000-acre park at
Holkham in Norfolk. However, the total size of a landowner's
property as much as its geographical location appears to have had
a bearing on the extent of amenity acreage. Landowners with
estates greater than 10,000 acres possessed, on average, amenity
lands extending over 500 acres while, in comparison, landowners
in the 3,000 to 10,000-acre group averaged just over 200 acres.

At the close of the nineteenth century the majority of country
houses on large estates were set in a landscape park. In layout
and design, in the disposition of trees and shrubs, the use of
prospects, vistas, and ornaments, in the creation of bodies of
water and the alignment of parks and gardens with the country
house, the hand of man had altered and adapted the scene to
form an idealised arrangement of nature. On some estates the
garden and park merged together being more or less large gardens
laid out as miniature parks, on others combinations of trees,
shrubs and flowers formed a series of changing landscapes both
park-like and garden-like, while for many the park and gardens
were quite separate and distinct. The estate amenity land, for the
most part, effectively segregated a landowner from the outside
world and provided an element of seclusion and privacy character-
istically sought by the upper classes. Such areas continued to
be expanded and maintained as long as landed estates flourished
and in the late nineteenth century the extent of estate amenity
lands was probably greater than it had ever been.[34]

NOTES

1   E.P. Shirley, 'Some Account of English Deer Parks' (J. Murray,
    London, 1867), p. 62.
2   O. Rackham, 'Trees and Woodland in the British Landscape'
    (J.M. Dent, London, 1976), p. 143.
3   Shirley, 'English Deer Parks', p. 28.
4   F. Moryson, 'An Itinerary written by Fynes Moryson, Gent.'
    (3 vols., J. Beale, London, 1617), vol. 3, p. 147.
5   J. Evelyn, 'Sylva, or a Discourse of Forest-Trees, and the
    Propogation of Timber', 3rd edn (John Martyn, London, 1679),
    p. 239.
6   J. Evelyn, 'Memoirs', W. Bray (ed.) (2 vols., H. Colburn,
    London, 1818), p. 426.
7   Evelyn, 'Sylva', p. 240.

8   Shirley, 'English Deer Parks', pp. 50-1.
9   Ibid., p. ix; includes 3 deer parks in Monmouthshire, a
     county outside the present study area.
10 J. Whitaker, 'Descriptive List of the Deer-Parks and Paddocks
     of England' (Ballantine, London, 1892).
11 A knot garden comprised a plot laid out in squares decorated
     with short clipped hedges, beds of flowers or herbs, gravels
     or coloured earths intertwined in intricate symmetrical
     patterns.
12 M. Binney and Anne Hills, 'Elysian Gardens' (SAVE Britain's
     Heritage, 1979), refer to the account of Nonsuch Palace which
     describes 'leafy woods glorifying in shady spots', p. 2.
13 A parterre was similar in materials to the knot but different
     in shape and composition, generally round rather than square,
     sometimes giving the appearance of patterns of embroidery
     upon the ground.
14 J. Kip, 'Nouveau Théâtre de la Grande Bretagne' (David
     Mortier, London, 1708), 'Britannia Illustrata' (2 vols., David
     Mortier, London, 1720), 'Nouveau Théâtre de la Grande Bret-
     agne' (Supplément, 5 vols., J. Smith, London, 1724-9).
15 A. Bagot, 'Levens Hall' (Levens, n.d.), however, states that
     there is no evidence that Beaumont worked at Hampton Court.
16 A 'ha-ha', also known as a sunk fence or fosse, was a device
     that separated the garden from the park or surrounding
     countryside. Usually a trench was dug and a retaining wall
     erected on one side while on the other the earth was sloped
     up to the original ground level. The appearance from a distance
     was of continuity between one landscape and another but
     cattle and sheep were prevented from gaining access to
     ornamental grounds.
17 Major works on the landscape gardening movement and its
     most celebrated practitioners include; J.D. Hunt and P. Willis
     (eds), 'The Genius of Place: The English Landscape Garden
     1620-1820' (Paul Elek, London, 1975); C. Hussey, 'English
     Gardens and Landscapes 1700-1750' (Country Life, London,
     1967); E. Hyams, 'Capability Brown and Humphry Repton'
     (Charles Scribner, New York, 1971); D. Stroud, 'Capability
     Brown', 2nd edn (Country Life, London, 1957); D. Stroud,
     'Humphry Repton' (Country Life, London, 1962); P. Willis,
     'Charles Bridgeman and the English Landscape Garden' (A.
     Zwemmer, London, 1977); H. Prince's publication, 'Parks in
     England' (Pinhorns, Isle of Wight, 1967) provides an invalu-
     able listing of the accredited works of Bridgeman, Kent,
     Brown and Repton.
18 Quoted from Horace Walpole's notebook in Stroud, 'Capability
     Brown', p. 202.
19 R. Fedden and R. Joekes (eds), 'The National Trust Guide'
     (Jonathan Cape, London, 1973), p. 87.
20 The picturesque movement gained impetus following the pub-
     lication of three notable works; Uvedale Price's, 'Essay on the
     Picturesque' (London, 1794); a poem titled 'The Landscape'

by Richard Payne Knight (Bulmer, London, 1794), and Humphry Repton's, 'Sketches and Hints on Landscape Gardening' (London, 1794).

21 H. Colvin, 'A Biographical Dictionary of British Architects 1600-1840', 2nd edn (John Murray, London, 1978), p. 632.

22 B. Jones, 'Follies and Grottoes' (Constable, London, 1953), p. 251.

23 N. Pevsner, 'The Buildings of England: Yorkshire, the North Riding' (Penguin, Harmondsworth, 1966), p. 141.

24 Jones, 'Follies and Grottoes', p. 227.

25 M. Girouard, 'The Victorian Country House' (Clarendon, Oxford, 1971), p. 2; See also p. 192.

26 It was the practice of Humphry Repton to prepare for each client a Red Book, a morocco-bound volume portraying in water-colour sketches the proposals for a country house and its setting. By 1816 it was estimated that he had prepared over 400. However, he had made no Red Book for Sheffield Park. Stroud, 'Humphry Repton', pp. 12 and 39.

27 Stroud, 'Capability Brown', pp. 136-7.

28 Stroud, 'Humphry Repton', p. 56.

29 Stroud, 'Capability Brown', p. 106.

30 Ibid., p. 67.

31 Prince, 'Parks in England', p. 14.

32 D.V. Fowkes, Nottinghamshire Parks in the Eighteenth and Nineteenth Centuries, 'Transactions of the Thoroton Society of Nottinghamshire' (1967), pp. 81-8.

33 Details of Paxton's work at Chatsworth are contained in, G.F. Chadwick, 'The Works of Sir Joseph Paxton 1803-1865' (Architectural Press, London 1961).

34 Prince, 'Parks in England', p. 10.

> But why not rather, at the porter's gate
> Hang up a map of all my lord's estate?
> Richard Payne Knight, *The Landscape* (Bulmer,
> London, 1794), Book 1, Lines 169-70.

In the broad panorama of the rural scene large landowners were
intimately involved in the development of the agricultural landscape, in shaping the growth of rural settlement, in the layout
of roads, canals and railways as well as in the emergence of
industrial landscapes associated with mineral exploitation. This
chapter intends only to touch on the nature of their role and to
illustrate some of the more common identifying features of the
landed estate in the landscape by the late nineteenth century.
Concern is primarily focused on the rural and agricultural landed
estate. The growth of the mining industry and the major communication networks that came into being as an adjunct of mineral
exploitation rank alongside the urban and industrial involvement
of large landowners, another dynamic beyond the range of the
present work.[1] Only in so far as physical lines of communication
directly affected, or were affected by, the layout of estate
property are they considered here.

Nevertheless, it is well to remember that large landowners were
the proprietors of the sub-surface minerals on their estates, the
increased exploitation of which expanded the wealth of many landed
families in the course of the late eighteenth and nineteenth centuries. For some the additional revenue was simply due to the
fortuitous status of ownership while others undertook vital entre-
preneurial roles not only in mineral exploitation but in a wide
range of industrial, transport and urban developments. Revenue
from non-agricultural sources, such as mineral royalties and urban
rents, broadened the income base of landed estates and carried
many properties through long-term periods of agricultural depression.

The economic interests of the majority of landowners, however,
were rooted in agriculture at least until the first half of the nineteenth century. It has been suggested that only a handful of
estate owners prior to 1850 derived half or more of their gross
income from non-agricultural sources, although the number
probably expanded as the tempo of the industrial revolution
gathered momentum.

THE AGRARIAN LANDSCAPE

Prior to the agricultural improvements of the eighteenth century
the landed estate was essentially a unit of consumption, and only
with the enhanced potential for profitability in farming did it
emerge as a unit of management.[2] Even so, maximisation of agricultural production did not appear to be a major landowning
motive for most eighteenth and nineteenth-century proprietors
who held land as much for political and pleasurable motives as
economic. Yet responsibility for major innovations and improvements in agriculture has largely devolved upon the large landowners. In addition, they have been accredited with considerable
initiative in the physical process of enclosure, whether in enclosure by agreement, or in enclosure by Act of Parliament in the
eighteenth century from which emerged the landscape, commonly
regarded as typical of England, with its chequerboard pattern
of fields bordered by hedgerows and interspersed with woodlands
and plantations. Far be it to claim that the sole initiative for
enclosure and land improvements came from the large-estate owners,
but it is generally accepted that they were in a better position to
afford the capital cost of undertaking enclosure and many were
motivated to do so by the possibility of increased profits from
rent.
  Landscapes of enclosure did not visually demarcate large-estate
properties from those of small landowners unless it was policy to
fence, hedge or ditch farm and field boundaries in a standard and
distinctive fashion. Notwithstanding this, however, in parts of
England the look of the land was completely transformed by the
process of enclosure, by reclamation and drainage and by changes
in the land management policies of the large estates.
  In the process of landscape change and associated agricultural
development a number of landowners stand out fundamentally because of the popularisation of their achievements as innovators
and 'improvers' by contemporary and subsequent historians. Two
of the most commonly cited names in this regard are 'Coke of
Norfolk' (Thomas William Coke, the Earl of Leicester) and 'Turnip
Townshend' (the Marquis Raynham). Their respective contributions have been well documented, analysed and somewhat deflated.[3]
Nevertheless, improvements on the Holkham Estate were held up
as a model by contemporary agricultural reporters, and although
many of the pioneering and revolutionary claims were exaggerated
it is still evident that during the eighteenth century a considerable area of land was enclosed, new farm boundaries were drawn,
trees planted and an essentially new landscape emerged on the
sandy soil of north-western Norfolk. In Lincolnshire, the changes
brought about in the early nineteenth century by the enclosure
of over 30,000 acres of wold land on Lord Yarborough's Estate
were no less dramatic[4] and a similar large-scale transformation
took place in the East Riding on wold land owned by Sir Christopher
Sykes at Sledmere.[5] In the far north of England the enclosed
landscape of the Wallington countryside was brought into being in

the late eighteenth century by the initiative of Sir W.C. Blackett.[6]
No less significant, however, were the more localised contributions
of large-estate owners outside the land-magnate class. Parallel
with developments at Wallington, the 7,000-acre Ford Estate,
property of Lord Delaval, underwent transformation from largely
unenclosed moorland to a landscape of regular fields fenced with
quickset hedges and interspersed with woodlands and coppices.[7]
Similar examples of such landlord initiative can be found throughout England whether drawn from the period of parliamentary enclosures or earlier enclosures of the sixteenth and seventeenth
centuries.

The once acclaimed innovative role of large landowners in agricultural development has been somewhat tempered by revisionist
views and there now appears to be a consensus that the so-called
agricultural 'pioneers' of the eighteenth century 'were more the
popularisers of the new methods of cultivation than the originators
of them'.[8] Their role was none the less important. 'Improving'
landlords, from the great-landowner and greater-gentry classes,
had the capital and incentive to experiment with new techniques
in farming and estate management and the dissemination of ideas
owes much to their initiative. Experimentation and agricultural
innovation continued to be a major interest of a group of landowners well into the nineteenth century. The founding of the Royal
Agricultural Society in 1839 was instigated by a body of rural
landlords who sought the creation of an organisation to further
the improvement of British agriculture by the application of
science to farm practice.[9]

TREES IN THE ESTATE LANDSCAPE

One of the most significant landscape contributions of estate
management policy was the planting of trees in parkland and elsewhere on the property. Before the creation of the Forestry Commission in 1919 the landed estates provided the principal source
of commercial timber in England.

Part and parcel of the new agricultural system and subdivision
of land into individually operated farms was the planting of hedgerows, woodlands, plantations and shelter belts, sometimes into a
formerly treeless landscape as was the case following the enclosure
of much of Northumberland.[10] The more notorious 'improvers'
were also famed for their tree-planting exploits. The nickname
'King Pine' was given to Thomas Coke who planted innumerable
pine trees on the sandy soils at Holkham.[11] A large area of the
north Lincolnshire landscape was similarly transformed by the
tree planting activities of the Earls of Yarborough. In the years
from 1787 to 1889 six generations of the Yarborough family planted
over $17\frac{1}{2}$ million trees on the estate at Brocklesby and by the late
nineteenth century the total extent of woodland, amenity and commercial, was 8,000 acres.[12] The landmark of Pelham's Pillar was
erected in 1849 on the highest point on the estate to commemorate

the planting of over 12 million trees by Charles Anderson, 1st Baron Yarborough (1748-1823), who initiated the timber enterprise on the estate.

Throughout the countryside the reintroduction of trees in the landscape, both native species and exotic, was a prominent feature in and around the heartland of the large landed estates; the more exotic trees were usually confined to garden and parkland locations though some were planted further afield to add variety to native woodland.

Areas of woodland, plantations, fox-coverts and spinneys outside park bounds were planted for pleasurable as well as commercial motives. It has been suggested that some landowners were reluctant to improve their property as it rid them of uncultivated lands ideally suited for the sports of fox-hunting and hawking.[13] The newly enclosed landscape provided so little natural cover in some Midland and southern counties that the large-estate owners deliberately set out plantations, fox-coverts and spinneys so as to help sustain the sport.

Aesthetic motives also extended tree planting beyond the park. In 1712, Addison wrote in the *Spectator* 'Why may not a whole estate be thrown into a kind of garden by frequent plantations. A man might make a pretty landskip of his own possessions'.[14] Indeed many owners took him at his word as was evident in the landscape garden movement of the eighteenth century, and picture-landscaping also took place on estate lands outside the park boundary, although usually within the vicinity of the estate heartland.

The planting of trees, the layout of fields and the design of farm buildings within the country-house panorama and along approach roads were undertaken as much with a view to their picturesque appearance as for anticipated economic returns. The *ferme ornée*, a precursor of the landscape park in the early eighteenth century was the epitomy of such a picturesque agrarian landscape.[15]

THE LANDSCAPE OF POWER AND PRESTIGE

The lines that introduce the chapter were a retort to the suggestion made by Humphry Repton to place milestones, bearing the arms of the estate owner, along the approach road to a country house.[16] His idea represented a practical way of conveying the 'greatness' of an owner's property, an impression otherwise gained from diverse facets in the rural landscape that subtly or overtly bore marks of ownership and association with a large estate and testified to the extent of territorial power and possessions of the landed family. The power wielded by the landed classes evident in the rural landscape can be effectively illustrated in two areas: first, in the manner by which they were able to alter or determine lines of communication, and second in their influence over settlement for the enhancement and aesthetic presentation of their property and for economic motives.

Communications: Roads and Railways
All over the countryside minor roads underwent drastic changes
as an outcome of the enclosure movement, many were straightened,
some were removed; but certain changes, from the sixteenth
century, were for aesthetic and prestigious rather than pragmatic
reasons, when, for example, a landowner rerouted a road, usually
by private Act of Parliament, in order to expand the open countryside around his residence to create or enlarge a park. Thus, at
Shugborough (Staffs.) Thomas Lord Anson diverted the Stafford-
Lichfield road in the early eighteenth century to increase the
privacy of his park;[17] in the latter part of the century Christopher
Sykes moved the York-Bridlington road to the outskirts of his
park at Sledmere (East Riding),[18] while in the early nineteenth
century the line of the Uffington road at Attingham (Salop) was
altered so that the park could be expanded.[19] These are just three
of numerous examples of minor and local road changes up and
down the country.

From the mid-nineteenth century few new parklands were
created and the tables somewhat turned as innovations in transport technology, namely railways, threatened to jeopardise the
integrity of existing estate parklands. But landed society remained
politically strong and the large landowners were usually able to
reroute unwanted lines to prevent interference with their property.

Many landowners welcomed the railways especially those for
whom they opened up new avenues of industrial and commercial
enterprises associated with the exploitation of minerals. A number
sat as directors on Railway Boards and some went so far as nego-
tiating for the construction of private stations or waiting rooms
in close proximity to their country house, but usually beyond
the park boundary. The Earl of Yarborough, a director of the
Manchester, Sheffield and Lincolnshire Railway Company, arranged
for Brocklesby Park Station to be built just two miles from the
hall and park.

Not all, however, were eager to embrace the new technology
and many undoubtedly shared similar sentiments to Ruskin who
wrote 'I detest railways. Your railway has cut through some of
the loveliest bits of scenery in the country'.[20] One landowner
vehemently opposed to railways was Lord Harborough of Stapleford Park (Leics.). When the Midland Railway in 1844 planned a
line from Leicester through Melton Mowbray and Oakham to
Peterborough, a proposed section was to pass through Stapleford
Park. The company offered to build Lord Harborough a station
at Saxby with a private waiting room and provision for trains to
stop whenever he so desired, but his Lordship would have nothing
to do with such a scheme and went as far as mounting an armed
guard to prevent company surveyors from entering the park.
What amounted to near warfare continued for over a year with
apparent victory for Lord Harborough when an alternative route
was finally approved by Act of Parliament. The new line curved

around the northern and eastern perimeter of the park and contained a sharp bend which became known as 'Lord Harborough's
Curve'.[21]

The 3rd Duke of Northumberland (1817-47) similarly refused to
let a railway penetrate the 5,000 acre park at Alnwick.[22] A branch
line serving Alnwick from the south east was eventually constructed
outside the park. Opposition also came from Earl Grey resulting
in the rerouting of a line that was planned to cut across his landscape park at Howick.[23]

Other landowners, however, were more accommodating and
allowed a line to penetrate the park, but negotiated with the railway company for cuttings, bridges or tunnels so as to minimise
the visual impact. One such line was planned at Shugborough
Park (Staffs.), the ancestral estate of the Earls of Lichfield. The
landscape park contained a rich variety of ornamental buildings
mostly erected by Thomas Anson from 1720 to 1773. When the Trent
Valley Railway was built across the estate in 1845-7 the Earl of
Lichfield negotiated for the line to occupy a half-mile tunnel
through a northern spur of Cannock Chase at a distance from the
house and to run in a deep cutting for the remainder of its course
through the park. In keeping with the character of the park, the
entrances of the railway tunnel, designed by Livock in 1847, were
decorated with turrets and battlements while a railway bridge over
the Lichfield Drive was designed as a bold classical structure.[24]

Rural Settlement
Perhaps more symbolic of the power of the large landowners was
their ability to influence rural settlement. They were instrumental
both in the physical destruction and creation of cottages, houses,
hamlets and entire villages and in the restriction and encouragement of settlement growth so affecting the distribution of population
and the settlement pattern in various parts of rural England.
Landowners were often ruthless in pursuit of their own goals
whether for economic or other motives to the extent of destroying
the habitation of the less fortunate members of rural society.

Medieval depopulation and the physical obliteration of many
hamlets and villages has been attributed to a number of causes,
but researchers have assigned a major role to the enclosure of land
for sheep pasture.[25] The profitability of sheep c. 1450 and the
growth of the wool-textile industry in England up to the mid-
sixteenth century motivated manorial landlords to evict villagers
and to demolish settlements in order to enclose extensive tracts
of land. Evidence from the work of Parker in Leicestershire shows
that in 37 out of 45 cases the lord of the manor was the encloser.[26]
There is no body of available evidence to indicate where the
evicted population went though it has been suggested that at the
time of greatest depopulating activity, many would have found
alternative employment in the expanding textile industry in neighbouring towns.[27]

As early as medieval times settlement was also destroyed in the
process of emparking. When a royal licence was granted to a

landowner to enclose an area of land for the creation of a deer park, settlement within the proposed boundary was removed. Such was the fate of the village of Fulbrook (Warwicks.) which found itself on the edge of a new park enclosed by the Duke of Bedford in 1421. By 1428 there were only four householders. Later the church was removed and only the deserted village site remained.

Early manor houses were usually situated adjacent to villages and hamlets and when in later centuries it became fashionable for a country house to be located in the privacy of an extensive formal garden or landscape park, one of two options were available to a landowner: either to relocate and build a new house elsewhere or to remove the existing settlement and empark the surrounding land. The latter was considerably less difficult when a proprietor had sole ownership of the village and its lands as was indeed the case on many of the large estates. A particularly interesting example was found on the Wimpole Estate (Cambridge.) where the village of Wimpole once stood around the hall and church with a series of hamlets, evident on a map of 1638, scattered in close proximity. When the new hall was built around 1640 for Sir T. Chicheley the village houses in its precincts were demolished to make way for an elaborate formal garden. Over the next two hundred years the setting around the hall was successively altered by Bridgeman (1730s), 'Capability' Brown (1767-73) and Humphry Repton (1801-9) and as the landscaped area was progressively expanded the remaining houses within its boundary were also removed.[29]

The demolition of individual cottages, houses and entire settlements was especially prevalent on estate lands as a consequence of emparking in the eighteenth century. In the majority of cases, removal was purely for aesthetic reasons, existing habitation presenting a potential 'eyesore' in a proposed landscape park. But by no means all emparking resulted in settlement loss. Research in Hertfordshire has shown that no villages in that county were destroyed. There, the major impact was to divert a few country roads as at Panshanger and Shephalbury, although evidence does indicate that in one or two cases, neighbouring gentry homes were purchased and demolished and their grounds incorporated into expanding country-house parks.[30] Nor are all deserted village sites within landscape parks the outcome of emparking. The tendency to select poorer land for park locations meant that many parks, newly formed after the Restoration, occupied areas of previously enclosed pasture and former scenes of population loss. Village sites of this nature have been noted, for example, in the estate parklands of Stapleford and Wistow in Leicestershire.[31] The presence of a parish church isolated in a park along with the country house sometimes has been cited as further indication of eighteenth-century emparking,[32] but a church was often the sole survivor of earlier settlement loss and cannot be taken, on its own, as clear evidence of later emparking except perhaps where eighteenth-century housing was constructed at the park gates.

A number of villages removed for purely landscaping reasons were rebuilt outside the park and constituted, as discussed below, a new form of settlement in the rural landscape. It has yet to be assessed how many landowners undertook to replace habitation which they swept away. In some cases the displaced population was relocated in neighbouring villages, as on the Stowe Estate (Bucks.) where many of the villagers evicted by the expansion of the park in the eighteenth century were rehoused at Dodford in an adjacent parish.[33] In other cases there appears to have been little regard for the immediate relocation of the homeless. At Easton Neston (Northants.), a village was removed from the park early in the eighteenth century but the building of the estate hamlet of Hulcote, on the park perimeter, was not undertaken until the early nineteenth century.[34]

It is appropriate at this point to make a distinction between 'estate' villages and 'freehold' villages, the former also referred to as 'closed' and the latter as 'open' villages. While 'closed' villages and in fact the entire parish in which such settlements were located were usually the property of a single landowner, or at most a few proprietors, the 'open' villages were owned by a large number of persons such that no individual could exercise power in control over building. This association between land-ownership and building became important from the early seventeenth century and led to a differential in population growth and village morphology between controlled and uncontrolled settlements a phenomenon strikingly evident in a number of counties in the Midlands and East England by the mid-nineteenth century.[35]

The need to restrict building, essentially cottage building, derived initially from the Act of 1601 which made each parish responsible for its poor and destitute.[36] The parish poor-rate fell heavily on occupiers of agricultural land and by limiting the number of cottages, whether in a village or throughout the parish, an estate owner could reduce the incidence of the rate for himself and his tenants. It is surprising that even in times of agricultural improvement, in the late eighteenth and early nineteenth century when the demand for farm labour was high, many estate owners were reluctant to build new cottages and went as far as to let those already in existence fall into disrepair and ruin. Contemporary evidence from Oxfordshire and Lincolnshire attests to the prevailing situation. Emery cites the examples of a survey undertaken by a Poor Law inspector in Oxfordshire in 1849 where it was found that in the ten-year period up to 1849 there had been an increase of 1,352 cottages in 86 'open' parishes whereas in 34 'closed' parishes only seven had been built.[37] In Lincolnshire, a surveyor of the Hainton Estate, in the 1790s, wrote that, 'The cottages are too numerous and should be reduced as the tenants die off',[38] while in a nineteenth-century Board of Guardians' report it was stated that

the exclusive proprietor (failing to provide the necessary accommodation for the increased population, and not only so,

but in some cases indeed pulling down the cottages upon his
estate, and in many cases suffering them to dilapidate in order
to get rid of the poor) had forced that portion of the population
which in common fairness belonged to him into the neighbouring
market-towns and villages (consisting of small freeholds).[39]

Agricultural workers removed from 'closed' parishes were com-
pelled to live in 'open' villages or neighbouring towns where
building restrictions were not applied. Such 'open' settlements
were characterised by sprawling and haphazard growth, cheap
and poorly constructed dwellings and stood in sharp contrast to
the neat and compact morphology of estate villages. 'Open' settlements provided the major source of surplus farm labour and itiner-
ant gangs of men, women and children travelled considerable
distances to work on the farms of 'closed' parishes. The operation
of the 'Gang System', as it came to be called, became a matter of
public moral concern and ultimately led to a parliamentary commission in 1867 on 'the Employment of Women and Children in
Agriculture'.[40]
    The issue of 'open' and 'closed' parishes was one of contemporary
debate from the early nineteenth century and resulted in the publication of the Poor Law Report of 1834 and a major revision of the
Laws of Settlement in the Poor Law Amendment Act later in the
same year.[41] The effect of the 'New Poor Law', however, did little
to change the housing problem and the impact of landed power on
settlement was still evident to contemporaries in the 1850s:

The population is very unevenly distributed; and the cause
invariably assigned is the unwillingness of parishes and proprietors to rebuild old houses or erect new ones, in consequence
of the "Law of Settlement". They wish to keep down the population in their respective parishes, with a view to having less
poor-rate to pay.[42]

In many cases building activity did not substantially increase
until the Union Chargeability Act of 1865 took the financial responsibility for the poor away from the parish.[43]
    At the time of rapid population growth in the early nineteenth
century estate villages tended to remain smaller and of more compact
morphology in comparison to freehold settlements. A brief examination of population data of the Lindsey division of Lincolnshire
from 1801 to 1861 (Table 5.1) clearly illustrates the differences in
growth between parishes that contained a principal estate nucleus
and estate village and those most frequently cited in contemporary
literature as being 'open' to settlement. While the poor-rate for
Brocklesby was assessed at 5½d in the pound in 1864, the rate-
payers of Donnington-on-Bain, Grasby and Keelby, similar in
population size in 1801, were paying 1/6d, 1/6¼d and 11d respectively; a simple illustration of the effect of population control on
the poor-rate.
    A similar situation to that found in Lincolnshire has been noted

Table 5.1: Population Growth of 'Closed' Estate-Village Parishes Compared with 'Open' Parishes, Lindsey, Lincolnshire 1801 to 1861

Estate-Village Parishes[a]	Population 1801	Population 1861	Per Cent Increase 1801-61[b]
Baumber	261	393	51
Brocklesby	207	232	12
Fillingham	242	316	31
Scrivelsby	92	168	83
South Ormsby	238	261	10
Tealby[c]	469	863	84
Open Parishes[d]			
Binbrook	498	1,334	168
Donnington-on-Bain	188	552	194
Grasby	168	433	158
Keelby	313	842	169
Kirkby-cum-Osgodby	123	477	288
Middle Rasen	463	1,063	130

Notes: a. Parishes containing at least part of the estate nucleus and all of the principal estate village of each large landowner in the sample estate population of Lindsey, Lincolnshire. Thonock is the only omission, the village population was not separated from that of the town of Gainsborough. b. The general trend in population growth 1801 to 1861 was one of increase. In Lindsey, population numbers rose by 97% during the period. c. Tealby is sometimes recorded as an open parish. d. The most frequently cited 'open' parishes of comparable population size to estate parishes in 1801.
Source: W. Page (ed.) *VCH of Lincoln* (Archibald Constable, London, 1906), vol. 2, pp. 356-79.

in other counties. In Oxfordshire, Nottinghamshire and the East Riding 'open' and 'closed' villages were found in all parts of the county and there is every reason to believe, from the published reports of Poor Law investigators, that the phenomenon was common throughout England in parishes where estate owners had sole ownership.[44] In 1845 Benjamin Disraeli made reference to the subject in his novel *Sybil*[45] which illustrates that the issue was topical enough to feature in contemporary literature, while a *Punch* cartoon of 1865 called 'Out of the Parish' published immediately prior to the passing of the Union Chargeability Act testified to the prevailing interpretation of the Poor Law at that time.

In consequence of the Laws of Settlement it can now be more readily appreciated why certain landowners, on clearing cottages from their parkland in the eighteenth century, chose not to rebuild the settlement elsewhere on their estate. While some owners appeared less adverse to rebuilding it was commonly the case that new estate villages comprised fewer dwellings than the original

demolished settlements and, it may be supposed, housed a more
select tenantry of permanent estate workers less likely to succumb
to poverty and destitution than the casual workers of neighbouring
'open' villages. Housing erected at the park gates to keep abreast
of fashion, in the late eighteenth and nineteenth century, was
thus unlikely to add to the incidence of the poor-rate in the
parish.

Planned Estate Villages. Settlement removed from a landscape
park in the eighteenth century and relocated by the landowner
was usually sited around one of the park entrances, but in a
location not visible from the country house. In some cases the
newly constructed cottages were of the same design and materials
and were arranged in a uniform pattern along either side of a
road leading from the park. The regular morphology of such
villages created a distinctive planned landscape and contrasted
markedly with the majority of rural settlements which were the
product of centuries of organic development. The formality and
regularity of plan reflected the classical symmetry and tastes of
the period, a fashion firmly established in the architecture of the
country house. At Nuneham Courtenay (Oxford.) Lord Harcourt
built such a formal village in the 1760s along the Oxford-Henley
turnpike. Uniform paired brick cottages faced one another in
mirror image on either side of the road. A similar style village was
built by the Earl of Dorchester at Milton Abbas (Dorset) in the
late 1770s, while at Harewood (West Riding) a formal settlement of
a different nature emerged in the 1760s when Edwin Lascelles
commissioned John Carr of York to rebuild both his country house
and estate village. The substantially built classical-style stone
houses were constructed in terraces outside a park entrance, the
whole scene producing an urban rather than a rural image.[46]
Relatively few examples of such 'regular-built' villages came into
being. Elsewhere in the countryside less formal estate villages
were constructed. As early as the late seventeenth century a new
village was built at the park gates of Euston (Suffolk) replacing
a settlement removed from the park.[47] Here the cottages were
irregularly sited singly or in blocks of two and three and constructed in the vernacular style of the area; timber-framed with
plaster walls painted white.[48] In Derbyshire, Kedleston village was
relocated following the enclosure and enlargement of the park in
the 1750s and 1760s and in the East Riding, a new Sledmere
village was built outside Sir Christopher Sykes's landscape park
in the 1780s.
    As embellishments of an estate seen by all visitors, the cottages
at the park gates were usually of a better visual quality compared
with their counterparts in the surrounding countryside though
little practical consideration was given to their internal design.
Concern for the living conditions of the village population was not
a common trait among estate owners in the eighteenth century and
the aesthetic appearance of the estate villages was not a priority
at a time when attention was principally focused on the adornment

and beautification of the landowner's country house and park. Master builders were employed for the construction of cottages and other estate buildings, and it was not until the late eighteenth century that architects became associated with small-scale estate housing and other rural domestic buildings. Some early estate villages thus came into being not as model settlements but only as a practical expedient that removed unwanted habitation from a park. Nevertheless, the building of such settlements along approach roads to a park was further testimony to the power and the status of the estate owner.

The formality of planned estate villages received considerable criticism in the late eighteenth century from the disciples of the picturesque. The ideology of the picturesque in turn had a significant impact on the design of estate housing and the development of model estate villages. Picturesque cottages were first built as ornaments in park landscapes to add a 'natural' rustic atmosphere to a prospect. While 'Capability' Brown had obliterated cottages and other buildings that obstructed his picture-landscapes, his successor, Humphry Repton, sought to enliven the rural scene with people and domestic buildings such that the cottage re-emerged as an integral part of planned park landscapes. Some were purely ornamental while others were habitable.

The picturesque movement emerged at the park gates in the form of gothicised and ornamental lodges, cottages and gateways and eventually was interpreted in the design of estate villages. An informal grouping of individually designed cottages around a village green was characteristic of model-estate villages of the nineteenth century, planned in the sense of being a deliberate creation but informal in layout. Such model villages were, in morphological terms, akin to organically evolved settlements yet distinguishable from them in that even though buildings were of different styles all were constructed within the same time period and of the same basic materials.

Only the more wealthy of the landed classes could afford the luxury of a 'model village' and relatively few entirely new settlements in picturesque style appeared in the landscape. Of the small group that came into being the most renowned of its day was undoubtedly Blaise Hamlet (Glos.) designed by John Nash in 1803 for J.S. Harford of Blaise Castle.[49] Here Nash excelled in the cottage *ornée* for practical use. No longer ornaments to grace a park landscape, the buildings at Blaise were designed as residences for elderly estate tenants. The village of Somerleyton (Suffolk) built for Sir Morton Peto in the mid-nineteenth century was closely modelled on Blaise Hamlet,[50] which probably also inspired the building of Edensor on the Chatsworth Estate, planned for the Duke of Devonshire by Paxton from 1838. An existing settlement at Edensor had already been substantially depleted by earlier emparking. When the new village was designed remnants of the former settlement were demolished to make way for a model village laid out in an irregular plan and composed of substantially built stone houses embracing a veritable compendium of architectural

styles.[51] On the Bearwood Estate (Berks.) the entirely new village
of Sindlesham Green was built, as the name implies, around a
green at the gates of the park at the same time that the Victorian
country house was being completed for John Walter, editor of
The Times (see p. 47). Other nineteenth-century picturesque
villages included Harlaxton (Lincs.) partially rebuilt by the
Sherwin-Gregory family and Old Warden (Beds.) built for Lord
Ongley owner of Old Warden Park Estate until 1877 when it became the property of Joseph Shuttleworth.[52]

Many rural settlements served as 'home' villages of large landed
estates through accident of location as much as design or intent.
Considerable building activity in the form of rebuilding and remodelling took place in these villages from the mid-eighteenth
and throughout the nineteenth century such that, even though they
were not planned as a composite settlement from the outset, they
nevertheless came to reflect the architectural tastes of the estate
owner.

General Building Activity. Despite the legislative impositions of
the Poor Law, a number of enlightened landlords built good
cottages and invested capital in estate buildings in the late eighteenth century although such individuals were undoubtedly in the
minority. Coke of Norfolk employed Samuel Wyatt from 1780 to
design farm buildings and cottages for the Holkham Estate.
Activity was first focused on the park, home farm and adjacent
park villages, but was later directed to the provision of substantially built houses and cottages over the entire estate such that
during Coke's lifetime every farm on his land was rebuilt, even
to the extent of replacing existing buildings on newly acquired
land.[53] Arthur Young reported that by 1804 around £100,000 had
been invested at Holkham on farm buildings.[54] Such investment,
underlain with the belief that improvement in estate buildings
was as important as improvement of land quality, was matched by
few landlords before the mid-nineteenth century. From that time,
however, notable changes took place in estate building policies as
an increased awareness of the poor living conditions of the rural
population in general, and agricultural workers in particular,
began to be reflected in the provision of better housing and other
community buildings. Not all landlords, however, shared the
opinion of Lord Tollemache of Peckforton (Cheshire) who wrote
that, 'The only real and lasting pleasure to be derived from the
possession of a landed estate, is to witness the improvement in the
social conditions of those residing in it.'[55] On his estate, up to
1881, he expended over £280,000 on the provision of farm houses
and new cottages. A benevolent autocrat of a similar vein was the
1st Duke of Westminster, who during his lifetime as owner of the
Eaton Hall Estate (Cheshire) built no less than 48 farmhouses,
360 cottages, 8 schools, 7 village halls and three churches.[56]

Philanthropy and paternalism became fashionable images for
Victorian landowners, most of whom took care to ensure that some
beneficent act was visible on their estate. To what extent increased

building activity was a philanthropic act and how much a response to a practical need or undertaken as a political expedient can only be surmised. At a time when the pull of industrial and urban growth at home and the expanding opportunities in the New World were attracting labour from rural areas, the provision of good housing was one means to maintain a permanent labour force. For whatever motives there was an increase in the number of cottages and a general improvement in farm buildings on a great many estates around the mid-nineteenth century. But the provision of housing in particular advanced dramatically following the passing of the Union Chargeability Act in 1865. Evidence from building accounts and other sources indicate that the ten-year period from the mid-1860s was one of heavy expenditure on farm buildings and cottages on a number of large estates.[57]

In certain areas the sparsity of cottage accommodation in the early nineteenth century was not only a consequence of the Laws of Settlement but was as much due to the relatively late enclosure of former waste land. Such was the case on the wolds of Lincolnshire and the East Riding of Yorkshire. The 2nd Earl of Yarborough expressed interest in the question of cottages on his Lincolnshire Estate in 1847 and it is evident that a number of cottages were built before the 1860s.[58]

> The late Lord Yarborough [the 2nd Earl] and the late Mr. Heneage [George Fieschi Heneage] built on their estates many cottages before the passing of the Union Chargeability Act, and more to their credit, as it would naturally be against the wishes and pecuniary interests of many of their tenants.[59]

Building activity was also much in evidence on newly acquired estates. Land at Lockinge (Berks.) purchased by the London banker Lewis Loyd in 1854 as an investment property became a residential estate in 1858 when it was settled on his granddaughter and Major R. Lindsey following their marriage.[60] The estate villages and farms were considerably improved in the 1860s. Part of Lockinge village was replanned and rebuilt and a number of model cottages were also erected in the village of Ardington. An estate yard was set up at Ardington to undertake the reconstruction, repair and construction of buildings over the entire property, and it was later recorded that the 'yard' employed over one hundred men.[61]

In general, estate buildings of the mid-nineteenth century were more substantial, functional and standardised than those of earlier decades. Widespread use of pattern-book designs, discussions and competitions in contemporary journals disseminated popular building styles throughout England.[62] The brick cottages and houses, for example, built on the Brocklesby Estate (Lincs.) displayed features common to designs of the day, notably steep-pitched tile roofs and superficial Tudor ornamentation.[63]

Around this time counteracting forces appeared to be at work, one to increase standardisation, another to return to more tradi-

tional local designs and materials. Standardisation in design
coupled with improved transport and the increased availability of
building materials had led to a decline in vernacular architecture,
yet beginning in the Victorian period were deliberate attempts to
reinstate local styles and materials for estate buildings. The work
of E. Nesfield for Lord Crewe at the estate village of Crewe Green
(Cheshire) in the 1860s has been pinpointed as a crucial turning
point in the move back towards regional styles in domestic architecture, even though George Devey had built vernacular cottages on
the Penshurst Estate (Kent) for Lord de L'Isle in the 1850s.[64]

Particularly in the nineteenth century a burst of activity occurred
in the provision of new and remodelled buildings for community
use on estate property. Price wrote in his *Essay on the Picturesque*
(1798) that 'There is no way in which wealth can produce such
natural unaffected variety, as by adorning a real village, and
promoting the comfort and enjoyment of its inhabitants'.[65] In 1830
Robinson illustrated Price's observations in a book titled *Village
Architecture* which itemised the principal landmarks in a village
and provided designs for 'the inn, the schoolhouse, almshouses,
market house, shambles, workhouse, parsonage, town hall and
church.'[66] Examples can be found throughout England of the provision of such facilities on large landed estates. Among them
occur interesting cases reflecting both prevailing architectural
styles and the character of the landowner who instigated them. A
case in point is the town hall at Ripley (West Riding) on the
Ingilby family estate, a mid-nineteenth-century gothic edifice and
a testimony to the personality of its creator whose love of European
travel became immortalised in the bold inscription 'Hotel de Ville'
on the front of the building.[67]

Estate owners particularly excelled in the provision of rural
churches and schools. In their role as lord of the manor, landowners had long patronised the construction and maintenance of
rural parish churches and from the early sixteenth century had
endowed almshouses for the poor to replace the charitable hospitality of the monasteries. Church building in the nineteenth
century may well have been motivated by political or even commercial reasons[68] but the religious zeal of the Victorian era and the
growing concern for the spiritual and moral welfare of the lower
classes was undoubtedly a motivating force behind the remodelling
and building of churches and chapels on many estates. On the
Sledmere Estate (East Riding), for example, as many as twelve
churches were built or rebuilt in the period 1863 to 1879 by the
5th baronet, Sir Tatton Sykes.[69]

Increased activity coincided with the rising tide of nonconformity
in England. Dissenting views preached against the orthodoxy of
the Church catechism found their greatest converts among the
working classes which threatened seriously to weaken the established order of rural society. It is probable that the resurgence
in church building was an attempt to attract the rural labourers
back into the fold of the Established Church. Nonconformist
chapels and meeting houses were more common in 'open' parishes

while the Anglican Church remained dominant in the 'closed' parishes of landed estates,[70] although strict demarcation was not universal. Wesleyan and Primitive Methodist chapels were found in parishes around the estate heartland at Brocklesby (Lincs.), but were less frequent in parishes where the Earl of Yarborough was the sole landowner.[71]

Education and religion were inextricably linked from early times, but it was not until the nineteenth century that considerable advances in educational facilities took place in the countryside. Two religious-based societies were founded at the turn of the century to build schools for the education of the lower classes; the 'National Society for Promoting the Education of the Poor in Principles of the Established Church' (1811) and the 'British and Foreign School Society' (1808-14). The former sponsored 'National' or 'Church' schools and tended to dominate in rural areas except where there was strong nonconformity, in which case a 'British' or 'Wesleyan' school might have been built by the latter. Supported after 1833 by grants from the government, both groups actively promoted the construction of education facilities in rural areas and directed the attention of estate owners towards education for their workers' children. The majority of new rural schools were built by church groups and local organisations, but a significant number were established in estate villages by benevolent landowners. Considerable activity was evident from the 1840s especially on the estates of the great landowners. Landlord initiative in the provision of schools is well illustrated by the 2nd Earl of Yarborough. Under his patronage a school was built at Housham in 1844 and in the same year he undertook negotiations with the Council of Education to construct a school at Brocklesby. Within the next decade or so, schools were erected at Brocklesby (1847), Broughton (1849), Cabourne, Swallow, Rothwell, Claxby by Normanby (1856) and Horkstow (1858).[72] The Duke of Bedford built eight schools on his estate at Woburn from 1840 to 1868[73] while from 1869 the same number were built by the Duke of Westminster on his estate at Eaton.[74] Gentry landowners were also providers of local schools. In 1856 the Rt Hon.Tennyson d' Eyncourt built 'commodious schools in gothic style' in the village of Tealby adjacent to his country house at Bayon's Manor (Lincs.).[75]

The number of schools endowed by local landowners rose after 1870 with the passing of the Education Act of that year, an Act designed to provide facilities for education in regions that were deficient.[76] The threat of greater external control and non-sectarian schools in their local community motivated many proprietors to build. Control that some landowners maintained over their schools was evident from the unwillingness to allow any inspection of their property for the purpose of school returns.[77] But, as education provision progressively moved into the hands of the State, fewer schools were built by estate owners.

Property Identification. The impact on the rural landscape of the building activity of large-estate owners, while important, should

not be exaggerated. Even though the total extent of their land holdings occupied over a third of England it would be incorrect to assume
that they made an identifiable imprint on so large an area by 1880. It
was on the land surrounding the estate nucleus that the greatest
visual association and composite unity of a landed estate was created.
Developments in this fringe area revealed much to the outside
world of the importance of the family who lived within the seclusion of the park. Here the more architecturally distinctive buildings were erected; at the park entrances, on the home farm and
in estate villages and settlements along the approaches to the
park. It is in fact observable that estate buildings were more
simple in style and ornamentation with increasing distance from
the country house and park, a probable reason being that in the
vicinity of the heartland, 'the life and taste of the tenant is not
so much indicated as the life and taste of the landlord and proprietor'.[78] Such a distance-decay was pointed out in an article on
estate farm buildings, in 1843, in which it was written that, 'the
farmsteads near the residence, or near the roads approaching to
it, may obtain some attention; but the remote ones are left to their
fate'.[79] Despite increased building activity in the latter half of
the nineteenth century the distance-decay factor remained evident
in the landscape. At one level it was apparent, for example, in
the school buildings on the Yarborough Estate. The schoolhouse
at Brocklesby Park, basic in plan, was quite ornate in external
detail, its carved brick chimneys being reminiscent of the picturesque fashion introduced early in the nineteenth century by
John Nash. It has no equal elsewhere on the estate.

Standard architectural styles taken from pattern books or distinctive styles designed by professional architects, the use of
bricks or local stone moulded or carved in estate yards sometimes
made possible the identification of buildings belonging to one or
another landowner, particularly on the vast and more compact
county estates such as exemplified in Eastern England by Holkham,
Brocklesby and Sledmere. On each of these great estates the
enclosure of extensive areas of previous waste land in the eighteenth and nineteenth centuries was followed by the layout of new
farms and considerable building activity. Where such sweeping
changes occurred, the likelihood of standardised building and
visual unity of the estate was greater. In older farm landscapes
building styles and materials were more likely to reflect the tastes
of a number of generations of estate owners, and have less apparent visual association.

Identification of a landowner's property was often assured by
the use of a datestone, cipher or distinguishing mark placed in a
prominent position on a building as testimony to future generations
as to its owner or benefactor. Such emblems were in some cases
the only feature by which to recognise the buildings of a particular
estate. The use of a mark of ownership had been in effect from
medieval times when families first began to adopt a coat of arms.
Estate size appears to have no bearing on this feature which was
used as much to identify ownership or to denote a philanthropic

act by the gentry and great landowners alike. The use of the Pelham Buckle or Pelham Peacock, parts of the family coat of arms identified buildings on the Yarborough Estate;[80] in the East Riding Lord Londesborough used a distinguishing cipher but one that was not derived from the coat of arms[81] and in Norfolk the 'T.W.C.' on datestones testified to the prolific building activity of Thomas William Coke, 'Coke of Norfolk'.[82] At Harlaxton (Lincs.) some houses bore the initials 'G.D.G.', the work of George de Linge Gregory in the period 1790 to 1820, and others were marked 'J.S.G.' signifying the building activity of John Sherwin Gregory who succeeded to the estate in 1860.[83]

Finally, mention should briefly be made of insignia of a different sort found in the English countryside. It was common for a village inn to be named after and indeed built by the local estate owner; the 'Yarborough Arms' at New Holland, the 'Walter Arms', at Bearwood, the 'Harcourt Arms' at Nuneham Courtenay, the 'Gregory Arms' at Harlaxton. A word of caution, however: the frequent occurrence of the 'Duke of Wellington' on inns outside the boundaries of the Stratfield and Saye Estate and the county of Hampshire is not testimony to the family's extensive landed wealth, but to the honours bestowed on the famous Duke by the English public and publicans!

NOTES

1 The role of landed society in industrial and urban development are the themes of a number of published works including; J.T. Ward and R.G. Wilson (eds.), 'Land and Industry' (David and Charles, Newton Abbot, 1971); S. Jenkins, 'Landlords to London' (Constable, London, 1975); D. Cannadine, 'Lords and Landlords' (Leicester Univ. Press, 1980).

2 F.M.L. Thompson, 'English Landed Society in the Nineteenth Century' (Routledge and Kegan Paul, London, 1963), p. 153.

3 See R.C. Parker, Coke of Norfolk and the Agricultural Revolution, 'Econ. Hist. Rev.', 2nd ser., vol. 8 (1955), pp. 155-66; and J.H. Plumb, Sir Robert Walpole and Norfolk Husbandry, 'Econ. Hist. Rev.', vol. 5 (1952), pp. 86-9.

4 P. Pusey, On the Agricultural Improvements of Lincolnshire, 'JRASE', vol. iv (1843), p. 299.

5 J.T. Ward, 'East Yorkshire Landed Estates in the Nineteenth Century' (East Yorkshire Local History Society, York, 1967), Local History Series No. 23, p. 13.

6 R. Newton, 'The Northumberland Landscape' (Hodder and Stoughton, London, 1972), p. 120.

7 Ibid., p. 120.

8 J.D. Chambers and G.E. Mingay, 'The Agricultural Revolution 1750-1880' (Batsford, London, 1966), p. 59.

9 J.A. Scott Watson, 'The History of the Royal Agricultural Society of England, 1839-1939' (Royal Agricultural Society of England, London, 1939); E.A. Wasson, The Third Earl Spencer and Agriculture 1818-1845, 'Agric. Hist. Rev.', vol.

26, pt. 11, (1978), pp. 89-99.

10   Newton, 'Northumberland Landscape', p. 119.

11   J.M. Robinson, Estate Buildings at Holkham - II, 'Country Life', 28 Nov. (1974), p. 1642.

12   LAO, Yarb. 5, Surveys and Valuations, Diary 1897-8, pp. 27 and 41.

13   D. Sutherland, 'The Landowners' (Anthony Blond, London, 1968), p. 15.

14   Quoted in C. Hussey, 'The Picturesque', 2nd edn (Frank Cass, London, 1967), pp. 128-9.

15   For the development of the *ferme ornée* see, Hussey, 'The Picturesque', pp. 130-4.

16   Repton's suggestion was contained in the Red Book produced for Tatton Park (Cheshire) in 1794.

17   D.M. Palliser, 'The Staffordshire Landscape' (Hodder and Stoughton, London, 1976), p. 136.

18   A. Harris, 'The Rural Landscape of the East Riding of Yorkshire 1700-1850' (Oxford Univ. Press, London, 1961), pp. 73-5. Christopher Sykes Esq., became Sir Christopher Sykes in 1783 when he succeeded to the estate at Sledmere.

19   T. Rowley, 'The Shropshire Landscape' (Hodder and Stoughton, London, 1972), p. 128.

20   Quoted in M. Robbins, 'The Railway Age' (Penguin, Harmondsworth, 1965), p. 57.

21   W.G. Hoskins and R.A. McKinley (eds) 'VCH of Leicestershire', 2nd edn (Dawsons, London, 1969), vol. 3, p. 118.

22   Newton, 'Northumberland Landscape', p. 118.

23   Ibid., p. 231.

24   Palliser, 'Staffordshire Landscape', p. 250; 'The Buildings of England: Staffordshire' (Penguin, Harmondsworth, 1974), pp. 236-8.

25   Other causes of depopulation and desertion included the Black Death, natural population decline and wars.

26   L.A. Parker, Enclosure in Leicestershire 1485-1607, unpublished PhD thesis, Univ. of London (Leicester), 1948, p. 83, footnote 176.

27   M. Beresford and J.G. Hurst (eds), 'Deserted Medieval Villages' (Lutterworth, London, 1971), p. 17.

28   M. Beresford, 'The Lost Villages of England', 4th edn (Lutterworth, London, 1971), pp. 205-6.

29   C. Taylor, 'The Cambridgeshire Landscape' (Hodder and Stoughton, London, 1973), pp. 164-5.

30   L. Stone and J.C.F. Stone, Country Houses and their Owners in Hertfordshire 1540-1879 in W.O. Aydelotte, A.C. Boque and R.W. Fogel, (eds), 'The Dimensions of Quantitative Research in History' (Princeton Univ. Press, New Jersey, 1972), pp. 77 and 109.

31   N. Pye (ed.), 'Leicester and Its Region' (Leicester Univ. Press, 1972), p. 256.

32   G. Darley, 'Villages of Vision' (Architectural Press, London, 1975), p. 2.

33   Beresford, 'Lost Villages', p. 342.
34   Darley, 'Villages of Vision', p. 142.
35   For a most comprehensive discussion on the differences be-
     tween villages owned by large landowners and those predomi-
     nantly in multiple ownership, see D.R. Mills, 'Lord and
     Peasant in Nineteenth Century Britain' (Croom Helm, London,
     1980).
36   The Poor Law Act 1601, 43 Eliz. I, c.2.
37   F. Emery, 'The Oxfordshire Landscape' (Hodder and Stoughton,
     London, 1974), p. 172.
38   LAO, Hen. 3/43, Estate Survey, 1790s.
39   'Stamford Mercury', 4 April 1845, Report of meeting of the
     Caistor Union Board of Guardians.
40   Hon. E. Stanhope (ed.), Report on the Employment of
     Children, Young Persons and Women in Agriculture, 'BPP'
     (1867).
41   'The Poor Law Report of 1834', reprinted and edited with
     introduction and notes by S.G. and E.O.A. Checkland
     (Penguin, Harmondsworth, 1974).
42   Census of Population 1851; Lincolnshire.
43   Union Chargeability Act 1865, 28 & 29 Vict., c.79.
44   Published reports are available for Bedfordshire, Berkshire,
     Buckinghamshire, Dorset, Essex, Hampshire, Norfolk,
     Northumberland, Nottinghamshire, Oxfordshire, Somerset,
     Suffolk, Surrey and Sussex; 'Reports to the Poor Law Board
     on the Laws of Settlement and Removal of the Poor'; 1850.
     Reports were not made for every county but this does not
     imply that the problems were not evident. See also, Harris,
     'Rural Landscape of the East Riding', pp. 192-4; Emery,
     'Oxfordshire Landscape', p. 176; D.R. Mills, The Poor Laws
     and the Distribution of Population, c. 1660-1860, with special
     Reference to Lincolnshire, 'TIBG', vol. 26 (1959), pp. 185-95;
     D.R. Mills, The Development of Rural Settlement Around
     Lincoln, pp. 83-97, and The Geographical Effects of the
     Laws of Settlement in Nottinghamshire: An Analysis of Francis
     Howell's Report, 1848, pp. 182-91, in D.R. Mills (ed.) 'English
     Rural Communities' (Macmillan, London, 1973); B.A. Holder-
     ness, Open and Closed Parishes in England, 'Agric. Hist.
     Rev.', vol. 20, (1972), pp. 126-39; D.R. Mills, 'Lord and
     Peasant in Nineteenth Century Britain'.
45   B. Disraeli, 'Sybil' (1845, reprinted Peter Davies, London,
     1927), p. 62; description of the rural town of Marney.
46   Darley, 'Villages of Vision', p. 10.
47   N. Pevsner, 'The Buildings of England: Suffolk', 2nd edn
     (Penguin, Harmondsworth, 1974), p. 185.
48   E. Sandon, 'A View into the Village' (Terence Dalton, Laven-
     ham, 1969) p. 108.
49   T. Davis, 'The Architecture of John Nash' (Studio, London,
     1960), p. 72; J. Summerson, 'John Nash', 2nd edn (Allen and
     Unwin, London, 1949), p. 100.
50   Darley, 'Villages of Vision', p. 144.

51   Ibid., pp. 38-40.
52   W. Page (ed.) 'VCH of Bedfordshire', 2nd edn (Dawsons, London, 1972), vol. 3, p. 253.
53   J.M. Robinson, Estate Buildings at Holkham - I, 'Country Life', 21 Nov. (1974), pp. 1554-7, Estate Buildings at Holkham - II, 'Country Life', 28 Nov. (1974), pp. 1642-5.
54   Ibid., p. 1642.
55   Quoted in M. Girouard, 'The Victorian Country House' (Clarendon, Oxford, 1971), p. 74.
56   Ibid., p. 1.
57   H. Fuller, Landownership and the Lindsey Landscape, 'Annals of the Association of American Geographers', vol. 66, no. 1, March (1976), p. 23; T.W. Beastall, A South Yorkshire Estate in the Late Nineteenth Century, 'Agric. Hist. Rev.', vol. XIV (1966), p. 44.
58   In a letter to his agent the Earl wrote 'the condition of the labourers' cottages on the estate is a subject to which I had had my attention drawn and that I intend to improve them - and to inspect personally the cottages attached to the farms', LAO, Yarb. 9, Letter Books, 1847, no. 82.
59   Stanhope, Employment in Agriculture, p. 73.
60   M.A. Havinden, 'Estate Villages' (Lund Humphries, London, 1966), p. 31.
61   Ibid., pp. 68-9.
62   One vehicle for discussion was provided in the 'JRASE'. In the 1840s a number of articles and prize essays dealt with the subject of estate buildings, particularly cottages. See, for example, J. Grey, On Farm-Buildings, pp. 1-16 and Rev. C. Hill, On the Construction of Cottages, pp. 356-69, 'JRASE', vol. 4 (1843); J. Grey, On the Building of Cottages for Farm-Labourers, 'JRASE', vol. 5 (1844), pp. 237-244; Duke of Bedford, On Labourers Cottages, pp. 185-7 and H. Goddard, On the Construction of a Pair of Cottages for Agricultural Labourers, 'JRASE', vol. 10 (1849), pp. 230-46. A number of pattern books of the late eighteenth and early nineteenth century are listed and described by J. Woodforde, 'The Truth About Cottages' (Routledge and Kegan Paul, London, 1969), pp. 23-8.
63   Features described by Darley, 'Villages of Vision', p. 52.
64   Ibid., pp. 56, 1 and 141.
65   V. Price, 'Essay on the Picturesque' (2 vols. London, 1978), vol. 2, p. 402.
66   P.F. Robinson, 'Village Architecture' (James Carpenter, London, 1830), The quotation is the sub-title of the book.
67   Darley, 'Villages of Vision', p. 16.
68   Thompson, 'English Landed Society', cites the case of Lord Monson who noted that, 'a church may induce the letting of land for building leases and church building is often an advantageous speculation', p. 208.
69   Ward, 'East Yorkshire Landed Estates', p. 14.
70   A. Everitt, 'The Pattern of Rural Dissent: the Nineteenth

Century' (Leicester Univ. Press, 1972), Department of English Local History, Occasional Papers, 2nd ser., no. 4, p. 21.

71 It cannot, however, be substantiated that the Earl of Yarborough, 'virtually never suffered nonconformity to appear', ibid., p. 49, as in the provision of estate schools the Earl took special note of the needs of dissenters.

72 R.C. Russell, 'A History of Schools and Education in Lindsey Lincolnshire 1800-1902' (Lindsey County Council, Education Committee, 1965), p. 68.

73 J. Godber, 'History of Bedfordshire' (Bedfordshire County Council, 1969), pp. 478-9.

74 Girouard, 'Victorian Country House', p. 1.

75 W. White, 'History, Gazetteer, and Directory of Lincolnshire' (1856, reprinted David and Charles, Newton Abbot, 1969), p. 488.

76 Education Act 1870, 33 & 34 Vict., c. 75.

77 Russell, 'A History of Schools', p. 69; Godber, 'History of Bedfordshire', p. 479.

78 A.J. Downing, 'The Architecture of Country Houses' (1850, reprinted Da Capo Press, New York, 1968), p. 42.

79 Grey, On Farm-Buildings, p. 2.

80 Fuller, Lindsey Landscape, p. 18.

81 D. Neave, 'Londesborough' (Londesborough Silver Jubilee Committee, 1977), p. 56.

82 Robinson, Estate Buildings, p. 1554.

83 J. Murden, 'Harlaxton Through the Ages' (J. Murden, 1976) pp. 9 and 17.

> The objects which men aim at when they become possessed of
> land . . . may I think be enumerated as follows:
> (1) political influence; (2) social importance, founded on
> territorial possession, the most visible and unmistakable form
> of wealth; (3) power exercised over tenantry; the pleasure of
> managing directing and improving the estate itself; (4) residen-
> tial enjoyment, including what is called sport; (5) the money
> return - the rent. 15th Earl of Derby, 'Ireland and the Land
> Act', *Nineteenth Century*, Oct. (1881), p. 474.

Landed estate owners for many centuries had conspicuously embellished the countryside with a landscape that reflected their
power and status in English society. In the nineteenth century an
unprecedented spate of activity preceded the demise of an era,
a final flourish and fanfare of opulence that heralded the end of
over three centuries of landed dominance in England. The extrava-
gances of large landowners throughout the Victorian period, their
lavish displays of wealth in the building and remodelling of
country houses, the laying out of new formal gardens, and acts
of beneficence in the countryside at large, masked the gradual
societal changes that had begun to undermine the very foundations
of landed society well before the end of the century. A new social,
economic and political order was evolving, but its impact on the
large landowners and their estate property was not felt until the
closing decades of the nineteenth century and not apparent in
the landscape until the twentieth.

The changing composition of landed society during the nineteenth century was in itself evidence of the developing milieu of
a capitalistic urban and industrial economy. While the English
landed classes since Tudor times had been expanded by the introduction of capital from trade and commerce, the impact was more
dramatic in the nineteenth century when possession of wealth,
whether from industrial, commercial or agricultural sources,
essentially replaced the values of birth and tradition as the symbol
of upper-class landed society. Increases in wealth were as characteristic for the 'established' landed families as for the emerging
commercial and industrial elite. The momentum of the industrial
revolution made fortunes for many landowners in the exploitation
of mineral rights, in the promotion of transport networks, in the
creation of port and harbour facilities and in the development of
urban property.

Bankruptcies were not uncommon in the high-risk period of

emerging capitalism and investment in land also afforded a more
stable and apparently secure foundation for newly acquired wealth.
But land remained a desirable commodity for its social value long
after its investment value had declined relative to expanding
commercial and industrial opportunities in the nineteenth century.
In 1870 it was written in *The Economist* that

> it would 'pay' a millionaire in England to sink half his fortune
> in buying 10,000 acres of land to return a shilling percent,
> and live upon the remainder, rather than live upon the whole
> without land . . . he would be a greater person in the eyes of
> more people.[1]

The *nouveau riche* thus invested newly amassed fortunes in
country houses and estate property and assumed the traditional
trappings of landed society. They embraced all aspects of the
'country-house culture', pursued the pleasures of hunting and
shooting and entertained on a par with their established counterparts.

As with previous entrants to landed society industrial and
commercial magnates sought landed status also as a possible means
to ennoblement, the ultimate symbol of social recognition. Ennoblement had long been associated with the possession of land yet this
apparent partnership was in decline by the late nineteenth century.
In his study of the new advancements in the British peerage during the reign of Queen Victoria and up to 1911, Pumphrey has
shown that, even though up to 1881 relatively few new families
had been elevated to the peerage from outside landed society,
during the period 1837 to 1885 the ratio between creations from
within landed society and those from without was gradually changing.[2] The established landed tradition in the House of Lords was
increasingly diluted as recognition for public service was awarded
to a growing number of commercial and industrial entrepreneurs.
From 1885 to 1911 over a third of the individuals receiving peerages
emanated from backgrounds outside landed society and just over
a quarter were from commerce and industry.[3] A large landed
estate, although still actively sought after for other motives, was
no longer an essential accoutrement for entry to the peerage by
the end of the nineteenth century.

Changes occurring in the rural environment progressively led
to a diminution of local power and authority of the landed classes.
The estate formed the nucleus of patriarchal rural society, of
communities in which the farmers, tradesmen, agricultural workers
and other rural folk were dependent on the 'big house' for their
livelihood and in which the landowner in turn relied on members
of the local society to work his land, to supply his daily needs
and to provide political support when called upon. The power in
the system was in the hands of the landowner, an authority inherited with the estate and accepted by the remainder of rural
society for the most part, without question.

> The position of landed proprietor, be he squire or nobleman is
> one of dignity. Wealth must always bring its responsibilities,
> but a landed proprietor is especially in a responsible position.
> He is the natural head of his parish or district. . .in which
> he should be looked up to as the bond of union between the
> classes.[4]

Dependency by the lower classes brought deference which
bolstered the political power of the landed elite. Autocracy in
rural England survived as long as this established order was maintained.

One of the key elements in the system was the relationship between a landlord and his tenants. The landlord was in the dominant position as long as the rural population continued to increase,
as it had at an unprecedented rate since the mid-nineteenth
century; so generating competition for farms among prospective
tenants. Even at times of agricultural depression in the 1830s
and 1850s when owners found difficulty in letting farms the tenants
did not seek to press their advantageous position, though evidence
shows that on many estates rentals were reduced as few landlords
at that time were willing to lose tenants and face the consequences
of taking land in-hand to farm it themselves.[5]

The Great Depression, of which much has been written,[6] effectively knocked the bottom out of the market in British agriculture,
more especially in the grain-growing regions of eastern England,
and significantly changed the landlord-tenant relationships on
many estates. Faced with economic hardship tenants were forced
to take a stronger stand and bargain for rent reductions or quit
their farms altogether. Many did leave which forced landowners
to take land in-hand or to obtain new tenants. In this manner
the long-established and traditional associations of many tenant
families with individual estates was broken. Newcomers had less
allegiance to the 'big house' and because of the depressed state
of the farm economy were less bound by restrictive covenants,
though on many estates covenants, or tenancy agreements, had
been noticeably relaxed during the nineteenth century. Clarke
noted of Lincolnshire, for example, in 1851 that 'the agents have
an increasing tendency to let the tenants do as they please with
respect to cropping, generally allowing them to break their agreements'.[7] By the late nineteenth century the supply of let land
exceeded the demand and tenants were unwilling to take up un-
economic holdings. Landowners were forced to lower rents in
order to keep land under cultivation and to retain tenants. The
security of rural land as an investment was called into question
as rental receipts were drastically reduced. On the Brocklesby
Estate revenue from let land fell from £89,000 in 1880 to £50,000
in 1895 and at different times during the intervening period rent
arrears were large, at one time amounting to £30,000.[8]

Legislation also became more favourably disposed towards the
tenant farmer, in the recognition of tenant-rights and in the provisions of the Game Laws. The Agricultural Holdings Act 1875

was the first attempt under law to compensate an outgoing tenant for unexhausted improvements made to the land during the term of tenure.[9] The Act, however, failed to make payment by a landlord compulsory and enabled owners to opt out of the terms of the Act. Tenant-right to compensation was not guaranteed by law until the Agricultural Holdings Act of 1883.[10] Even then landlords could instigate reciprocal claims for damage to property or failure to comply with a tenancy agreement, claims that could negate and exceed the value of a tenant's claim. In a court decision of 1895, however, judgment was ruled in favour of the tenant such that if a landlord counter-claim exceeded the amount awarded to the tenant the landlord was not entitled, under the provision of the 1883 Act, to recover the difference.[11]

The Game Laws, introduced in 1770 to preserve the shooting of game as the exclusive prerogative of the landowner, had long been a bone of contention for estate tenants and a source of political agitation in the early nineteenth century.[12] Crops were destroyed by the ravages of rabbits and hares, and to a lesser extent by game birds, but tenant farmers were legally prohibited from killing game that encroached on their land. The old Game Laws were severe. In the early nineteenth century poaching was a criminal offence with harsh penalities for those caught. The grim use of man-traps and spring guns on some estate game-preserves testified to the extent to which landowners would go to assert their rights for the pleasurable pursuit of sport. By the 1830s the severity of legal penalties for poaching had been somewhat relaxed and the use of inhuman devices had been abolished. The more enlightened landlords hired rabbit catchers to kill game on tenants land, reduced rents on farms adjacent to game preserves, or granted concessions to their tenants for the killing of ground game. In this respect the 2nd Earl of Yarborough provided a good example. When he succeeded to the Brocklesby Estate in 1846 'he allowed his tenants to shoot game as long as they did not disturb the fox coverts'.[13]

Few went as far as the successive owners of the 5,000-acre Elveden Estate (Suffolk) who acquired the estate primarily for sporting purposes, reared large numbers of birds for the shooting season and deliberately retained land in hand to avoid possible conflict with tenants.[14]

In 1880 the Ground Game Act was passed which made it legal for all tenants to kill game trespassing on their farms. Concessionary power of the landlord was removed and replaced by legislation. In this manner the traditional landlord-tenant relations were again thrown out of balance as tenants gained greater proprietory rights over let land.[15]

Rural labourers too gradually became less dependent on the large estates. As the momentum of the industrial revolution accelerated, workers were attracted from the overpopulated countryside to the expanding towns and cities. From the first quarter of the nineteenth century rural migration began to affect the absolute size of rural communities[16] and the abundant and cheap labour supply of the 1820s and 1830s, was gradually replaced, particularly as the twentieth century progressed, by a shortage of agricultural labour in the countryside.

This long-term trend appears to have had little immediate impact on landed society, except in so far as the increase in estate housing from the 1840s to the 1870s may have been partially in response to the exodus of labour and an attempt to retain a permanent body of workers on the large estates. It was, nevertheless, another factor in the changing rural milieu that contributed to the decline of landowner control.

In other aspects the role of the landowner in the rural community was changing. Increased patronage in the institutional fabric of the countryside, evident in the building and remodelling of churches and in the support for new schools, can be seen as a final attempt to reassert and confirm the established order in rural society. The spread of nonconformity, largely outside the control of the landed interest, challenged the religious and social dogma of Anglicanism which was staunchly upheld in the majority of rural parishes by the local landowners. Even so, nonconformity was necessarily tolerated and patronised by landowners, many of whom were obliged to do so in order to maintain the political affiliation of their tenants and the allegiance of good estate workers. In North Lincolnshire 'the Methodists were some of the best tenants Lord Yarborough had'.[17] Thompson has suggested that, among other activities, Earl Fitzwilliam had to 'support the chapels of Dissenters' in order to retain political control over Malton in the North Riding.[18]

The provision of rural schools was practically devoid of any landlord control by the end of the century as the state increasingly intervened in educational provision, particularly following the 1870 Education Act (see p. 89). As standards for educational facilities were raised and greater financial support was required to maintain existing structures the landed classes for the most part retired from the field and handed educational responsibility to the state to be nurtured into a national system.

Other authority positions in rural administration, previously held by the landed interest, had been opened up to other classes or replaced by new organisations by the 1880s. Traditionally, landed society had virtual control over the judicial system at the county and local level. The Lord Lieutenant and the local magistrates were appointments initially based on landed wealth and class status; the former an aristocratic position, the latter generally the role of a landed gentleman. Even though the landed interest retained effective control over the judiciary until the 1880s, the Quarter Sessions, presided over by the Lord Lieutenant and the Justices of the Peace, became less powerful in their control of county government as various duties were handed over to newly instigated local bodies throughout the nineteenth century. It was the setting up of County Councils in 1888, however, that took much of the decision-making in rural affairs out of the hands of the landed interest.[19]

In all new offices, however, including the Board of Guardians set up following the 'new' Poor Law in 1834, the School Boards and the Sanitary District Boards established in 1870, or the County Councils, the landowners for the most part retained a role as elected officials. But while their previous position of power was autocratic the changes of the nineteenth century instituted more democratic control.

At the national level the opening up of the Civil Service and the university system with the introduction of competitive examinations in 1870 and the abolition of purchased commissions in 1871 curtailed the virtual landed monopoly of the Civil Service, the army and the professions, although the impact of such legislation took time to work through the established system.

In the political arena landed society also gradually lost power throughout the nineteenth century. In county society the political hold of the landed interest essentially derived from the deferential characteristics of the rural classes in which the allegiance of tenant farmers to the landlord, or his chosen candidate, played a vital part in local elections. Tenants were a numerically significant proportion of the enfranchised population of rural areas in the early nineteenth century. There is, however, little evidence to support the notion that selection of tenants was in any way linked to their political affiliations, or that coercion was brought to bear on the voting of farmers. In fact the 2nd Earl of Yarborough had twice publicly denied any attempts to influence tenant voting on the Brocklesby Estate. He declared in 1832 to be proud 'that my father has allowed his tenantry to vote as they please, and I wish every landlord in the country would do the same', and later, in 1850, in a letter to the *Stamford Mercury* he stated that, 'I am satisfied no person can say that I have attempted at any time to control the free expression of opinion in politics by my tenantry'.[20] Nevertheless, it was repeatedly apparent in election results that the majority of tenant farmers on the Brocklesby Estate, as on other landed property throughout the countryside, voted with their landlord.

The deferential aspect of nineteenth-century rural society remains a controversy amongst political and social historians and sociologists.[21] How much was tenant voting, if not a response to direct coercion, a form of psychological coercion from fear of eviction or future reprisal, or to what extent was allegiance given in the expectation of landlord favours in rents or other allowances remain questions of debate. Whatever the basis of tenant voting their enfranchised status played a considerable part in the retention of political power by the landed classes. When this changed, and landowners were faced with new challenges in order to secure parliamentary seats, legislation contained in three Reform Bills progressively undermined their ability to retain political control. Successive Acts in 1832, 1867 and 1884 broadened the base of the voting population to embrace a wider spectrum of English society.[22] The 1867 Act enfranchised middle and working-class householders in the towns. It was not until 1884, however, that agricultural

labourers were accorded the same rights. Parliamentary representation was given to many new towns and cities for the first time.
Adjustments in electoral boundaries broke the traditional ties of
landlord patronage over parts of the English countryside and
finally, with the introduction of the secret ballot in 1872, the
reality of coercion was effectively undermined.[23]

The middle class acquired a political voice and increasing
strength as representatives of commerce and industry were voted
into parliament. Attacks on the power of the land aristocracy
became more vocal from middle-class radicals (see p. 19). Anti-
Corn-Law agitation was seen as an attempt to break the monopolistic hold of the landed aristocracy and even though its repercussions were not drastically felt till the 1870s, the repeal of the
Corn Laws in 1846 effectively heralded the end of agrarian dominance in the political arena and with it the demise of traditional
landed society.[24]

After 1885 the landed interest no longer dominated the House of
Commons and became relatively less representative of the aristocracy in the House of Lords. The power of the latter was in any
case considerably curtailed with the passing of the Parliament Act
in 1911.[25] By the late nineteenth century the interests of landed
society were no longer protected by Parliament and the tables
were soon to be turned in the twentieth century when the demands
for greater economic equality that accompanied emerging socialism
focused government policy on the elimination of private wealth,
especially landed wealth.

The currents of change that were undermining the power of
landed society had little repercussion on the estate itself until
the advent of the Great Depression in the period after 1875. Even
so, at the close of the nineteenth century and point of entry into
the twentieth, the impact was more apparent in the abstract sense
pertaining to changes in ownership than in any profound manner
visible in the landscape. The depression largely brought to an end
any further expansion of the great agricultural estates and had
important effects on both the agricultural industry and the life-
styles of landed society. The degree of impact varied throughout
England from county to county and from estate to estate. In terms
of a declining agricultural market the arable eastern counties from
the East Riding to Kent and as far west as Hampshire and parts
of Gloucestershire, and the county of Wiltshire, bore the brunt of
the depressed state of agriculture, although counties where livestock was dominant over grain production were not entirely unaffected. The price of meat and dairy products fell in the 1880s
and 1890s, but downswings in the livestock market were not as
prolonged nor as intense as those affecting arable agriculture.
Fletcher in fact showed that during the course of the depression
the value of gross output from livestock farms in Lancashire rose
by a third.[26]

For many landlords the reduction in the rental and capital value
of estate property, as an outcome of the depression, led to economies in estate management and personal life-style. Expenditure

on estate buildings was drastically curbed and investment in agricultural improvements and capital maintenance slowed down. Some landed families went bankrupt largely as an outcome of the increased indebtedness that the loss of agricultural revenue brought upon the estate. Such appears to have been the cause of the break-up of the Manners-Sutton property at Kelham, (Notts.). In the 1850s the family had rebuilt their country house. It has been suggested that the grand scale of the new mansion was not justifiable for the estate of 5,500 acres that yielded only £11,500 per annum.[27] It is possible to speculate that if the agricultural economy had remained as buoyant as it was in the period 1840 to 1870, the family may have 'held on', but as it turned out the estate was heavily mortgaged at the onset of the depression and when J.H. Manners-Sutton died in 1898 the mortgage was fore-closed and the estate went into Chancery.[28] A similar fate transpired for the Buckworths of Cockley Cley (Norfolk), who mortgaged the estate to rebuild the country house in the 1870s and were subsequently hit by falling grain prices. In 1900 the estate of around 3,600 acres was sold following bankruptcy. It is probable too that the agricultural depression contributed to the decline of the Carlton Towers Estate (West Riding). The 9th Lord Beaumont went bankrupt after rebuilding the country house at Carlton Towers in the 1870s, which resulted in the sale of most of the nearly 6,000 acre estate in 1888-9. By 1892 all land except 800 acres had been sold.[29]

Many estates became encumbered by financial indebtedness that burdened the property well into the twentieth century. The Settled Land Act of 1882 was passed in an attempt to liberate the proprietory rights of entailed owners and to permit greater flexibility in the disposal of land. As an outcome more owners were able to put land into the market. But the market was glutted, land prices were poor and the demand for agricultural property low. None the less, evidence from the sample population indicates that a number of estate sales were made. The Carew-Gibson Estate at Sandgate (Sussex) was broken-up by sale in 1887; in 1888 Jeremiah Coleman, the 'mustard king', purchased Gatton Park (Surrey) from Viscount Oxenbridge (7th Baron Monson); in 1889 the Berkswell Hall Estate (Warwicks.) was sold; in 1890 W.D. James purchased the 8,000-acre West Dean Estate (Sussex) from F. Bower; in 1892 the Maer Hall Estate (Staffs.) comprising some 4,000 acres was sold in its entirety by Henry Davenport to Mr F.J. Harrison, a Liverpool shipowner; in Salop the 4,000-acre Condover Estate owned by R. Cholmondeley was sold by auction in July 1895, and in Somerset and Dorset the entire property of Viscount Bridport comprising 5,683 acres was put up for sale in 1895, and by 1897 a Mr Fry of Bristol was the owner of its heartland at Cricket St. Thomas comprising 1,370 acres including the country house, park and home farm.[30]

Not all landowners were fortunate in their ability to sell land and some property put on the market was later withdrawn.[31] Others sold, or attempted to sell, portions of estate land. On Lord

Yarborough's Estate two large farms in the parish of Thorganby,
ten miles from Brocklesby Park, were sold to their tenants in
1891.[32] Economies were also made in other ways by the land magnates and gentry alike. Lord Yarborough in 1895 leased his London
residence in Arlington St to Lord Wolverton and let the shooting
rights at Manby for £800. He also sold all his horses and one pack
of the famous Brocklesby hounds.[33] Some families let the country
house and lived elsewhere while others sold or leased their town
house and retreated to the quieter life on their home estates.

Not all suffered to the same extent or even at all. It has already
been indicated that the impact on estates in the livestock counties
was small in comparison to the effect in the arable areas of England.
Throughout the country, however, landowners with substantial
non-agricultural sources of income were more readily able to
weather fluctuations in the agricultural economy. Even where the
depression induced a high turnover of tenants, lower rental
income and the need to take land in-hand, owners with income
from outside agriculture were able to maintain their family estates
throughout the period; some on the basis of urban ground rents,
others from mineral royalties or capital resources from industrial
and commercial associations. Landowners not dependent on agricultural income, sublimely unaffected by the impact of the depression, maintained the opulence and landed traditions of the
high-Victorian era. The pleasures of hunting and shooting, of
seasons in London and lavish entertainment at the country house
devolved to the *nouveau riche* and to the more wealthy established
landowners. The late-Victorian and Edwardian days were the
'Indian summer' of the large landed estates. Some owners lived
beyond their means in attempting to maintain the image befitting
their social standing. In some cases it is a matter of conjecture
as to whether a property was more affected by the agricultural
depression or whether its decline was an inevitable consequence
of the incumbent owner's extravagance. Such is the case with the
Hawkstone Estate (Salop). Like his father before him Lord Rowland
Hill, who inherited the property in the 1870s, was a man of expensive tastes who gradually dissipated much of the family income and
was declared bankrupt a year before his death in 1894. The
estate at Hawkstone was put on the market and sold by his son
in 1895.

The major impact of the Great Depression was irrevocably to
confirm that the economic and political power in England had moved
away from the agrarian sector. As agricultural estates became
increasingly indebted more landowners attempted to sell peripheral
or outlying lands or to quit the landowning tradition entirely, but
the market was not receptive and the comment made by the Duke
of Marlborough in 1885 that, 'were there any effective demand for
the purchase of land, half the land in England would be in the
market tomorrow'[34] did not prove a reality in the 1880s or 1890s,
but was delayed until after the turn of the century.

NOTES

1 'Economist', 16 July 1870.
2 R.E. Pumphrey, The Introduction of Industrialists into the British Peerage: A Study in Adaptation of a Social Institution, 'Amer. Hist. Rev.', vol. 65, no. 1 (1959), pp. 1-16.
3 Ibid., estimated from Table III and Table IV, pp. 7 and 9.
4 Sir G. Scott, 'Remarks on Secular and Domestic Architecture Present and Future' (John Murray, London, 1857).
5 F.M.L. Thompson, 'English Landed Society in the Nineteenth Century' (Routledge and Kegan Paul, London, 1963), p. 197.
6 T.W. Fletcher, The Great Depression of English Agriculture, 1873-1896, 'Econ. Hist. Rev.', vol. 13, no. 2 (1960), pp. 417-32; C.S. Orwin and E.H. Whetham, 'History of British Agriculture 1846-1914', 2nd edn (David and Charles, Newton Abbot, 1971), pp. 240-88.
7 J.A. Clarke, On the Farming of Lincolnshire, 'JRASE', vol. 12 (1851), p. 337.
8 Brocklesbyana, unpublished document relating to the Lincolnshire estate of the Earls of Yarborough, Estate Office, Brocklesby Park, p. 106.
9 Agricultural Holdings (England) Act 1875, 38 & 39 Vict., c. 92.
10 Agricultural Holdings (England) Act 1883, 46 & 47 Vict., c. 61.
11 S.B.L. Druce, The Agricultural Holdings (England) Act, 1883, 'JRASE', 3rd ser., vol. 6 (1895), p. 182.
12 Game Laws, 10 Geo. 3, c. 19, 1770; 13 Geo. 3, c. 80, 1773. The Game Laws were used by the Anti-Corn Law League in an attempt to cause a rift between landlords and farmers; see Orwin and Whetham, 'History of British Agriculture' p. 47.
13 'Stamford Mercury', 20 Nov. 1847.
14 G. Martelli, 'The Elveden Enterprise' (Faber and Faber, London, 1952).
15 Ground Game Act 1880, 43 & 44 Vict., c. 47.
16 J. Saville, 'Rural Depopulation in England and Wales 1851-1951' (Routledge and Kegan Paul, London, 1957), p. 5.
17 R.J. Olney, 'Lincolnshire Politics 1832-1885' (Oxford Univ. Press, London, 1973), p. 40, note 31.
18 Thompson, 'English Landed Society in the Nineteenth Century', p. 274.
19 County Councils were established under the Local Government Act 1888, 51 & 52 Vict., c. 41, Part 1.
20 Taken from Olney, 'Lincolnshire Politics', pp. 33-4. Original source 'Stamford Mercury', 21 Dec. 1832 and 18 Jan. 1850.
21 See, for example, D.C. Moore, 'The Politics of Deference' (Harvester, London, 1976); H. Newby, 'Property, Paternalism and Power' (Hutchinson, London, 1978).
22 Representation of the People Act 1832, 2 & 3 Will. 4, c. 65; Representation of the People Act 1867, 30 & 31 Vict., c. 102; Representation of the People Act 1884, 48 Vict., c. 3.
23 Ballot Act 1872, 34 & 35 Vict., c. 33.
24 The impact of free trade resulting from the repeal of the Corn

Laws did not hit the agricultural sector until the import of
cheap grain from North America flooded the market after 1875,
a primary cause of the Great Depression.

25 Parliament Act 1911, 1 & 2 Geo. 5, c. 13, limited the power of
the House of Lords to block legislation.

26 T.W. Fletcher, Lancashire Livestock Farming during the
Great Depression, 'Agric. Hist. Rev.', vol. 9 (1962), p. 37.

27 M. Girouard, 'The Victorian Country House' (Clarendon,
Oxford, 1971), p. 111.

28 Ibid., p. 111.

29 Information provided by J.M. Robinson, archivist to the Duke
of Norfolk at Carlton Towers, Dec. 1977.

30 Sale catalogues, 30 and 31 Oct. 1895, Somerset Record Office,
DD/SAS c 2401 No. 87; DD/SAS c 2273 I/B 14.1.

31 A number of cases are cited by F.M.L. Thompson, 'English
Landed Society in the Nineteenth Century', p. 320.

32 Brocklesbyana, p. 108.

33 Ibid., p. 108.

34 'The Times', 3 Oct. 1885.

PART TWO: A CENTURY OF CHANGE 1880 TO 1980

7 PRIVATE LANDOWNERSHIP AND ESTATE DECLINE

> Nor can it be said that our experience of corporate adminis-
> tration, in the case of lands held by collegiate, ecclesiastical
> and municipal bodies...is such as to recommend the substitu-
> tion of public for private ownership on a much grander scale.
> G.C. Brodrick, *English Land and English Landlords* (1881,
> reprinted David and Charles, Newton Abbot, 1968), p. 105.

Throughout the past hundred years many privately owned landed
estates have ceased to function as operating units, ownership has
changed, component parts have been broken-up, country houses
demolished, and amenity land ploughed up, sub-divided and built
over. As a corollary new agricultural estates have come into being,
many owned by private families, but an increasing number have
been assembled, or taken over, by public, semi-public and institutional bodies. This study, however, does not seek to establish
the present-day structure of landownership but only to examine
the fate of the private estate properties that were in existence in
the late nineteenth century.

The reasons for changes in ownership and the break-up of historic estates[1] are numerous and for each property comprise a complex set of circumstances related to events in the national economy, particularly in the agricultural sector, and the impact of
various government policies, as well as personal family misfortune.
The location of estate property *vis-à-vis* urban and industrial
development has also entered the picture, but such locational factors, related to changes in land use and function, are dealt with
at length in succeeding chapters. It is intended in this chapter to
discuss the ongoing process of decline that has continued over the
past century and to examine in some detail the present-day ownership of the 500 sample estates.

HISTORIC ESTATE DECLINE IN THE TWENTIETH CENTURY

By the 1880s the landed estate as a focal point of English country
life had reached its zenith. Already the political and economic dominance of the landed interest was in decline, the status attached to
owning a landed estate had begun to lose prominence and landowner control in rural society, and indeed over their own tenants,
had diminished. Forces for change apparent in the nineteenth
century have been entrenched and augmented in the twentieth.

With the onset of the Great Depression there had begun a

renewed interest in land reform and the pressure of radical opinion against the 'landed monopoly' was an important influence on political policy in the period 1885 to 1914. As a consequence landed estates were increasingly viewed as a potential source of revenue and taxed accordingly. Estate duty was first introduced by Harcourt in 1894, the maximum rate being 8 per cent on estates worth £1 million.[2] In 1909 Lloyd George sought, unsuccessfully, to introduce the so called People's Budget which included a state valuation of land and a 20 per cent tax on the future unearned increment to be levied when property changed hands, and a ½d in the £ on the capital value of undeveloped land and minerals.[3] In comparison with modern rates of taxation, those either proposed or implemented in the late nineteenth and early twentieth centuries were excessively moderate. But legislation against landed society was seen to be getting progressively harsher. The fiscal policies of the period, coupled with the portent of worse to come and the ultimate threat of nationalisation, advocated by the more ardent reformers as the most equitable and only long-term solution to the land question, have been cited as major causes of the increase in land sales from 1910 to 1914 and the flood of sales that took place in the period 1918 to 1922. It has been suggested, however, that landowners chose to act on the scares of 1909 as self-justification for a course of action that had long seemed wise.[4] Many properties remained heavily mortgaged and encumbered by indebtedness incurred during the Great Depression, and the favourable market for land after 1909 enabled owners to liquidate landed assets, increase net incomes by reinvesting former land-based capital and clear estate indebtedness by selling outlying property. The market was favourable for both buying and selling and for some a buoyant market allowed scattered estates to be tidied up through sale of peripheral land and purchase of more adjacent property. Not only estate break-up but also consolidation was a feature of the period, and a number of large estates were able to enter the inter-war decades cleared of indebtedness, more compact and in a healthier financial position than in the pre-war years.

Some proprietors chose to retire from landownership at a time when the economic and social advantages of holding land was seemingly less beneficial, while others entrenched their landed status. The Joicey family, in common with other Northumberland landowners in the nineteenth century, greatly increased their wealth through the exploitation of coal on their property and in the years 1907 and 1908 Lord Joicey purchased the two adjacent estates of Ford Castle and Etal Manor, properties with a combined extent of over 10,000 acres.[5]

In the period up to the outbreak of World War I it has been estimated that over 800,000 acres of land were sold.[6] A reduced number of sales took place during the war years but with peace the land market revived and a flood of sales were recorded in 1918 topped by a veritable avalanche in 1919 and 1920; many sales occurring prior to, and possibly in anticipation of the 1919 budget, which raised death duties to 40 per cent on estates over £200,000 value.[7] In the boom of 1918-22 calculations suggest that over one quarter of the land area of England and Wales changed ownership.[8] The extent and rapidity of land transfer occurred at an unprecedented rate.

Death in a family, often an untimely cause of estate sales, was compounded in the post-war period. Traditional ties of landed society with the commissioned ranks, though no longer their exclusive domain, meant that a high number of estate owners and their successors served in the war. The death of an heir to a property often brought to an end family associations with an estate, and in other cases land sales were necessary to pay double death duties in quick succession during and following the 1914-18 period. The Public Schools Club recorded that 800 of its members, most of whom were from landed families, had been killed in action by 1918, just one indication of the extent of loss from the ranks of the upper classes.[9]

The forty or so years from 1880 to 1922 witnessed important changes for many sample properties. The complete record of land sales is not known, but more comprehensive data are available for estate heartlands and fragmentary evidence exists of the sale of outlying property and the break-up of secondary estates. Over the entire period ending 1923 at least 106 (21 per cent) of the sample estate heartlands underwent at least one change of ownership. For some such changes meant total break-up while for others the land area was sold in one lot (see p. 103). On other property the heartland was retained, but individual farm holdings were sold from principal estates and the sale of secondary estate and peripheral land reduced the total holdings of many landed families. Examination of a handful of cases is illustrative of the sales that occurred. Over 2,000 acres, nearly two-thirds of the Barttelot Estate at Stopham House (Sussex), were sold in 1911; in 1914 approximately 4,500 acres were sold off from the 8,600-acre Rigmaden Estate in Westmorland and the Antrobus family sold all but 150 acres, comprising the Abbey and park, when the entire Abbey Estate (Wilts.), a property of 6,420 acres, was offered for sale in 1915.[10] Two secondary estates, each extending over 1,000 acres were sold by the Fitz-Herbert-Brockholes family who retained the principal estate at Claughton Hall (Lancs.); the 4,309-acre Denton Park Estate was sold in 1902 by the Wyvill family, who still occupy the ancestral home at Constable Burton (North Riding).[11] Similarly, the Earl of Derby disposed of 4,224 acres of outlying property at Burscough in 1916, the Earl of Harewood sold property at Barforth and Stainsby amounting to 2,685 acres in 1919 and the Earl of Pembroke sold over 8,000 acres, comprising outlying portions of the Wilton Estate (Wilts.), in 1918.[12]

Many estates in the 3,000 to 10,000-acre range were drastically reduced in size, while great landowners and land magnates holding property in a number of counties, or spread throughout a single county, were more often in a position to place detached portions in the market without affecting the major part of the principal estate.

In 1917 the government introduced the Corn Production Act[13] which encouraged increased output and supported the agricultural economy by means of a system of minimum guaranteed prices. In 1921 the repeal of the Corn Production Acts[14] heralded the onset of a recession in the agricultural sector which continued through much of the inter-war period. Consequently, the third and fourth decades of the century saw comparatively little activity in land sales as compared with the post-war boom. Sales to raise capital for estate maintenance and improvements were few as prices were low, rents low and the cost of labour had steadily risen after the war such that estate owners had little incentive to invest in agricultural property. The period has been described as the nadir of the privately owned agricultural estates and for many it was a crucial turning point.[15] It was time for change as agriculture entered the realms of business enterprise and increased capitalisation of farming became the order of the day, more especially after 1945. In the years immediately prior to World War II land prices began to pick up, especially as investment in land became an attractive form of security and hedge against inflation for private and institutional proprietors and by 1945 prices were higher than they had been for seventy years.

Taxation underwent further changes in this period. As early as 1925 an abated rate of estate duty had been introduced for agricultural land though, as a corollary, by 1939 the maximum rate of estate duty had risen to 60 per cent. In this era too, particularly up to 1940, the creation of private estate companies became a popular means of tax avoidance, but legislation contained in the 1940 Finance Act effectively terminated many of the financial advantages in this form of land holding.[16] The practice of 'gifting', whereby property was exempted from taxation if passed to the next generation three years before the death of the owner, became a popular means of reducing the impact of estate duty.[17] Not all landed families, however, were far sighted in the gifting of estates. The untimely death of the 6th Earl of Harewood in 1947 led to the sale of some 13,000 acres of the Harewood Estate (West Riding) as well as part of the contents of Harewood House.[18] When the 10th Duke of Devonshire died in November 1950 only a few weeks short of the legal gifting period (then five years) his successor became liable for duties in excess of £6 million. The Treasury accepted Hardwick Hall and its contents, 2,305 acres of park and adjoining farmland and the Hope Woodlands Estate of 16,000 acres in lieu of part payment of death duties;[19] the property was transferred to the National Trust in 1959. Some 3,500 acres of the Lockinge Estate (Berks.) were sold in 1944 following the death of A.T. Loyd; 6,500 acres of land, principally in Somerset and Wiltshire, belonging to the Marquis of Bath were put up for sale in 1946 and 1947 'solely for the purpose of paying death duties'; the Constable Burton

Estate (North Riding) was reduced from 4,000 to 3,000 acres after the death of M.F. Wyvill in 1953; and in the same year, death duties of over £400,000 resulted in the sale of 31 of 61 farms on the Ashburnham Estate (Sussex), a few of the numerous examples of land sales made necessary to finance death-duty liabilities, one of the most consistently cited causes of the decline of privately owned estates.[20]

Many of the traditional agricultural estates suffered from under-capitalisation in the inter-war years and landlords made little gain in the inflationary period of World War II when rents remained frozen by government legislation. In the aftermath of war another round of sales took place as entire estates encumbered by debt and lack of capital, and particularly estate heartlands bearing large and uneconomical country houses, were put on the market. The impact of the latter is discussed in the following chapters, but suffice it to say at this point that over one hundred heartlands, 20 per cent of the sample group, entered and re-entered the market in the ten-year period ending in 1955. Other owners sold part of their land in order to raise development capital to improve the remainder.

In an attempt to assist the recovery of agriculture in the post-war period the Labour Government introduced a fiscal policy in 1945 to provide rebates on income tax and surtax for capital invested in agricultural improvements. Landowners with high taxable incomes could potentially convert former tax losses into real wealth by investing in land improvements. Inducements to landownership provided by legislation contributed to the growing demand for land, the continual rise in land prices and the increase in land transfers that characterised the post-war period. Consolidation, rationalisation and expansion took place on a number of the large landed estates as the agricultural industry revived.[21] Outlying land was sold and adjacent land purchased, encouraged by roll-over tax relief for investment in agricultural land; an incentive for the reinvestment of capital gains derived from the sale of development land.[22]

Land prices continued to rise during the 1950s and 1960s and from the mid-1960s successive governments imposed additional capital taxes on landed wealth. In 1965 long-term capital-gains tax was introduced. Even though capital-gains tax has had, in combination with estate duties, considerable impact on privately owned property the use of legal devices such as Discretionary Trusts, the practice of gifting and roll-over tax relief in the 1960s and early 1970s could be effectively combined to reduce tax burdens on landed property.

In the years 1971 to 1973 land prices boomed both for urban-fringe development land and farm land.[23] Demand for land was high but the supply entering the market relatively low. The rise in prices has been partly attributed to the increased activity of financial institutions seeking investment in land. The estimated holdings of financial institutions in 1971 was 120,000 hectares (296,400 acres) or some 3 per cent of the agricultural area held by public and semi-public bodies.[24] In 1972 financial institutions increased their holdings by 40 per cent.[25] Though becoming more active in the land market the role of such institutions in the total picture remained proportionally small.

Demand was highest from the agricultural sector itself as the over-capitalisation of farming in the 1950s and 1960s had led to the growth of larger farm holdings over which to spread fixed costs. Six out of every seven purchasers of agricultural land were in fact farmers.[26] The inflationary spiral of prices was undoubtedly a stimulus to legislation introduced in the 1975 Finance Act even though in 1974 the artificially high prices had already begun to fall.[27]

In 1975 a heavy blow was dealt to the remaining large landed estates with the introduction of the capital transfer tax (CTT) and the stated intent of the government to impose an annual wealth tax. The latter, up to 1981, has not yet come into being, but there is no reason to suppose that it will not be introduced if a socialist government is reinstated.[28]

An early comment following the Finance Act 1975 declared that 'the results of the capital transfer tax will be the break-up of a land pattern which has existed for a thousand years'.[29] Unlike the former estate duty that it replaced, capital transfer tax is fundamentally unavoidable, being a progressive tax levied at the time of land transfer whether land is gifted or passed by inheritance. The measure of transfer is assessed on the basis of loss to the transferor rather than gain to the transferee, an important distinction for valuation. It is assessed as a multiple of rental value, or imputed value in the case of owner-occupiers, that is, 'the price which the property may reasonably be expected to fetch if it was sold on the open market at that time'.[30] There is a lower limit at death below which the tax does not apply and gifts of £2,000 per donor per annum are tax free, while gifts between spouses are not taxable.[31] Discretionary Trusts also incur notional period distribution, with some exemptions, such that this means of avoiding estate duty is no longer inviolate. In addition, the former 45 per cent alleviation of duty that applied to all agricultural property has been replaced with a differential valuation on farmland and working assets for full-time working farmers, that is, owner-occupiers who have been in possession for a minimum of two years.[32] Such tax concessions do not apply to agricultural landlords and have been regarded by many as heralding the end of the landlord-tenant system in British agriculture, the characteristic land organisation of a traditional estate. It is not the intention here to discuss the advantages and disadvantages of the let-land system, arguments that are well documented elsewhere.[33] It should be noted, however, that let land is not the exclusive domain of the large private estates. Harrison, Tranter and Gibbs have estimated that approximately 18 per cent of rented farmland in England is under public and semi-public institutional ownership.[34] Yet the impact of CTT, particularly in combination with other capital and income taxes,

is expected to hit privately owned tenanted estates harder than
institutional land holdings.

With the gradual break-up of the large landed estates during
the past century the structure of agriculture has been moving
towards greater owner-occupation of land. CTT will undoubtedly
accelerate the process. In 1914 only 11 per cent of farm holdings
were owner-occupied, by 1927 the figure was 36 per cent, by
1960 it was 49, by 1975 around 60 and by 1979 the approximate
figure was 65 per cent.[35] Much of the increase has been the outcome of the break-up of the large landed estates, whereupon
individual farm units have been sold to the sitting tenants or
other farm operators. When the Ashton Court Estate (Somerset)
was sold in 1948 a newspaper report on the sale noted that with
only one exception all the tenants bought their farms.[36] Where
tenants could not raise capital to purchase their individual holdings they formed a syndicate to facilitate acquisition. Such was
the case with the sale of the 3,259-acre Wrottesley Estate
(Staffs.) in 1963 sold for £453,000 to a tenant syndicate.[37] In
other cases a land speculator became the middle man in the transfer of a property from single ownership into individually owned
units. The break-up of the 15,000-acre Bewerley Estate (West
Riding) appears to have been in this manner. *The Times* of
August 1924 indicated that an offer of £150,000 was accepted
for the entire property and in October of the same year the
estate was again for sale broken into lots ranging from 25 to
280 acres.[38]

The increase in owner-occupation of land does not entirely
reflect a decline in the ownership of private landed estates. The
traditional agricultural estates have adapted and are in the process of adapting to the changing economic conditions of the
twentieth century and, especially since World War II, landowners
are turning to management of their land as a business enterprise. The ranks of the owner-occupiers are being swollen by
a growing number of estate owners who are taking former let
land in hand as occupation becomes vacant. This action may well
have been induced in the post-war period by the poor level of
rental income in comparison with the potential profitability from
agriculture, but is now reinforced by the added incentive of
tax concessions on owner-occupied land. The process of transfer for owners of let land, however, is slow as legislation, particularly following World War II, has further protected the proprietory rights of tenant farmers and as of 1976 has given
security of tenure to the second generation.[39] It is no longer
an easy matter to appropriate one's own land.

Capital taxation from the mid-1960s and especially from 1975
has brought about further sales of estate property. Over sixty
estate heartlands have been sold or transferred in ownership
since 1965, but by no means all can be attributed directly to
capital taxation. Many were resales and fewer than half represented initial transfers from descendants of the c. 1880 landowning family. Nineteen heartlands, however, have changed

hands from 1976 to late 1979 and a look at those of 1,000 or more acres will show that only one out of six was purchased by a private family, two were acquired by financial institutions, one was a transfer to the National Trust, one a purchase by Manchester University and the last recorded sale was an acquisition by a roadstone company who plan to quarry over much of the remaining estate.

Little information was obtained concerning piecemeal sales from home estates still owned by the original landed family, but evidence indicated the prevalence of sales to the non-private sector, and continuing compulsory acquisition of small land areas by local authorities. For example, 1,000 acres have been sold from the Merton Estate (Norfolk) in 1977/8 mostly to Fisons Ltd Pension Fund.[40] The nature of comments made on a large number of the survey questionnaires testifies to the general apprehension of private landowners concerning the future and the belief by many that if present taxation policies are maintained the next generation will see the end of the privately owned landed estate.

As early as June 1922 it was written that, 'These are the days in which the greater residential properties of the country can only be owned and kept up by those whose income is from sources apart from the property itself and then of very substantial character.'[41] In the estate survival stakes Harbury concluded in his work in 1962 that, 'the chance of leaving an estate valued at over £100,000, or even over £50,000, was outstandingly enhanced if one's father had been at least moderately well-off';[42] a statement that supports the premise that survival has been greater when additional sources of non-agricultural wealth, usually inherited wealth, have been available to bolster estate capital and to pay death duties and other tax liabilities.

Ground rents from urban property have provided an important means of support for a number of rural estates since the nineteenth century, but private owners of urban land in the twentieth century have been under pressure to relinquish property both directly with increases in local authority planning and development controls and indirectly through taxation. The great transfer of land after World War I was urban as well as rural and many owners sold their town houses and other urban assets for what were, at that time, considered high prices offered by a growing class of property speculators. For some the sale of urban land has helped to meet the burden of death duties. Such was the reason for sales in Skegness after 1945 and again in 1969 by the Earl of Scarbrough and for the sale of part of the Portman Estate in London in the early 1950s.[43] In London the area owned by the landed aristocracy has diminished throughout the century though in 1967 Marriott wrote that, 'The idea that these ancient estates have been broken up and scattered by taxation is largely a myth'.[44] The Grosvenor, Portman, Portland, Cadogan and Bedford estates were still in family ownership and elsewhere the Grosvenors owned land in Chester and Liverpool, the Norfolks owned part of Sheffield and the Seftons and Derbys were still major landowners in certain Midland counties in the late 1960s.[45] Those who retained urban estates after World War II were in a position to capitalise in the property boom of the 1950s and 1960s, but the ownership of urban land and prospective development land in the rural-urban fringe appeared to offer little future potential of increased revenue for the private landowner following the introduction in 1975 of the Community Land Act (now repealed) and in 1976 of the Development Land Tax; the former attempted to provide for the compulsory acquisition of development land, primarily urban, by public authorities while the latter is a tax on incremental gains accruing from property development.[46]

Little evidence came to light in the study of the five hundred principal estates to indicate the extent of urban property presently held by landed families. Certainly a few own small areas from which they still derive ground rents, though the work by Massey and Catalano suggested that in fact only a very small sub-group of aristocratic landowners continue to possess lucrative urban holdings.[47]

Revenue from mineral royalties, the key to the growth and longevity of a number of landed estates, particularly in the North and industrial Midlands, has been considerably reduced since the inter-war period with the imposition of Mineral Rights Duty and Excess Mineral Rights Duty, and with the nationalisation of the coal industry in 1946. Compensation paid by the government in lieu of coal royalties did, however, provide an important injection of development capital for a number of estates at a time of general capital scarcity.

Little will be said in the context of this work concerning the private collections of art that have been accumulated over the centuries in country houses throughout England, but such collections have proved invaluable as sources of revenue in times of financial need both for estate improvements and to cover taxation payments. Death-duty settlement amounting to £6 million for the Chatsworth Estate (Derby.) in the 1950s necessitated the sale of eight paintings from the family collection, and in early 1978 Lord Scarsdale sold a Guido Reni painting from his Kedleston collection for a sum believed to have been around £100,000.[48] The break-up of collections of furniture, pictures and other valuable items is in itself another facet in the cultural loss associated with the decline of private landed estates. To the extent of financing CTT historic connections with a property have also proven to be an asset. In 1978 the family archives of the Lyttletons of Hagley Hall (Worcester.) that date from the twelfth century were sold at Sotheby's for an estimated £164,000.[49]

THE OWNERSHIP OF SAMPLE ESTATES c. 1980

To date few studies have attempted to review, at the national level, the extent of the demise of historic landed estates and consequently there is considerable divergence of opinion as to the degree and nature of their survival; some suggest that private landed estates have been broken-up and that few now remain, while others point to a number of properties still owned by titled families as evidence of persisting inequalities of wealth and the continuing existence of a 'landed elite' in England. Lack of public knowledge clouds the issue and comparison of c. 1980 with c. 1880 presents no simple task. Regarding basic landownership statistics there has been no equivalent survey in the twentieth century to that of the 1873 New Domesday and hence no published data from which to compile a comparable Bateman-like listing.[50] It is something of an anomaly that in the late nineteenth century there was a more complete state of knowledge on landownership in England than exists in the present era of sophisticated survey techniques and computer technology. Until there is a publicly accessible comprehensive land register, the question of historic estate survival can only be partially examined through piecemeal evidence. Such is the nature of the present analysis.

The following classification is based on the definition of the home estate as *comprising all or part of the 1880 estate heartland (principal country house and amenity land) with or without supporting acreage, the total being greater than or less than 1,000 acres.* The latter is somewhat arbitrarily taken as the minimum acreage for a landed estate in the present day to give a base-line measurement for a notion of estate survival.[51]

At this point no further qualification is made concerning the physical condition of the estate heartland; for example, the country house may be still standing or it may have been demolished. The pertinent fact in the immediate context is the ownership of the land, that is, how many estate heartlands and supporting acreage remain in private ownership,[52] how many have been transferred to public, semi-public or institutional ownership,[53] and how many have been broken-up in some manner that has divorced all or part of the heartland from the remainder of the estate land area.

Two interrelated classifications of ownership have been devised, the first to examine the continuing association of the original family[54] with the estate, and the second to identify the present-day ownership and extent of land owned in association with all estate heartlands in the sample.

Continuity of Estate Ownership

The present-day relationship between the original family and the 1880 estate has been grouped into five categories which more or less define a continuum of unbroken association to complete severance with the estate property.

(a) *Original Family Own a Minimum of 1,000 Acres Centred on the Estate Heartland.* Out of 500 properties 172 (34 per cent) are known to fall within this category which represents the highest level of estate survival[55] (Table 7.1). Yet even here extensive sales of peripheral land and secondary estates have taken place and the land area of the home estate in many cases has also been substantially reduced. The proportion of land area still owned varies enormously, but only 13 original family owners indicated that their present acreage was equal to or greater than their total family acreage held c. 1880, while for a further eleven the acreage c. 1980 was more than the area of the nineteenth-century home estate but less than their previous total family acreage in England. In most cases it was apparent that the figure provided was the total acreage owned in England. For example it was pointed out by the agent that considerable land sales had reduced the Longford Castle Estate (Wilts.) from the 17,000 acres recorded in 1880, to less than 9,000, but two nearby estates, each over 3,000 acres, have been purchased by the family since World War II, one in Wiltshire and one in Hampshire, bringing the total area owned to over 15,000 acres.[56] In some cases, however, especially for the great-landowner group, it was not always clear whether the acreage figure provided referred only to the principal estate or was the total land area now owned in England.

Table 7.1: Number and Extent of Historic Estates, Minimum Area 1,000 Acres, in Original Family Ownership c. 1980[a]

Estate Size Group c. 1880	Estate Area c. 1980			
	≥10,000 acres No.(%)	3,000-9,999 acres No.(%)	1,000-2,999 acres No.(%)	Total No.(%)
≥ 10,000 acres[b]	25 (25)	29 (23)	5 (4)	59 (48)
3,000-9,999 acres[c]	- -	59 (16)	54 (14)	113 (30)
Total	25 (5)	88 (18)	59 (12)	172 (34)

Notes: a. In all cases the estate heartland, the country house or its site, is the core of the property. b. Great landowners, 100% in 1880 = 124 estates. c. Greater gentry, 100% in 1880 = 376 estates.
Source: Questionnaire Survey.

A number of respondents indicated that the land owned in 1980 was not entirely synonymous with the estate layout c. 1880. In the intervening period many land holdings were expanded and were subsequently reduced again at a later date. The Ingleborough Estate (West Riding) is a notable example. In the late nineteenth century it comprised some 1,500 acres, by 1950 it was 30,000 acres though much was woodland and commons. It has since been reduced by two major land sales and a number of minor sales to the present 10,000 acres.[57]

Other proprietors have purchased adjacent land to consolidate the principal estate, sometimes selling outlying land or secondary estates in the process. Consolidation and expansion has been evident on the Graythwaite Estate (Lancs.[58]) where adjoining land has been purchased piecemeal over the years to add to the 1880 property. In 1946 1,500 acres were sold, part of which, however, was later repurchased and the present day estate now extends to 5,500 acres as compared to 3,300 acres at the end of the nineteenth century. The estate is owned and administered by a family-held private company.[59]

It is apparent that a higher proportion of owners whose ancestors held over 10,000 acres in 1880 retain land in the present day compared with the descendants of the 3,000 to 9,999-acre group. In fact a little under 50 per cent of the former great-landowner class still own all or a substantial area of the principal family estate. Only 16 per cent of the greater-gentry group, however, continue to own property extending over 3,000 acres comprising at least all or part of the historic principal estate and, in the majority of cases, probably representing the total family acreage in England.

(b) *Original Family Own Less than 1,000 Acres Centred on the Estate Heartland.* In the great-landowner group not one example was recorded where an original family retain the heartland with less than 1,000 acres and only 15 cases, less than 4 per cent, were recorded in the greater-gentry group.[60] It would appear, therefore, that the historic landed families either retain a substantial land area, worthy to be classed an estate, or have completely broken their association with the land, whether by necessity or choice. This is further reinforced when one examines the number of original families who have retained land but sold all or part of the estate heartland, namely the country house and an associated acreage (see below). Perrott, who in 1968 reached a similar conclusion in his work on the aristocracy, interpreted it to mean that 'the nobleman expects to have an estate big enough to allow him to live on rents paid by tenants rather than on primarily farming the land himself. In other words, the nobility's traditional attitude to the land is still basically there'.[61]

(c) *Original Family Own a Minimum of 1,000 Acres but have Sold or Transferred the Ownership of that Part of the Estate Heartland which Includes the Country House, or its Site.* Out of the total sample as many as 51 original families (10 per cent) are known to retain over 1,000 acres of land although no longer being in possession of the country house or its former site; comprising 17 per cent of the great-landowner class and 8 per cent of the greater-gentry class (Table 7.2). This group included ten estates where ownership of the country house had been transferred to the National Trust, but where the original family still occupy the house and retain over 1,000 acres of land beyond that

Table 7.2: Number and Extent of Historic Estate Land Areas, Minimum 1,000 Acres, in Original Family Ownership c. 1980 from which the Heartland has been detached by Sale or Transfer

| Estate Size Group c. 1880 | Estate Land Owned c. 1980 | | | |
	≥10,000 acres No.(%)	3,000-9,999 acres No.(%)	1,000-2,999 acres No.(%)	Total No.(%)
≥10,000 acres[a]	5 (4)	12 (10)	4 (3)	21 (17)
3,000-9,999 acres[b]	– –	10 (3)	20 (5)	30 (8)
Total	5 (1)	22 (4)	24 (5)	51 (10)

Notes: a. Great Landowners, 100% in 1880 = 124 estates.
b. Greater gentry, 100% in 1880 = 376 estates.
Source: Questionnaire Survey.

transferred to the Trust, as at Antony (Cornwall), Knightshaye's Court (Devon), Petworth (Sussex), Scotney Castle (Kent) and West Wycombe House (Bucks.). A slightly different situation is presented by the Luttrell family property in Somerset. Here the home-estate land at Dunster Castle passed to the Commissioners of Crown Lands in 1950 and the family retained only the castle and its immediate environs as well as an older seat at East Quantoxhead. In 1976 Dunster Castle and grounds were given to the National Trust and the family relocated at East Quantoxhead, a property of around 5,000 acres.[62]

(d) *Original Family Own Less than 1,000 Acres and have Sold or Transferred the Ownership of that Part of the Estate which includes the Country House.* While information is more readily obtainable on the ownership status of the heartland and of large acreages of estate property, the survival of original-family proprietory rights to smaller portions are less easy to ascertain. In a number of cases it would be reasonable to expect that parcels of land may be kept in the family possession for investment purposes because of their location as potential development land.[63] The complete picture in this category is the most uncertain. In fact only 18 cases were recorded where the original family retain less than 1,000 acres of home-estate land from which the heartland has been detached; four from the former great-landowner group and 14 from the greater-gentry group.

(e) *Original Family has no Apparent Ownership Association with any Part of the Home Estate.* Of the remaining 241 estates (48 per cent) it is known that the original family no longer own the heartland[64] and that in the majority of cases they have no association whatsoever with the property. Questionnaire respondents for 204 estates indicated that, to their knowledge, the original family had no land. In some cases the respondent was a descen-

dant of the original family but the greater number bore no relation to the original owner. Evidence of complete disassociation
is, therefore, not confirmed in all cases and for 37 of these
estates it is only possible to state with certainty that the original
family no longer own the country house or its site.

In summary (Table 7.3) there is some, if limited, continuity in
land ownership for at least 259 original families (52 per cent), a
high number considering the popular conception of the break-up
of private estates. Yet it could justifiably be put forward that,
in terms of land area, only categories (a) and (c) should be
considered as a continuing estate while in terms of an historic
estate as a unit only category (a) represents continuity. Even in
the latter case survival in all senses is dependent, as will be
seen in successive chapters, on the physical condition of the
country house and use of the amenity land.

Table 7.3:   Summary: Original Family Ownership c. 1980

	Category	No. of landowners (%)
Historic	(a) ⩾ 1,000 acres	172(34) + 3 for which acreage
Estates	(b) < 1,000 acres	15(3) not known
Estate Land	(c) ⩾ 1,000 acres	51(10)
without Heartland	(d) < 1,000 acres	18(4)
	Total	259(52)

Source: Questionnaire Survey.

There is also an association between the original landownership
class and survival with a much higher proportion of great-
landowner property retained by the original family. Estate loss
has been more apparent among the greater-gentry group. It is
important to remember that size of property, both in 1880 and in
the present day, provides little indication of its value. A 1,000
acre estate of barren moorland bears no comparison to 1,000
acres of good-quality agricultural land, or land adjacent to an
expanding urban centre. None the less, the total extent of property in the nineteenth century tended to be a reasonable indicator of the wealth and social status of the landowner and as such
it would not be unreasonable to hypothesise that in periods of
economic hardship, whether a national recession or family misfortune, those with greater land resources and wealth would be
more likely to survive, even if at the expense of some land.

In Denman's analysis of the incidence of estate duty on 2,750
estates in the 1950s the breakdown of properties revealed that
the higher-size classes were dominated by what he termed 'old
title' properties, that is, historic estates, pre-1900. Of the 216
estates that were over 5,000 acres nearly 86 per cent were of
'old title'. Such evidence testified to the survival of large and
old inheritances in the mid-twentieth century. From the analysis

Denman concluded that 'lower figures than these will be necessary before we can speak of the passing into history of the large
country estate'.[65]

Ownership of All Sample Estate Heartlands
Transfer of ownership has taken place for 310 (62 per cent) of
the sample estate heartlands since c. 1880 whether to a different
family[66] or a public, semi-public or institutional body. For some,
transfer has occurred on more than one occasion and the static
comparison of c. 1880 with c. 1980 does little to reflect the
ownership history through which a number of properties have
gone to reach their present status. Only a few cases can suffice
as illustration. The 6,000-acre estate at Woolverstone Park
(Suffolk) was sold by the Berners family in 1938 to Oxford University Chest and was resold in 1958 in 185 lots; the country
house and at least 63 acres of grounds have been owned since
that time by the Greater London Council.[67] In 1938, the Harlaxton
Manor Estate (Lincs.) was broken-up and the heartland purchased by Mrs Van der Elst, who resold it in 1948 to the Society
of Jesus who, in turn, transferred the ownership of 100 acres
to the University of Evansville, the present owners.[68] Finally,
there is the example of Buscot Park (Berks.[69]), an estate of
over 3,000 acres bequeathed to the National Trust by Ernest
Cook in 1949. The estate had passed by sale from the executors
of Robert Campbell in 1889 to the 1st Lord Farringdon and from
the latter to Ernest Cook in 1948. Similar patterns of ownership
change have been repeated on many of the sample properties,
79 of which are recorded as changing hands at least twice and
a further 43 have been transferred in ownership three or more
times over the past century.

The present-day ownership of all estate heartlands can be
divided into those in private hands and those now in public,
semi-public or institutional ownership.

Private Ownership. Apart from the 190 estate heartlands remaining in original-family ownership a further 86 heartlands, many
with a substantial supporting acreage, have been sold to a different family since 1880 (Table 7.4).

Table 7.4: Number and Extent of Estate Heartlands in Private
Ownership c. 1980

	Estate area c. 1980					
Estate size group c. 1880	≥10,000 acres	3,000- 9,999 acres	1,000- 2,999 acres	1-999 acres	Not known	Total
	No.	No.	No.	No.	No.	No.(%)
≥10,000 acres[a]						
Original family	25	29	5	–	2	61(49)
Different family	–	3	3	3	2	11(9)

Estate area c. 1980

Estate size group c. 1880	≥10,000 acres	3,000- 9,999 acres	1,000- 2,999 acres	1-999 acres	Not known	Total
	No.	No.	No.	No.	No.	No.(%)
3,000-9,999 acres[b]						
Original family	–	59	54	15	1	129(34)
Different family	–	16	22	30	7	75(20)
Total						
Original family	25	88	59	15	3	190(38)
Different family	–	19	25	33	9	86(17)
Total	25	107	84	48	12	276(55)

Notes: a. Great landowners, 100% in 1880 = 124 estates.
b. Greater gentry, 100% in 1880 = 376 estates.
Source: Questionnaire Survey.

The purchase of entire estates by private families took place more in the late nineteenth and early decades of the twentieth rather than later in the present century. Examples have already been given of properties that changed hands as an outcome, directly or indirectly, of the Great Depression (see p. 103) and the volume of turnover from original owners to other private families is well illustrated in the analysis of country-house sales in Chapter 9.

Seventeen per cent of sample estate heartlands remain in private hands but are owned by a different family. Of the total of all heartland sales or transfers over 60 per cent of those above 1,000 acres and 50 per cent above 3,000 acres are presently in private ownership.

As a group private owners retain 55 per cent of estate heartlands in the sample of which 216 (43 per cent) are properties of over 1,000 acres.

Public, Semi-public and Institutional Ownership. The majority of heartland sales or transfers have been to public, semi-public and institutional bodies, including 32 properties now held by the National Trust (Table 7.5). For the most part this situation has arisen from the increasing inability of private families to maintain large country houses as the century has progressed, a topic discussed at length in following chapters.

Apart from five estates transferred to the National Trust, each with over 3,000 acres of land as an endowment, only eleven of the historic estates now in public or institutional ownership comprise 3,000 or more acres. This small group nevertheless represents a range of landowner types with the notable exclusion of ownership by central government and the local authorities.[70] Two are owned by the Crown; the Crewe Hall Estate (Cheshire) and Newton Park (Somerset), are properties of the Duchy of

Table 7.5: Number and Extent of Estate Heartlands in Public, Semi-public and Institutional Ownership c. 1980

Estate Size Group c. 1880	Estate area c. 1980					
	≥10,000 acres	3,000-9,999 acres	1,000-2,999 acres	1-999 acres	Not known	Total
≥ 10,000 acres[a]	No.	No.	No.	No.	No.	No.(%)
Public Body[b]	–	5	1	30	2	38(31)
National Trust	1	1	4	5	–	11(9)
Others[c]	–	–	–	–	3	3(2)
3,000-9,999 acres[d]						
Public Body	–	6	5	108	12	131(35)
National Trust	–	3	3	15	–	21(6)
Others	–	–	–	4	16	20(5)
Total						
Public Body	–	11	6	138	14	169(34)
National Trust	1	4	7	20	–	32(6)
Others	–	–	–	4	19	23(5)
Total	1	15	13	162	33	224(45)

Notes: a. and d. (see Table 7.4, a. and b.) b. Includes semi-public and institutional owners. c. Includes multiple owners and cases where heartland occupies a built-up area. In fifteen cases ownership was not known.
Source: Questionnaire Survey.

Lancaster and Duchy of Cornwall respectively. One, Cresswell Hall (Northld.) is an 8,000-acre estate now owned by the National Coal Board. Four are classed as educational establishments; the West Dean Estate (Sussex) and Old Warden Park (Beds.) are educational trusts. The former, the Edward James Foundation established in 1964, comprises the country house, now West Dean College, farms and cottages on a 6,000-acre estate; the latter was set up in 1944 in commemoration of Richard Ormonde Shuttleworth; 1,000 acres are occupied by the Shuttleworth Agricultural College and a further 3,500 acres comprises let land and woodland.[71] Wytham Abbey Estate (Oxford.) since 1958 has been owned by the Oxford University Chest and more recently in 1976 the Tabley House Estate (Cheshire) was acquired by Manchester University after being turned down by the National Trust. Gunthorpe Hall Estate (Norfolk) was purchased in 1976 by the Sun Alliance Insurance Group, the only financial institution represented in this size category. The three remaining estates were classed under Miscellaneous. The 3,000-acre Chevening Estate (Kent) was established as a Trust, with Coutts and Company as Custodian Trustees, under the Chevening Estate Act, 1959.[72] Stoughton Grange (Leics.) was purchased by the Co-

operative Wholesale Society (CWS) in 1919 and has grown from
its original 4,321 acres to 5,333 acres; one of the largest CWS
holdings which now total 38,000 acres of commercial farmland.[73]
Another entirely agricultural property is the 5,000-acre Laver-
stock House Estate (Hants) made into a public company in 1946
by Viscount Portal who died in 1949 without issue.[74]

The vast majority, nearly 80 per cent, of estate heartlands
held by the non-private sector are less than 1,000 acres and
represent only remnants of former historic properties rather than
complete units. The disintegration of traditional estates as complete units accelerated when public and institutional buyers
entered the land market in greater numbers after World War II.
Especially from this time, heartland areas were sold separately
from the remaining estate land and the market has become basically divided between private and institutional buyers seeking
blocks of agricultural land or development property without a
country house, associated outbuildings and ornamental grounds,
and those that have sought the heartland in order to make specific use of the house or its site. Closer examination of all those
in the non-private sector that presently own estate heartlands
shows that the majority comprise local authorities and various
educational establishments (Table 7.6). Although recorded
elsewhere as possessing an increasing share of England's agricultural land,[75] financial institutions holding complete estate
heartlands are few. Research has shown that they have concentrated investment in high-quality arable land in the counties

Table 7.6: Classification of Public, Semi-public and Institutional
Bodies Owning Sample Estate Heartlands c. 1980[a]

		No. of estate heartlands owned
1.	The Crown	3
2.	Central government	16
3.	Local authorities	52
4.	Statutory agencies and nationalised industries	6
5.	Educational establishments	39
6.	Conservation authorities	33[b]
7.	Financial institutions	4
8.	Religious institutions	9
9.	Miscellaneous and unclassified	39
	Total	201

Notes: a. See Appendix 4 for more detailed breakdown of categories 1-9. b. See note 78.
Source: Questionnaire Survey.

of eastern England, but also hold considerable acreages in other counties.[76] Most have sought only land and not the added liability of a large country house, which if acquired has been resold or leased.

The 3,000-acre estate at Gunthorpe (Norfolk) owned since 1976 by the Sun Alliance Insurance Group is a case in point. Here the house and approximately 20 acres of parkland were to be resold on a 150 year lease in 1978.[77] In 1963 over 3,000 acres of the Thicket Priory Estate (East Riding), with the exception of the Priory and a few acres which had been sold in the 1950s to a religious community, were sold along with the small mansion of Thorganby Hall to Sir John Eastwood. In October 1978 the estate, then a total of nearer 6,000 acres, was resold to the central fund of the Gas Staff Pension Schemes.[78] A pension fund also now owns around 2,000 acres of the heartland of the West Grinstead Estate (Sussex), but in this case the country house was demolished in the 1950s long before the fund acquired the land.[79] Both the Guardian Royal Exchange Assurance Group, that owns 2,000 acres of the former Clifton family estate at Lytham (Lancs.) purchased in 1965, and the National Westminster Bank, that owns 440 acres of the Heythrop House Estate (Oxford.) purchased in 1969, have retained the country house for an adapted use; in the former case part is used as office space though the majority is unoccupied, while in the latter the house is used as the National Westminster Bank Staff College.[80]

Despite the lack of a comprehensive land register a picture none the less emerges of continual and steady decline in the overall number and extent of privately owned historic estates. Though the results of the sample survey need to be treated with caution, as the study has focused on principal estates rather than total lands held by private families, it is clear that the extent of decline has been greater for estates of private landowners in the 3,000 to 10,000-acre size range, that is, the greater gentry. For many in this group agriculture provided the principal source of family income that failed to yield sufficient revenue in times of economic recession or to cover estate duties occasioned by the untimely death of the landowner. The break-up of estate property appears to have been less severe for the great landowners, especially the long-established landed aristocracy, though here too the predominant trend has been one of decline in total acreage, with many selling secondary estates and peripheral lands and concentrating their enterprises on the principal estate.

While the changing economy of the twentieth century has deprived some landowners of former sources of non-agricultural revenue, new opportunities and enterprises have emerged particularly linked with the heritage value of traditional estates. The preservation of historic property in association with the growth of tourism and recreation has become for many landowners a facet of estate management policy. In the light of current concern for England's heritage it is apparent, nevertheless, that little attention has been paid towards treating a landed estate as a complete unit since grants, allowances and tax concessions for heritage purposes become immaterial at a time of estate transfer following the death of an owner when the entire property is threatened with break-up. Failure in the past to treat the landed estate as an integral whole has already led to the separation of historic heartlands from the rest of the property, often with disastrous consequences for heritage preservation, a topic to be examined at some length in following chapters.

NOTES

1   Historic estate and traditional estate refer to all estate properties that were in existence in the late nineteenth century no matter when their date of origin.
2   Finance Act 1894, 57 & 58 Vict., c. 30, Pt. 1, sec. 17.
3   The People's Budget failed in its passage through the House of Lords. For a complete analysis see, B.K. Murray, 'The People's Budget 1909/10' (Clarendon, Oxford, 1980).
4   F.M.L. Thompson, 'English Landed Society in the Nineteenth Century' (Routledge and Kegan Paul, London, 1963), p. 325.
5   Questionnaire respondent, Lord Joicey, Etal Manor, Northumberland, Nov. 1977.
6   Thompson, 'English Landed Society', p. 322.
7   Finance Act 1919, 9 & 10 Geo. 5, c. 32, Pt. III.
8   'Estates Gazette', 31 Dec. 1921.
9   A. Lejeune, Gentleman's Estate, in Burke's 'Landed Gentry', 18th edn (Burke's Ltd, London, 1972), p. xvi.
10   Questionnaire respondents, Barttelot, Stopham, Sussex, Nov. 1977; C.E. Wilson, Rigmaden, Lancashire, March 1978; P. Antrobus, Amesbury Abbey, Wiltshire, June 1978.
11   Questionnaire respondents, M. Fitzherbert Brockholes, Claughton Hall, Lancashire, June 1978; M.C.A. Wyvill, Constable Burton Hall, North Yorkshire, March 1978.
12   Questionnaire respondent, R.B.B. Warwick, The Estate Office, Knowsley, Merseyside, July 1978; Sale Catalogues, Yorkshire Archaeological Society, Claremont, Leeds; Thompson, 'English Landed Society', p. 329.
13   Corn Production Act 1917, 7 & 8 Geo. 5, c. 46. Amending Acts were passed in 1918 and 1920.
14   Corn Production Acts (Repeal) Act 1921, 11 & 12 Geo. 5, c. 48.
15   D. Sutherland, 'The Landowners' (Anthony Blond, London, 1968), p. 54.
16   Finance Act 1940, 3 & 4 Geo. 6, c. 29, Pt. IV.
17   Later changed to 5 years.
18   Questionnaire respondent, N.A. Ussher, Estate Manager, Estate Office, Harewood, Yorkshire, Feb. 1978.

19   'Country Life', vol. 122, 22 Aug. (1957), p. 334; vol. 123, 26 June (1958), p. 1408.

20   M.A. Havinden, 'Estate Villages' (Lund Humphries, London, 1966), p. 131. Somerset Record Office, Sale Catalogues, DD/KW 1946/2; 1947/9; 1947/27; 1947/42; Questionnaire respondents, M.C.A. Wyvill, Constable Burton Hall, North Yorkshire, March 1978; The Rev. J.D. Bickersteth, Ashburnham Place, East Sussex, June 1978.

21   D. Massey and A. Catalano, 'Capital and Land' (Edward Arnold, London, 1978), p. 77 cites the example of estates purchased by the Duke of Westminster in 1949 and 1950.

22   Roll-over tax relief in this context is a deferral of capital gains tax on land purchases that are classed as a 'replacement of business assets'. See the Finance Act 1965, Eliz. 2, c. 25, Pt. III, sec. 33; Capital Gains Tax Act 1979, Eliz. 2, c. 14, Pt. VI, sec. 115-21.

23   R.J.C. Munton, Agricultural Land Price Survey in England, 1971-73: some preliminary results, 'Chartered Surveyor: Rural Quarterly', vol. 2, no. 4 (1978), pp. 59-64.

24   R.S. Gibbs and A. Harrison, 'Landownership by Public and Semi-public Bodies in Great Britain' (Dept. of Agric. Econ., Univ. of Reading, 1973), Misc. Study no. 56.

25   A. Harrison, R.B. Tranter and R.S. Gibbs, 'Landownership by Public and Semi-public Institutions in the UK' (Centre for Agricultural Strategy, Reading, 1977), Paper no. 3, p. 31.

26   I am grateful to A. Harrison (Dept. of Agric. Econ., Univ. of Reading) for drawing my attention to this point.

27   Munton, Agricultural Land Price Survey, p. 60.

28   The inflationary spiral of the 1970s has all but converted the Capital Gains Tax into a Wealth Tax.

29   G.R. Judd, Capital Taxation and the Farmer, 'Estates Gazette', 5 April (1975), p. 35.

30   Finance Act 1975, Eliz. 2, c. 7, sec. 38.

31   It is possible to lower the incidence by dividing ownership between spouses and through a gradual system of lifetime transfers for smaller area estates.

32   These concessions also apply to valuation for capital gains on land gifted during a farmer's lifetime.

33   A recent discussion on the let-land system is found in, 'Report of the Committee of Inquiry into the Acquisition and Occupancy of Agricultural Land', the Rt.Hon. Lord Northfield (Chairman) (HMSO, London, 1979), Cmnd. 7599, pp. 204-9.

34   Harrison, Tranter and Gibbs, 'Landownership', p. 19.

35   C. Sandford, Inflation, Taxation and Landownership, 'Estates Gazette', vol. 237, 6 March (1976), p. 713; D.K. Britton, A.M. Burrell, B. Hill and D. Ray, 'Statistical Handbook of UK Agriculture' (Wye College, Kent, 1980), p. 70. The distinction between owner-occupied and tenanted land is not clear cut. Even some full agricultural

tenancies may be *de facto* owner occupation as, for example, when a tenancy is held by the son of the land-owner.

36   Somerset Record Office, DD/KW 1948/49, Sale Catalogue, 1948 containing local newspaper cutting, n.d.

37   'Estates Gazette', 9 Nov. (1963), p. 527.

38   'The Times', 2 Aug. 1924; 6 Oct. 1924.

39   Provision for greater security of tenure involving notices to quit and succession following the death of the tenant are found respectively under the Agricultural Holdings Act 1948, 11 & 12 Geo. 6, c. 63, sections 23-33; and Agriculture (Miscellaneous Provisions) Act 1976, Eliz. 2, c. 55, Pt. 11.

40   Questionnaire respondent, Lord Walsingham, Merton Hall, Norfolk, May 1978.

41   'Estates Gazette', 10 June (1922), p. 841.

42   C.D. Harbury, Inheritance and the Distribution of Personal Wealth, 'Economic Journal', vol. 72, no. 288 (1962), p. 867.

43   Questionnaire respondent, Earl of Scarbrough, Sandbeck Park, Rotherham, South Yorkshire, Nov. 1977; O. Marriott, 'The Property Boom' (Hamish Hamilton, London, 1967), p. 84.

44   Marriott, 'The Property Boom', p. 80.

45   Sutherland, 'The Landowners', p. 97.

46   Community Land Act 1975, Eliz. 2, c. 77; Development Land Tax 1976, Eliz. 2, c. 24.

47   Massey and Catalano, 'Capital and Land', p. 76.

48   'Country Life', vol. 122, 22 Aug. (1957), p. 334; 'Guardian', 21 May 1978.

49   'Guardian', 24 Dec. 1978. The sale was occasioned by the death of Lord Cobham in 1977.

50   J. Bateman, 'The Great Landowners of Great Britain and Ireland', 4th edn (1883, reprinted Leicester Univ. Press, 1971).

51   The CLA has demarcated a major estate as comprising over 6,000 acres, a large estate from 3,000 to 6,000 acres and a medium estate from 1,000 to 3,000 acres. Below 1,000 acres has been defined as a large farm. 'The Future of Landownership' (CLA, London, 1976), A 438, pp. 6-7. It is not inconceivable that an estate heartland alone may be more than 1,000 acres as a number of parks in 1880 exceeded this size.

52   Private ownership has been defined as any form of legal status whereby an individual member of a landed family, or number of family members together retain power in the administration of an estate property. This can be single ownership, joint ownership or partnership, a family limited estate company, a property held in trust whether as part of a settled estate or a discretionary trust. The one exclu-sion from this category is the private charitable trust

which has been accorded institutional status. Identification of ownership status was, where possible, left to the discretion of the present landowner.

53 Public, semi-public and institutional bodies include private charitable trusts and the National Trust. The latter is acknowledged as a separate category in the text on the basis of its important role in the preservation of historic buildings and landscapes. For more precise classification the non-private sector has been sub-divided into nine categories which are listed in Appendix 4 along with a more detailed breakdown of public and institutional bodies owning estate land in the sample group c. 1980.

54 Original family refers to descendants of the 1880 family who have inherited the estate property, either in the male or female line, by marriage or through settlement of an entailed estate. Two cases were recorded where the estate passed from original family hands through sale and was later repurchased; The Grange (Hants) and Hannington Hall (Wilts.). Both have been classed under the original family category even though continuity in strict definition was broken.

55 For three properties still owned by the original family the acreage was not known.

56 Questionnaire respondent, P.H.D. Jenkins, Estate Office, Longford Castle, Wiltshire, June 1978.

57 Questionnaire respondent, J.A. Farrer, Ingleborough Estate, Clapham, Yorkshire, Jan. 1978.

58 Now Cumbria.

59 Questionnaire respondent, M.E.M. Sandys, Graythwaite Hall, Ulverston, Cumbria.

60 In only one case was the principal estate in 1880 less than 3,000 acres.

61 R. Perrott, 'The Aristocrats' (Weidenfeld and Nicolson, London, 1968), p. 156.

62 Questionnaire respondent, Lt. Col. W. Luttrell, East Quantoxhead, Somerset, Feb. 1978.

63 The future financial benefits from holding development land have been somewhat negated since the imposition of the Development Land Tax in 1976.

64 At minimum this implies a change of ownership of the country house, but generally when the house was transferred a quantity of land accompanied the transaction.

65 D.R. Denman, 'Estate Capital' (Allen and Unwin, London, 1957), p. 122.

66 Different family status is accorded to private owners who have purchased all or part of an estate in the sample since c. 1880.

67 Questionnaire respondent, B. Mann, Woolverstone Hall School, Suffolk, May 1978.

68 J. Murden, 'Harlaxton Through the Ages' (J. Murden, 1976), pp. 21-2, and correspondence with G.R. Rowlands,

Principal, Harlaxton College, Lincolnshire, Aug. 1978.

69   Now Oxfordshire.

70   For the complete list of public, semi-public and institutional bodies owning sample estate heartlands see Appendix 4.

71   Questionnaire respondents, M. Heyman, Agent, The Edward James Foundation, West Dean Estate, West Sussex, Dec. 1977; J.E. Scott, Principal, Shuttleworth Agricultural College, Biggleswade, Bedfordshire, Oct. 1978.

72   Chevening Estate Act 1959, 7 & 8 Eliz. 2, c. 49.

73   Correspondence, P. Rodgers, Manager, Manchester Office Estate and Property Group, Co-operative Wholesale Society Ltd., Aug. 1980. Document titled CWS Farms Group, p. 1.

74   Questionnaire respondent, J.V. Sheffield, Laverstoke House, Whitchurch, Hampshire, May 1978.

75   R.J.C. Munton, Financial institutions: their ownership of agricultural land in Great Britain, 'Area', vol. 9, no. 1, (1977), pp. 29-37; Harrison, Tranter and Gibbs, 'Land-ownership', p. 32.

76   Munton, Financial Institutions, p. 34.

77   Questionnaire respondent, J.H. Ellson, Assistant Manager, Estates Department, Sun Alliance Insurance Group, London, June 1978.

78   In a strict definition of ownership based on possession of the heartland, that is, country house and amenity land, the Thicket Estate was classed under religious institution, even though only a few acres are retained with Thicket Priory.

79   Questionnaire respondent Sir. W. Burrell Bt., Knepp Castle, Horsham, Sussex, n.d.

80   Questionnaire respondents, C.J. Bailward, Principal Estates Surveyor, Guardian Royal Exchange Assurance, Lytham, Lancashire, Jan. 1980; W.R.S. Hodson, Principal, National Westminster Bank Staff College, Heythrop Park, Oxfordshire, June 1978.

In succession
Houses rise and fall, crumble, are extended,
Are removed, destroyed, restored...
T.S. Eliot, *East Coker* (Faber and Faber, London, 1940).

Over the past century there has been a steady and continuous decline in the private ownership of traditional landed estates, even though to date the loss has not been as extensive, particularly for the great estates, as popular rhetoric would have one believe. From a landscape and heritage point of view, however, there have been considerable changes in the physical make-up of estate heartlands involving the country house and amenity lands, the extent and nature of changes being related to, but not entirely synonymous with, the altered pattern of landownership. For many country houses the consequences have been drastic leading to abandonment, ruination and demolition. Why have some survived while others of equal architectural or historical merit have been demolished; when did they disappear from the landscape, and for what basic reasons? Such questions are some of the more important to be addressed in the present chapter, which examines country-house losses in the sample group over the past hundred years; from a landscape perspective perhaps the greatest physical change to occur on a landed estate.

In total, 106 sample houses (21 per cent) have been demolished since 1880, although 32 were replaced by a new house.[1] An additional thirteen are uninhabited and in a ruinous condition and many others have been reduced in size through partial demolition or have undergone changes through remodelling and adaptation. Bearing in mind that the sample houses were the principal residences of large-estate owners, who often held more than one country house, it is reasonable to suppose that they would be the last to be let go and for families with a strong landed tradition would certainly be retained as long as possible.

For some houses destruction was accidental. At least 20 were razed to the ground by fire, while Trafford Park (Lancs.) and Sandling Park (Kent) were bombed beyond repair in World War II and were later completely dismantled. But for the most part demolition has been the deliberate choice of the owner. It is of interest to observe that over 50 per cent of the houses were torn down while still in private hands[2] and part of an ongoing estate, but nearly half of these demolitions were undertaken to make way for a new house, while in a number of other cases the family flag had been transferred to another estate building.

At least 40 per cent of the deliberately demolished houses had been unoccupied and had undergone considerable deterioration prior to demolition. In Lincolnshire, for example, Scrivelsby Court, ancestral seat of the Dymokes, Knights Champion of England, was abandoned after World War II and from 1946 to 1955 it became increasingly dilapidated and riddled with dry rot. It was levelled in 1956 and the site is now a garden. The present Scrivelsby Court is the original gatehouse of the mansion that was destroyed by fire in 1760.[3]

The ultimate stage of clearance from the landscape has yet to be realised for some abandoned buildings which stand as roofless shells in varying stages of dilapidation and decay. One or two ruinous houses are fossilised under the protection of the state. Sutton Scarsdale (Derby.) is a case in point. The house was built in 1724 by Francis Smith for the 4th Earl of Scarsdale and later in the eighteenth century it became the property of the Arkwright family. William Arkwright, who died in 1925, was the last to occupy the house. He sold the greater part of the estate including the house in 1920, having no children to succeed to the property.[4] Part of the house was sold to a buyer from the United States and three rooms are now in the Philadelphia Museum of Art.[5] The remainder, after being stripped of saleable parts including the lead roofing, was abandoned to decay. Over thirty years later what remained of Sutton Scarsdale was purchased by Sir Osbert Sitwell ostensibly to preserve the eighteenth-century classical ruin as part of the Derbyshire landscape, of special nostalgia to Sir Osbert who lived nearby at Renishaw and had known the property all his life. The ruin was transferred in 1971, after much negotiation,[6] to the care of the Ministry of Public Building and Works[7] and is now scheduled as an Ancient Monument. The Grange (Hants) has undergone a similar fate. In 1934 the house was sold by the Baring family but was bought back in 1964 in a dilapidated state. It was intended to demolish the house, but after partial demolition in 1972 public outcry prevented further work. As an outcome the house, described as one of the most remarkable neo-classical revivals in Britain, was transferred to the custody of the Department of the Environment and is now also scheduled as an Ancient Monument.[8]

At least two country houses were abandoned as ruinous after being gutted by fire, Carclew (Cornwall) in 1934 and Lulworth Castle (Dorset) in 1929, and Rougham Hall (Suffolk) has remained in a ruinous state since it was bombed during World War II.

By 1980 Hasell's Hall (Beds.) had been empty for over ten years, its owner Mr Francis Pym, whose ancestors had occupied the house since the mid-eighteenth century, lives in a modern residence nearby. The old hall had reached such a state of decay that it was estimated as much as a quarter of a million pounds would be required to restore it.[9] Nevertheless, listed-building consent to demolish has not been granted and the house remains

standing awaiting restoration and possible conversion to flats.
Butleigh Court (Somerset) is another of a growing number of
unoccupied houses that may be saved by being turned into
residential units. After its sale in 1946 the house became derelict, but at the time of the survey was undergoing a second
attempt at conversion. Other houses still standing but unoccupied and in varying stages of dilapidation as yet have an
undetermined future. These include: the Mynde (Hereford.),
Shelswell Park (Oxford.) and Balcombe Place (Sussex).

THE CHRONOLOGY OF DEMOLITION: c. 1890 TO c. 1980

The dates of demolition for sample houses can be differentiated
according to whether loss was accidental or deliberate (Figure
8.1). Fire continues to be an indiscriminate destroyer of country
houses but it is of interest to observe that 19 of the 22 recorded
accidental demolitions occurred prior to 1945. Fifteen of these
houses were subsequently rebuilt. Presumably as safer methods
of heating have developed, with less reliance on open fires, and
as the wider use of fireproof materials has been adopted, so
the number of houses accidently razed to the ground has diminished; the hazard, however, can never be eliminated.

Figure 8.1: Country-house Demolitions c. 1875 to c. 1980

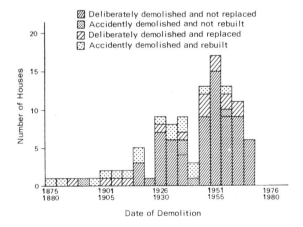

Source: Questionnaire Survey. See also Note 2.

There were two major intervals during which deliberate demolition was most prevalent on sample estates; 1926 to 1940, and
1946 to 1965. Only after the mid-1960s did the number of demolitions per five-year period fall back to the pre-World War II level.
What in fact is revealed is a steady and continual increase in

the number of demolitions per decade up to 1940, interrupted
by the war when houses were readily converted to alternative
uses, and resumed in the aftermath of war at an unprecedented
rate reaching a peak in the mid-1950s. The 1920s through to
the early 1950s have been appropriately referred to as the black
decades in architectural history.[10]

Demolitions to 1940
All demolitions on sample estates prior to World War I were either
accidental or deliberate acts in order to replace the existing
house with one more suited to the tastes of the owner. Only after
the war were country houses deliberately demolished and not
replaced, reflecting either the choice to occupy another estate
building, usually of a smaller size, or the break-up of the estate.
It is generally upheld that once divorced from the estate a
country house, prior to legislation in the 1950s, had less chance
of long-term survival. The fact that over the whole period to
1980 as many as 50 per cent were demolished, for whatever reason, when still part of an ongoing estate somewhat refutes this
belief, but even so the number of house demolitions certainly
began to increase coincident with the break-up of estates after
World War II.
  Throughout the late Victorian and Edwardian era and into the
inter-war years, even though underlying trends were towards
the abandonment of the so-called 'country-house culture', it
was possible for many owners to lease their country houses as
an alternative to sale or demolition. As the costs of house
maintenance increased or estate revenues declined, a number of
families vacated the principal seat and moved to a smaller house.
Leasing provided additional revenue in times of financial hardship and became a more common practice in the early decades of
the twentieth century. At this time tenants were not hard to
find and houses on good sporting estates were let with little
difficulty for a season or on a more permanent basis.
  It was not uncommon to find advertisements in journals or
newspapers offering country seats for lease. Three of the sample
properties for instance were advertised in 1928 in *Country Life*.
In July, Ingestre Hall (Staffs.), a house rebuilt in 1882 following loss by fire, was offered for lease for seven years, with
the option of shooting on over 7,880 acres.[11] In December Kedleston Hall (Derby.) was available with fishing and 6,000 acres
of shooting,[12] while later in the same month Levens Hall
(Westmorland) was on the market to be let with 1,814 acres of
shooting, one-and-a-half miles of salmon and trout fishing,
and a grouse moor of 5,200 acres.[13] The emphasis on sport was
the key to leasing many country houses, the fashion of shooting
being heightened particularly in the Edwardian era by the
popularity of the sport in the royal household. Of the three
houses, only Ingestre was later sold, the other two are today
occupied by descendents of their original owners.
  Leasing or sale were not viable alternatives to demolition for

all landowners, nor for all houses, and as costs of house maintenance increased and the agricultural economy continued in a
relatively depressed state throughout much of the inter-war
period, the incidence of demolition steadily increased as more
houses became an added burden on estate property.

The Country House in War (1940 to 1945)
War brought a temporary reprieve for a number of houses and
no planned demolitions occurred on sample estates from 1940 to
1945. This does not hold true for all of England's country houses,
but it is apparent that few large buildings were destroyed at a
time when they could be put to use in the war effort.

It would be as well to pause for a moment to consider the impact
of World War II on country houses in spite of the fact that few
were actually demolished at this time. It is without doubt that the
role of the country house was of immense value on the home front.
A number of houses had been offered as convalescent homes and
hospitals in World War I, but far more were brought into
service during World War II. Surprisingly few were destroyed
by direct enemy action (see p. 133) yet many requisitioned for
wartime use suffered considerable physical abuse in their adapted
role. Country houses, parks and entire estate properties were
requisitioned under the Compensation Defence Act 1939[14] and were
put to a multitude of uses. Many houses in the sample were used
as convalescent homes including, Hawkstone (Salop), Preston
Hall (Kent), Lynford Park (Norfolk), Stapleford Park (Leics.);
others were used as military hospitals including Harewood House
(West Riding), Carlton Towers (West Riding), Leeds Castle
(Kent), Ford Castle (Northld.); while a group far too large to
enumerate were taken over by the armed forces for various military uses. A small number including North Seaton Hall (Northld.)
were bases for prisoner of war camps. In the history of World
War II a few country houses and estates had a special role;
Southwick Park (Hants) served as the headquarters for Supreme
Allied Command, Merton Hall (Norfolk) and a large area of the
estate land was used for the training of Montgomery's forces for
the Normandy landings and much of the planning for D-Day took
place in Inigo Jones's double cube room at Wilton (Wilts.); vignet-
tes of the country house in war time, a complete history of which
has yet to be written.

Prior to being requisitioned, a number of country houses had
already changed hands, many were unoccupied and some had
undergone adaptation for uses other than residential. For example, Keele Hall (Staffs.) and Felton Park (Northld.) were unoccupied prior to being taken over for army use in 1939; Longridge
Towers (Northld.) had been sold by the Jerningham family and
was in use as a school before being made over to the army; Sand-
hill Park (Somerset) had been sold to the County Council in 1921
for use as a home before being occupied by the American Armed
Forces as a hospital. Gopsal (Leics.) had been purchased by
the Land Commission in 1927 and Newton Park (Somerset) by the

Duchy of Cornwall in 1940; both were occupied by the army till the end of the war. Of these six houses, Gopsal and the major part of Felton Park were subsequently demolished and none of the remainder have since been occupied as private residences.

Many requisitioned houses, however, were still owned and occupied as private homes. A number suffered considerable and often irreparable damage and were eventually demolished including Sudborne Hall (Suffolk), Redgrave Hall (Suffolk), Garendon Park (Leics.), Easton Hall (Lincs.) and Warnford Park (Hants). Others underwent damage or decay through abuse and general lack of upkeep during wartime occupation and were restored by their owners at considerable expense after 1945. Compensation was paid under the Requisitioned Land and War Works Act 1945[15] but the amount gave no recognition to the cost of re-adapting premises to their former use. Only with the formation of the Historic Buildings Councils (HBCs)[16] in 1953 was additional government assistance made available to help meet the costs of restoration and renovation for country houses of historical and architectural significance.

The Aftermath of War (1945 to 1980)
Faced with the poor condition of country houses following wartime occupation and combined with the additional capital outlay required not only for renovations, but also to meet the rising costs of maintenance and daily upkeep, a number of owners gave up the attempt to preserve their ancestral home; houses were put up for lease or sale or, as a last resort, if no suitable offer was made, were demolished. For an increasing number of families the size of the house was far in excess of modern-day requirements and added to this a major factor in the problem of upkeep was the rising cost and shortage of domestic staff. In the nineteenth century the staffing requirements of large country houses provided an important source of employment for the sons and daughters of local labourers and tradesmen. While wages were not necessarily high, a position in the 'big house' usually entailed room and board and was one that offered considerable security at a time of an over-abundance of cheap, unskilled labour. By the late nineteenth century the general staff complement of a good number of country houses had already been lowered, many owners being forced to cut estate costs in times of economic hardship. Not only were fewer staff hired, but as time passed the attraction of alternative employment and often better wages elsewhere meant that a reduced number were available for hire; a decline exacerbated in the twentieth century by an apparent social stigma identified with being 'in service'. As labour costs have progressively risen so more owners have been faced with the necessity to make additional cut-backs. Certainly many no longer maintain staff to cater to their personal needs, but while modern domestic appliances have reduced the help needed for daily housekeeping there is a point below which employee numbers cannot be reduced without leading to the potential deterior-

ation of the contents, if not the houses themselves. Cornforth
pointed to the fact that even in the 1950s when alterations were
being made to country houses, extensive staff accommodation
remained an important consideration.[17] Thus, even though owners
had begun to face serious problems in cost and recruitment of
staff, the full impact of the domestic revolution had not hit by
the 1950s, but has been more strongly felt in recent decades.
However, there is little doubt that the problem of staffing was
a contributory factor in the increased number of country-house
demolitions in the immediate post-war period.

The ten years from 1945 to 1955 witnessed the greatest loss to
date of any decade of the twentieth century, at least 30 houses
in the sample were completely demolished and many others were
reduced in size at this time. In 1953 with the establishment of
the HBCs, country houses of outstanding architectural or historic
interest were eligible to receive financial assistance for repairs
and maintenance. The injection of exchequer funding,[18] coupled
with the growth of country-house tourism and a generally more
buoyant economy undoubtedly saved a number of important
country houses from going under. There were, however, as
many sample houses demolished from 1955 to 1960 as in the five
years from 1945 to 1950. Only after 1960 was there a decline, but
it was not until the late 1960s that demolition fell to the pre-war
level. On sample estates no principal residences have been completely demolished since 1970, undoubtedly related to the controls introduced in the Town and Country Planning Act 1968,
of which more will be said shortly. A number of owners, however,
have attempted to acquire listed-building consent for demolition.
The fate of Hasell's Hall (Beds.) has already been discussed
(pp. 134-5). Here permission to demolish was turned down in 1972
as well as in 1980. In the 1970s the owner of Hylands Hall (Essex)
was similarly refused demolition consent and the property was
transferred to the Department of the Environment and is now
held by the Chelmsford Borough Council. In 1977 the owner of
Balcombe Place (Sussex) was also denied the go ahead to demolish. It should nevertheless be noted that for England as a whole
a number of demolitions have taken place since the 1970s of which
at least six were recorded in *The Destruction of the Country
House*.[19] More recently, in an *Annual Report* of the HBCE it
was stated that no listed-building consent was given for the total
demolition of a Grade I building in 1978.[20]

COUNTRY HOUSE LOSSES ACCORDING TO ARCHITECTURAL
PERIOD OF ORIGIN

As early as 1877 William Morris founded the Society for the
Protection of Ancient Buildings (SPAB), the first public pressure group of its kind.[21] Its basic emphasis concerned the preservation of medieval buildings in the light of adaptations and
alterations being made to 'modernise' or 'Victorianise' them. For

the most part, houses of the Tudor and Elizabethan period that
survived the rebuilding mania of the Georgian and Victorian
eras have, with the exception of those consumed by fire, endured
to the present day; not solely because of the work of SPAB, but
as much due to a general appreciation of medieval buildings as
part of English architectural tastes.[22]

At the end of the nineteenth century the construction of large
country houses had not entirely ceased, but investment had
been in sharp decline since the 1880s. New houses of the late
Victorian and Edwardian eras tended to originate from the proceeds of urban or industrial wealth as was the case of Bryanston
(1890) in Dorset (see p. 48), one of four houses built in the
period 1880 to 1916 following the demolition of an earlier building. Pickenham Hall in Norfolk, a house of the early nineteenth
century, was entirely rebuilt in 1903 to 1904 as was Hampworth
Lodge in Wiltshire and Gargrave House in the West Riding.
Seven other sample houses burned down in the period from
1875 to 1916, some completely but others to the point where
rebuilding was still possible. The eighteenth-century core of
Duncombe Park (North Riding) was gutted in 1879, but rebuilt
to its original design as was Ingestre Hall (Staffs.), a house
that dated from the 1630s but which was altered by John Nash
from 1808 to 1810. Most of Nash's work was destroyed in the fire
of 1882, but the hall was reinstated over the next three years.
Wrottesley Hall (Staffs.), a late-seventeenth-century house was
ruined by fire in 1897 and later rebuilt on a reduced scale. Lees
Court (Kent) was similarly rebuilt following a fire about 1911
and here the eighteenth-century work of Soane was lost.[23] Hengar
House (Cornwall) was completely rebuilt in Elizabethan style
after being destroyed by fire in 1904, while one of the tragedies
of the period was the destruction of Aqualate Hall in Staffordshire, a country house that was largely the work of John Nash.
It was completely gutted in 1910 and replaced by a new house in
the period 1927 to 1930.[24] Brookman's Park (Kent), a house of
the seventeenth century, was an early casualty that was not
replaced after being destroyed by fire in 1892.

From 1916 to 1945 35 sample houses were demolished (Table
8.1) of which at least ten were as a result of fire and two due
to wartime bombing. Few of those destroyed originated prior
to the Commonwealth. Cassiobury (Herts.) was a house with Tudor
origins, but it was more associated with the later designs of
James Wyatt in the early nineteenth century and the interior
work of Grinling Gibbons. The house was dismantled following
the sale of the estate in 1922 and by 1927 parts of its interior
as well as the furnishings and art work had been sold to col-
lectors at home and abroad.[25] Shobden Court (Hereford.),
designed in 1705 by William Talman, was demolished in 1933.

The inter-war years witnessed the first onslaught in the
demolition of Georgian houses; at least eleven in the sample built
from 1715 to 1840 were torn down prior to World War II. Of particular note can be mentioned the loss of Kirby Hall (West Riding),

Table 8.1: Date of Country-house Demolition Cross-tabulated
with Period of Origin

Date of Demolition	Pre-1560	1561-1660	1661-1715	1716-1760	1761-1840	1841-1890	No Data	Total
1875-1900	–	1	3	–	1	–	–	5
1901-1915	1	1	–	–	2	–	2	6
1916-1945[a]	–	2	3	6	14	4	6	35
1946-1980	4	6	4	3	24	9	10	60
Total	5	10	10	9	41	13	18	106[b]

Notes: a. Only 3 houses were demolished from 1939 to 1945,
none deliberately. b. Includes 22 known accidental demolitions.
Source: Questionnaire Survey and miscellaneous secondary
sources, Chapter 3, see note 2.

built in the 1740s to the designs of Lord Burlington, demolished
in 1920; Norton Priory (Cheshire) an early eighteenth-century
house remodelled by James Wyatt in 1790, demolished in 1928;
Debden Hall (Essex) designed by Henry Holland in 1796, demolished in 1936; Cresswell Hall (Northld.) a neo-Grecian house
built by John Shaw in the 1820s, demolished in 1930; and Drayton Manor (Staffs.) built by Robert Smirke in the 1830s, but
more well known as the home of the Rt Hon. Sir Robert Peel.
Despite its historic significance the Manor was demolished in
1926, one of many Georgian, and predominantly classical houses,
removed from the landscape in the inter-war period. Such losses
eventually stimulated the formation in 1937 of the Georgian
Group, an organisation with concern for the protection of buildings of that era.

A further 27 houses of the Georgian period have been lost
since the war, of which 21 disappeared between 1946 and 1960.
The list is too long to enumerate but as with earlier decades
included the work of a number of England's more famous architects and buildings of considerable architectural merit. Another
house designed by John Nash, West Grinstead Park (Sussex)
was destroyed in 1968, while High Legh (Cheshire), which also
incorporated his work, was demolished in 1963. Cadlands (Hants),
demolished in 1953 and Redgrave Hall (Suffolk) burned in 1946
and demolished in 1960, both embodied the work of Lancelot
Brown. Panshanger (Herts.), built by William Atkinson in 1806,
was demolished in 1953 and Sundorne Castle (Salop), also in
part attributed to Atkinson, was demolished in 1953. Roundway
Park (Wilts.), a house designed by James Wyatt, was destroyed
in 1955.

Within such a gloomy picture of loss it is of interest to record
one example of a notable house, largely of Georgian creation,
saved from demolition at this time. Arbury Hall (Warwick.), a
house remodelled in rococo gothic style in the mid-eighteenth

century and referred to as 'the Strawberry Hill of the Midlands',[26] a Grade I listed building, was threatened with demolition in 1954 when the National Coal Board planned to mine beneath it. Government intervention prevented the Coal Board scheme and the house was saved. It remains in the ownership of the Newdigate family, whose association with the property extends back to the sixteenth century, and is today one of the country houses of England regularly open to the public.

Houses of earlier origin suffered fewer casualties in the post-war period although two of note were removed from the Lincolnshire landscape, namely Scrivelsby Court (see p. 134) demolished in 1956, and Bloxholme, built in 1650 and demolished in 1963.

And what of Victorian houses? Certainly at the beginning of the century all were of fairly recent origin and one or two still in the process of completion. Demolition of such houses was delayed until after World War II although a few disappeared in the inter-war years. In the sample group, out of nine recorded post-war demolitions, six were in the 1950s, the worst decade for most English country houses. Among these losses were Birch Hall (Essex), built by Thomas Hopper in 1884, and Bishop Burton High Hall (East Riding), rebuilt in the period 1865 to 1872, both demolished in 1951; Denbies (Surrey), designed for himself by Thomas Cubitt in the 1850s, demolished in 1953, and Longden Manor (Salop), built in the 1860s and demolished in 1954.

One of the largest, if not the largest, country house to be demolished in the post-war period was Eaton Hall (Cheshire), principal residence of the Dukes of Westminster. The original house built by William Samwell from 1675 to 1682 had been much altered by the mid-nineteenth century, but from 1870 to 1882 it had been completely rebuilt by Alfred Waterhouse. The result has been described as a 'Wagnerian palace...the most ambitious instance of Gothic Revival domestic architecture anywhere in the country.'[27] Eaton Hall was demolished in the period 1961 to 1963.[28] Marbury Hall was another notable loss in Cheshire. The original house had been totally remodelled by Salvin in the 1850s in a French style after the Palace at Fontainebleau. It was torn down in 1968.

True to form of the English character as the loss of Victorian buildings, urban and rural, became more evident, another action group was born, the Victorian Society, which from 1958 drew attention to many pending demolitions, especially of buildings in the London area.

No matter what period of origin, the characteristic most common to country houses that have been demolished was their large size. Generally, the more modest seventeenth-century creations have endured longer than many houses constructed at a later date. The fate of the majority of the colossal late Georgian and Victorian edifices, for the most part, has been either demolition or conversion to other uses; few remain as private homes.

LOCATION OF COUNTRY-HOUSE DEMOLITIONS

The distribution of country-house losses is shown on Figure 8.2.

Figure 8.2: Sample Estates: Country-house Demolitions since 1880

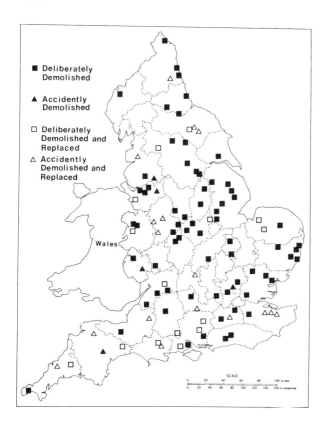

Source: Questionnaire Survey.

On a proportional basis the number of demolitions in the sample group has been broadly similar for all regions, ranging from a low of 19 per cent in the South West to a high of 25 per cent in the North West and East. Taking only demolitions where the house was not replaced, that is, the data for absolute loss, the South East and South West have by far the lowest proportions of 8 and 13 per cent respectively, while the East of England has the highest recorded loss of 22 per cent. The latter continues to be principally an agricultural area and a relatively remote region *vis-à-vis* industrial development and urban settlement. Thus, large country houses that burden an agricultural estate, in the past and in the present, have had less potential for sale or adaptation from urban or industrial generated sources. While on the one hand remoteness would seem, therefore, to be important in accounting for the pattern of demolition, notable losses have also been concentrated in the industrial environs of the central Midlands, North and North West.

Replacement and rebuilding activity has been more prevalent in the South of England, especially since World War II, though the overall number of new houses has been small and the majority of estate owners have made use of an existing building rather than construct a replacement for a demolished country house.

PARTIAL DEMOLITION OF COUNTRY HOUSES

While some owners have resorted to wholesale demolition, others have undertaken partial demolition and remodelling in order to retain the house as a family residence, or to adapt it for another purpose. Reconstruction following fire has also led to some houses being drastically reduced in size, as with Clovelly Court (Devon) in 1944 and Merton Hall (Norfolk) in 1956. The vast majority that have undergone partial demolition since 1880 were reduced in the post-war period, particularly in the 1950s. Brocklesby Hall (Lincs.) is a case in point. The Hall was rebuilt in 1710 and enlarged with the addition of a picture gallery in 1807, another wing was added in 1827 and a further two storeys above the gallery in 1868. Fire in 1898 substantially damaged much of the main building which was reconstructed by Sir R. Blomfield. In 1958 the whole was reduced by Claude Phillimore leaving only the early-eighteenth-century block and the one storey gallery.[29] The more drastic reductions of the 1950s include Rufford Abbey (Notts.), Felton Park (Northld.), of which only the kitchen wing remains, Morton Hall (Norfolk) partially demolished in 1951, Somerley (Hants) in 1955, Stanley Hall (Salop) and Garnons (Hereford.) in 1957, and Ashburnham Place (Sussex) in 1959. More recent have been Maer Hall (Staffs.) in 1966, Pentillie Castle (Cornwall) in 1968, Hall Barn Park (Bucks.) in 1969; a list by no means inclusive of all partial demolitions that have been undertaken. In many cases late-Georgian and Victorian extensions, service wings built to accommodate extra staff and guests at a time when country-house entertainment was the height of fashion, have also been removed as at Dingley Park (Northants.) in 1972. Such offices were more often cheaply constructed and of little architectural merit and a number of houses have no doubt been visually improved following the removal of such superfluous appendages.

NEW COUNTRY HOUSES

During the past century at least 32 country houses have been demolished on sample estates to be replaced by a new house on the same site or in close proximity to the original.[30] Between 1880 and 1916 the newly constructed house may well have been on a larger scale than its predecessor, as at Bryanston, but as the twentieth century progressed, country-house building has been on a smaller scale to provide more manageable family homes. This course of action reflected similar choices made in the past when, through changing needs, fashions or personal tastes, a landowner chose to demolish and rebuild the principal estate residence. Thus, many Tudor and Elizabethan houses disappeared in the eighteenth century. While the motives are somewhat different in the twentieth century, predominantly reflecting economic constraint rather than the pursuit of fashion, the outcome has been the same. However, in previous centuries the right of an owner to remodel or demolish his country house remained unchallenged, while in the present day the introduction of legislative protection for historic buildings has made it more difficult for an individual owner to exercise proprietory freedom of choice in either the external remodelling or demolition of the country house on his estate.

PROTECTION OF THE COUNTRY HOUSE

Despite the work of early pressure groups to curtail the demolition of historic buildings, their impact was more directed towards urban areas than the countryside, and little protection was afforded the country house until the introduction of legislative controls. The first step in government responsibility can be dated from the Town and Country Planning Act 1932 which permitted local authorities to 'make an order with respect to any building of special architectural or historic interest...directing that without their consent the building shall not be demolished'.[31] Even though the Act appears to have had little impact on country-house preservation in its formative years, it provided the foundation for further legislation in the post-war period.

Statutory listing of buildings of special architectural and historic interest was introduced in the Town and Country Planning Act 1944 to provide a guide for local authorities in the implementation of the 1932 Act.[32] Buildings were graded in three categories; Grade I were considered to be of such exceptional interest that greatest importance was to be given to their preservation; Grade II were also deemed of national importance and were to be preserved where possible, while Grade III were of less importance and included, for example, buildings of which only a part was of architectural value, or small-scale examples of local vernacular architecture. Grade II* was introduced in 1968 to demarcate the more significant buildings in Grade II, and since 1971 Grade III has no longer been used; most of the buildings previously listed in this category have been accorded Grade II status.

In the Town and Country Planning Act 1947 demolition control was further defined with the introduction of the 'building preservation order'[133] but it was not until the creation of the HBCs in 1953 that grants were made available to assist the preservation process.[34] Local authorities could acquire funding to repair and maintain neglected buildings of outstanding merit, and private landowners likewise could receive financial assistance for important buildings on their estates.

Even so, loopholes in the system of building preservation orders failed to prevent the demolition of many listed country houses in the immediate post-war years.[35] New provisions that tightened the gaps in the existing laws were enacted in the Town and Country Planning Act 1968.[36] Building preservation orders were abolished and in their place legislation made it compulsory for an owner to have written consent, 'listed building consent', from the local planning authority or Minister before demolition, alteration or extension of a listed building could take place.[37]

Successive revisions and amendments have further strengthened central and local government control over the demolition of listed and unlisted buildings. 'Building preservation notices' for unlisted buildings were introduced in the Town and Country Planning Act 1971, and permitted any building considered of architectural or historic interest but previously unlisted to be accorded listed status by a local authority subject to Ministerial approval.[38] In 1974 protection from demolition was also extended to include all unlisted buildings in conservation areas.[39]

Certainly, stricter controls have prevented the needless demolition of a number of country houses, the majority of which are listed buildings. But the fact that a building is listed, or protected due to its location, does not guarantee its survival; at minimum the law only ensures that the case for preservation is examined.

However, the number and strength of groups and organisations, local and national, concerned with heritage preservation has grown tremendously in recent years and few country houses of note have been let go without considerable protest. Demolition decisions have been reversed due to public pressure, but the struggle to retain what is left continues and is likely to become more difficult given the prevailing economic situation in Britain since the mid-1970s. Country houses are becoming a greater financial liability, especially for private estate owners, and annually more difficult to maintain given the escalation in the cost of repairs and maintenance at around 15 to 25 per cent per annum.[40] Further, as the impact of capital taxation on private landed estates is increasingly felt in the 1980s, more country houses will inevitably come on the market. In the past, local authorities were important purchasers of country houses, but costs are rising for public as well as private owners. In fact, a large country house costs more to be maintained by the public sector. Recent estimates have put the annual average running cost of a country house in public ownership at £62,000 compared with £31,400 for private ownership.[41]

The government has not been willing to intervene in all cases to save a building or its contents. The much publicised case of Mentmore Towers (Bucks.) offered to the nation by Lord Rosebery in 1976 for the sum of £2 million was, it is believed, rejected by the government because of the continuing costs of maintenance.[42] And more recently, Heveningham Hall (Suffolk) has been listed for sale, a property acquired by the government in 1970 through the Land Fund.[43] In the mid-1970s there was much apprehension among those concerned with heritage preservation, particularly with the introduction of CTT, that another round of devastation akin to that of the post-war period would inevitably follow. Yet it appears that the government is becoming more conscious of heritage preservation. Certain historic buildings were given conditional exemption from CTT in the Finance Act 1975, which also introduced the principle of establishing maintenance funds.[44] Further legislation concerning maintenance funds was contained in section 84 of the Finance Act 1976, but early legislation was unattractive to private owners in that the settlement to set up a fund was irrevocable and would terminate at the end of a Perpetuity Period (80 years) at which time the property would devolve to a designated non-profit making body.[45] The Finance Act 1980 has gone a long way to extend the coverage of maintenance funds and to overcome previous drawbacks and can be seen as a genuine attempt to assist further the survival of historic country houses and other heritage property.[46]

It can be argued, as indeed it is by preservationists, that demolition in the present day is needless when a country house can be adapted to alternative uses, but for many houses long-term survival will depend in the first instance on finding new owners. This problem is not new, but was recognised in the early 1950s by the HBCs and led in 1954 to the formation of the Historic Buildings Bureau. Initially the Bureau was concerned only with buildings of outstanding interest, but since 1967 its mandate has included all listed buildings. It is not a government substitute for an estate agent, but has been set up to facilitate contact between interested parties through the quarterly publication of a list of buildings in need of new tenants or purchasers. It has been estimated that since its inauguration, at least 80 country houses in England have found new uses or users.[47]

It is appropriate to conclude on this positive note in a chapter that has dealt with destruction and loss. At present throughout the English countryside many country houses remain standing, but in whose ownership, in what use and with what potential for long-term preservation is the subject of the following chapter.

NOTES

1   Fifteen were completely rebuilt following accidental demolition by fire, while 17 were deliberately demolished to be replaced by a new house.

2   Includes all private families, new owners as well as original owners.

3   Information from Lt.-Col. Dymoke, Jan. 1979.

4   Burke's 'Landed Gentry', 18th edn (3 vols., Burke's Peerage, London, 1965), vol. 1, p. 23.

5   H. Colvin, 'A Biographical Dictionary of British Architects 1600-1840', 2nd edn (John Murray, London, 1978), p. 751.

6   Some of the background concerning the transfer of Sutton Scarsdale to the Ministry of Public Building and Works is described by J. Cornforth in Uncertain Future of Sutton Scarsdale, 'Country Life', 16 April (1970), pp. 850-1.

7   The Ministry of Public Building and Works was incorporated into the Department of the Environment in 1970.

8   The Grange is presently undergoing renovation.

9   'Guardian', 10 June 1979.

10 R. Strong, M. Binney, J. Harris, 'The Destruction of the Country House', (Thames and Hudson, London, 1974), p. 16.

11 'Country Life', 28 July (1928), p. 148.

12 'Country Life', 16 Dec. (1928), p. 886.

13 'Country Life', 22 Dec. (1928), p. 918.

14 Compensation Defence Act 1939, 2 & 3 Geo. 6, c. 75.

15 Requisitioned Land and War Works Act 1945, 8 & 9 Geo. 6, c. 43.

16 Historic Buildings Councils are statutory bodies set up by the Secretary of State for the Environment under the Historic Buildings and Ancient Monuments Act 1953, 1 & 2 Eliz. 2, c. 49, an Act that came into being following the recommendations of 'The Report of the Committee on Houses of Outstanding Historic or Architectural Interest', 1950, chaired by Sir E. Gower. Separate councils have been set up for England, Scotland and Wales.

17 J. Cornforth, 'Country Houses in Britain - can they survive?' (Country Life, London, 1974), p. 18.

18 Provision was also made under the Local Authorities (Historic Buildings) Act 1962, 10 & 11 Eliz. 2, c. 36, for local authorities to make grants available for any building considered of architectural or historic interest without it having to be either of outstanding status or listed. Funding from this source for country houses has been negligible.

19 Strong, Binney, Harris, 'The Destruction of the Country House', pp. 188-90.

20 HBCE, 'Annual Report 1978-79' (HMSO, London, 1980), p. 3.

21 Interest in medieval buildings extended back to the eighteenth-century Society of Antiquaries.

22   Observation made by J. Harris in 'The Destruction of the
      Country House', p. 16.
23   In most cases the data were clear cut, as when a house was
      demolished to be replaced with a new house, but problems
      arose over classification following damage by fire. Certain-
      ly some houses in this category were completely destroyed
      and replaced while for others part of the original structure
      remained. When a house was reinstated in its original form
      it was nevertheless classed as demolished since the house
      that came to occupy the site was not the one that existed
      c. 1880. The number of cases in which this applies is
      so few as to make little difference to the overall pattern
      of demolition.
24   N. Pevsner, 'The Buildings of England: Staffordshire'
      (Penguin, Harmondsworth, 1974), p. 133.
25   A Grinling Gibbons staircase from Cassiobury is on dis-
      play in the Metropolitan Museum of Art in New York.
26   Colvin, 'Biographical Dictionary', p. 558.
27   N. Pevsner and E. Hubbard, 'The Buildings of England:
      Cheshire' (Penguin, Harmondsworth, 1971), p. 208.
28   Only the clock tower, chapel and stables remain; ibid.
      p. 209.
29   N. Pevsner and John Harris, 'The Buildings of England:
      Lincolnshire', 2nd edn (Penguin, Harmondsworth, 1973),
      p. 200.
30   At least two country houses were demolished to be replaced
      with another type of building. Bishop Burton (East Riding)
      demolished in 1951 was replaced by a purpose-built college
      and Wilton Park (Bucks.) demolished in 1967 was replaced
      by a modern building used as the officers' mess of the
      Royal Army Educational Corps. Neither has been included
      in the replaced category which is defined as being houses
      only.
31   Town and Country Planning Act 1932, 22 & 23 Geo. 5,
      c. 48, sec. 17(1). Ancient monuments had received a
      degree of protection under Acts of 1882 and 1900 but to
      qualify a building had to be uninhabited.
32   Town and Country Planning Act 1944, 7 & 8 Geo. 6,
      c. 47, Pt. 1, sec. 42, 43.
33   Town and Country Planning Act 1947, 10 & 11 Geo. 6,
      c. 51, Pt. 111, section 29(1).
34   Historic Buildings and Ancient Monuments Act 1953, 1 & 2
      Eliz., c. 49, Pt. 1, section 4(1).
35   W. Kennet, 'Preservation' (Temple Smith, London, 1972),
      pp. 75-8, discusses the three major loopholes in the early
      legislation; the 'Silhill Gap', the 'Sick Typist Gap' and the
      Development Value Compensation Gap'.
36   Town and Country Planning Act 1968, Eliz. 2, c. 72,
      Pt. V, 40(4).
37   Additional planning control such that a building could not
      be altered or extended without local authority or

Ministerial consent was first introduced in the Town and Country Planning Act 1944.

38   Town and Country Planning Act 1971, Eliz. 2, c. 78, Pt. IV, section 58(1).

39   Town and Country Amenities Act 1974, Eliz. 2, c. 32, section 1(1), 277A.

40   Strong, Binney, Harris, 'The Destruction of the Country House', p. 9.

41   J. Butler, 'The Economics of Historic Country Houses' (Policy Studies Institute, London, 1981), pp. 47 and 51.

42   S. Andreae and M. Binney (eds) 'Save Mentmore for the Nation' (Save Britain's Heritage, London, 1977), p. 4.

43   Department of the Environment Historic Buildings Bureau, Quarterly List of Buildings which are for Sale or to be Let, Summer 1980, pp. 77-9.

44   Finance Act 1975, Eliz. 2, c. 7, Pt. 111, section 34 and Pt. 11, schedule 6.

45   Finance Act 1976, Eliz. 2, c. 40, Pt. IV, section 84. Designated bodies are listed in schedule 6 of the Finance Act 1975.

46   Finance Act 1980, Eliz. 2, c. 48, Pt. IV, section 88.

47   Cornforth, 'Country Houses', pp. 39-40.

The great houses remain but only half are inhabited,
Dusty the gunrooms and the stable clocks stationary.
Some have been turned into pre-schools...,
Others into club-houses for the golf...
W.H. Auden and C. Isherwood, *The Dog Beneath the Skin*
(Faber and Faber, London, 1935).

This chapter seeks to clarify the current situation pertaining
to country houses that remain as integral components of landed
estates and as independent physical structures. The principal
questions analysed concern their ownership and their use:
knowledge that is essential for any policy formulation regarding
the long-term future of country houses.

COUNTRY-HOUSE OWNERSHIP c. 1980

Of the 500 sample houses that existed c. 1880, 394 (78 per cent)
are still standing, in part or in whole, but only 381 (76 per
cent) are occupied or presently capable of being occupied. At
least 210 are in private hands (Figure 9.1) including two houses
owned jointly by a number of families, while 169 are in public or
institutional ownership of which 32 are held by the National
Trust[1] (Figure 9.2).
    While it has been shown that as many as 259 (52 per cent)
original families still hold some of the principal estate land, many
have chosen not to retain the heartland. Only 190 (38 per cent)
in fact continue to own the heartland and within this number,
20 own the site previously occupied by the country house, 16
have rebuilt or replaced the house, and a further four own
houses in a ruinous or highly dilapidated state. Thus, realistic-
ally only 150 (30 per cent) continue to hold the original country
house (Table 9.1). As with estate land a higher proportion have
been retained by the great-landowner group, 41 per cent of
whom still own the original family house compared with only 26
per cent of those classed as greater gentry. It is evident that
the sale and break-up of estates has had even greater impact
on country houses than on the ownership of estate land. For
the majority of private estate owners their landed interest
apparently has priority over the country house such that even
though a substantial number have attempted and continue to
hang on to the house, some selling land to do so, few in the

Figure 9.1: The Sample Estate Country Houses in Private
Ownership c. 1980

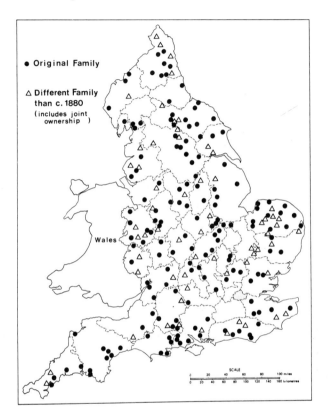

Source: Questionnaire Survey.

long run are prepared to maintain the house over and above
the land. Revenue from the estate can help to support a country
house but not vice versa. In the nineteenth century it was
thought that over 10,000 acres was needed to maintain a large
country house.[2] In the present day substantial capital is still
required and its availability, whether from land or alternative
sources, is a critical determinant of the future of the country
house. Faced with a choice, when a country house becomes a
financial liability, or simply too large to maintain, many owners,
as evident from the previous chapter, have resorted to demolition rather than burden their landed interest. Others have
opted for sale or transfer to another owner.

For the total sample over 300 country houses, 52 of which were
subsequently demolished, have changed hands over the past

Figure 9.2: The Sample Estate Country Houses in Public, Semi-public and Institutional Ownership c. 1980

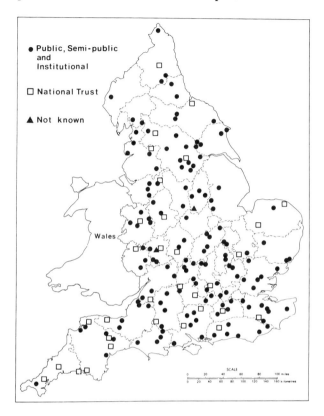

Source: Questionnaire Survey.

hundred years. It would appear from Tables 7.4 and 7.5 that excluding sales to a different family, only relatively small areas of principal estate land were transferred with or have remained attached to, the country house. In fact, excluding demolished, rebuilt and ruinous houses, only 30 original country houses, of which half are held by a different family, are part of estates greater than 3,000 acres, while this number is increased to 58 if 1,000 acres is taken as the acreage minimum. One hundred and sixty-one country houses, of which the vast majority are owned by public or institutional bodies including the National Trust, comprise part of estates of less than 1,000 acres, the average land area being just under 200 acres. Transfer of owner-ship to public bodies or institutions has occurred in all parts of the country (Figure 9.2). More detailed examination of location

Table 9.1:   Original Family Ownership of the Country House,
Former House Sites, Replaced and Ruinous Houses, in Relation
to the Principal Estate Land Owned c. 1980

	Estate Area c. 1980					
	≥10,000 acres No.	3,000- 9,999 acres No.	1,000- 2,999 acres No.	1- 999 acres No.	Not Known No.	Total No.
Country house						
Great landowners[a]	19	26	6	–	–	51
Greater gentry[b]	–	46	37	13	3	99
Total	19	72	43	13	3	150
Sites, ruins and replacements						
Great landowners	6	3	1	–	–	10
Greater gentry	–	13	15	2	–	30
Total	6	16	16	2	–	40
Total	25	88	59	15	3	190

Notes: a. ≥10,000 acres in c. 1880. b. 3,000-9,999 acres in
c. 1880.
Source: Questionnaire Survey.

reveals that the majority of country houses no longer in private
hands are in close proximity to or have been enveloped within
urban centres, whether large city agglomerations or county
towns, or lie in the more heavily industrialised zones. For
instance, in an area bounded by Leeds, Sheffield and York, predominantly within the coalfield belt of the former West Riding,
no less than eleven of the 15 country houses still standing have
been transferred from private ownership. Most notable changes
are in the counties of central and south eastern England, especially in the vicinity of London where few houses are now retained
in private ownership. Generally in the North and East regions,
excepting the Newcastle conurbation, fewer country houses have
been transferred out of private hands, possibly a reflection of
the comparative lack of urban centres from which the demand for
alternative uses can be generated. Such is well evidenced by
Norfolk where changes in ownership have tended to be within
the private sector (Figure 9.1), the remaining country houses
in the vast majority of cases still lying at the heart of an agricultural estate.
     By no means all transfers to public or institutional ownership,
however, have been conditional upon proximity to a built-up
area. Outstanding country houses preserved by the National
Trust, for example, are found adjacent to urban centres and in
the heart of rural areas. Certain adaptive uses such as religious
retreats and public schools have tended to favour rural settings.

For example, in Dorset and Wiltshire, predominantly rural counties, transfers to institutional ownership have tended to be associated with adaptation for public-school use and apart from this the majority of country houses are still in private hands.

THE CHRONOLOGY OF OWNERSHIP TRANSFER

Two graphs of recorded dates of legal transfer of country houses other than by inheritance after 1880 have been plotted, to show the first date of transfer from the original family to another family, and the first date of transfer from private to public or institutional ownership[3] (Figure 9.3). Transfer to the latter has not always been directly from the original family. Many houses initially sold to a different family were later resold by them to public or institutional buyers. Once out of private hands it has been very infrequently, with the exception of the war years, that a country house has been later reinstated as a single-family private home.

Figure 9.3: Country-house Changes of Ownership on the Sample Estates c. 1880 to c. 1980

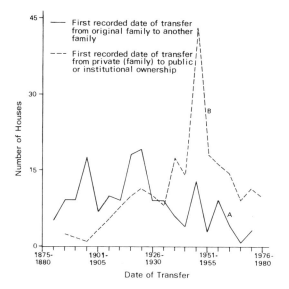

Source: Questionnaire Survey.

A number of distinct peaks are evident on both graphs. Sales before 1914 were predominantly between private families. In the late Victorian era the demand for country residences, particularly

by wealthy urbanites was evident both in house leasing and
sales. A peak of sales activity occurred around the turn of the
century but declined somewhat prior to World War I possibly,
it can be speculated, a reflection of uncertainty over the future
of private ownership given the political climate of the decade.
From 1916 to 1925 there was a perceptible rise in house sales,
still predominantly to other private families, but for the first
time public or institutional acquisitions were notable. The pattern
coincides with the increased volume of estate land entering the
market (see p. 110), but not all country-house sales necessarily
meant either the complete break-up or the sale of an entire
estate property. In many cases, then as now, only the house and
grounds were disposed of.

In the inter-war years the major recipients of sales reversed,
with private transfers falling consistently until after World
War II and sales to public and institutional bodies rising noticeably in the 1930s. The last apparent peak of private purchases
occurred in the years immediately following the war, when an
increased number of country houses were put on the market,
but the volume of sales to public bodies over-shadowed all previous transfer activity and reached an unprecedented height in
the five years from 1945 to 1950. Local authorities in particular
were purchasing large country houses for schools and other
institutional uses at a time when restrictions imposed by the
government of the day made it difficult to construct new buildings for such purposes.[4] Since the peak of the late 1940s there
has been an overall decline in initial transfers to both private
and public ownership although sales to the latter have been consistently higher in number. The small flurry of activity in the
five years from 1956 to 1960 in sales to private buyers may well
reflect a willingness to undertake the responsibilities of country-
house ownership following the creation of the HBCE and the
provision of grants to assist in the repair and maintenance of
listed buildings.

Costs have risen so fast since the 1960s, however, that few
individuals are now prepared to invest in the purchase and
maintenance of a large country house as a home. There are, as
always, exceptions. Sheffield Park (Sussex) was purchased by
Mr and Mrs P.J. Radford in 1972 and considerable renovation has
been undertaken. The house, however, is not only the Radford's
home, but is also the location of the family business as well as
being open to the public for part of the year. Hampton Court
(Hereford.) was purchased in a dilapidated state in the early
1970s by Mr Hughes, owner of the Hughes International coach
building firm, and has undergone extensive restoration and
repair to become a family home and location for business entertainment.

A number of country houses have been sold many times. The
recorded rate of all transfers increased from an average of two
per annum from 1880 to 1910, to five from 1911 to 1940, to over
eight per annum from 1941 to 1960. The rate has declined since

1961 to a litte under five per annum in the 1960s and 1970s.
While it is possible that the resale data were incomplete for some
country houses, it is nevertheless clear that the general level
of transfer activity reached a peak in the 1940s and 1950s. It has
remained fairly high and fallen only gradually throughout the
1960s and 1970s. The vast majority of sales and resales, or other
forms of transfer, have been to public and institutional bodies
whether from private owners or amongst institutions.

THE COUNTRY HOUSE AS A RESIDENCE c. 1980

Whatever motives of prestige and status underlay each landowner's decision to erect or rebuild a country house, they were
built to be residences. Only 41 per cent of country houses in
the sample continue to serve the purpose for which they were
originally constructed[5] (Table 9.2), but only half of these are
strictly the private residences of single families.[6] Others have
been adapted to serve a multiple-residence function, that is,
either a section of the house has been sub-divided into rental
accommodation, of which at least 25 cases were recorded[7], or
the entire house, sometimes including the outbuildings such as
former stables, has been converted into flats or a number of
separate houses, of which fifteen cases were noted.

Over one-third of the total are also open to the public, hence
outside the 'strictly private' category, even though in the
majority of cases public access is seasonal. Included in the latter
group are 13 houses in the care of the National Trust for which
it has become practice to make an agreement with the former
owner, or a tenant, to live in at least part of the house.[8]

Greater continuity of residential use tends to be found in the
more prosperous agricultural areas, parts of the arable Eastern
region, notably in the county of Norfolk, in the mixed farming
area of the Midlands and in the countryside of Dorset, Hampshire
and Wiltshire (Figure 9.4). Houses in residential use in the
South East are, for the most part, outside the immediate environs
of Greater London.

The age of a country house appears to hold less significance
than its size as a determinant of residential continuity. Relatively
few large houses, especially of the Victorian era, remain exclusively as private homes.

Nearly 90 per cent of the country houses still occupied as
residences, whether in part or in whole, whether in single or
multiple occupancy, are in private hands, and well over half are
retained in the ownership of the original family.

In the past it was not uncommon for an entire country house
to be leased as a residence (see p. 136), but in the present day
this practice has all but ceased as there are few tenants to hand
who are willing or able to assume the responsibilities of staffing
and maintaining a large country house. Residential leasing nowadays is an entirely different phenomenon and tends to be for

Table 9.2: Major Present-day Uses of Country Houses

| | Owner of Country House 1980 | | | | | |
	Original family	Different family	Public body institution	National Trust	Other	Total
Pre-1880 houses	150	58	137	32	4	381
Replaced houses[a]	16	9	7	–	–	32
Total	166	67	144	32	4	413[b]
Major uses[c]						
1. Residential						
Pre-1880 houses	129	54	6	13[d]	3	206
Replaced houses	14	9	1	–	–	24
Total	143	67	7	13	3	230
2. Recreation and tourism	51[e]	12	29[e]	29	–	121
3. Education	9[e]	2	80[f]	3	–	94
4. Business	2	2	8	–	–	12
5. Health	3	–	6	–	–	9
6. Religious	–	–	6	–	–	6
7. Other	3	2	4	–	1	10

Notes:
1. Private residential use only; excludes college dormitories etc.
2. Includes museums, art galleries, libraries, record offices, hotels and social clubs, as well as houses open to the public on a regular basis.
3. All schools including special schools and borstals, colleges, universities, conference and field-study centres.
4. Excludes estates offices; includes company headquarters, research establishments and offices.
5. Hospitals, clinics and convalescent homes.
6. Seminaries, convents and retreats.
7. Unoccupied at time of survey, no data.

a. Country houses replaced by a new house, 1880 to 1980.
b. Excludes 13 ruinous or dilapidated at time of survey, and 74 demolished. c. Column totals do not equal the total number of country houses as many have more than one major function, most notably combining residential and tourism uses. d. Excludes use for staff flats. e. Includes one 'replaced house'. f. Includes four 'replaced houses'.

Source: Questionnaire Survey.

multiple occupancy. Sections of houses have been modified by private owners, while entire buildings have been converted by private owners, property companies and housing associations. One of the foremost in the field has been the Mutual Households Association, a non-profit-making body that was established in 1955 with two principal aims: to preserve houses and to convert them into apartments for retired or semi-retired people. Today, the Association owns or leases around 20 houses in England, the majority of which are of historic or architectural note. Two were in the sample; Aynhoe Park (Northants.) purchased c. 1960 when the remainder of the former Cartwright Estate was broken up, and Danny, a house on lease to the Association by the Campion family who continue to own around 2,000 acres of the Danny Estate in Sussex. Both houses are listed Grade I.

Figure 9.4: Country Houses still in Residential Use: Single and Multiple Occupancy

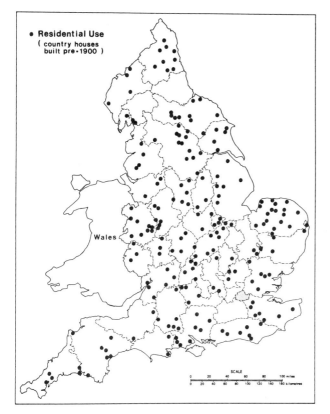

Source: Questionnaire Survey.

Other houses converted into flats are co-operatively owned or co-owned by families who occupy them. A case in point is Hunstanton Hall (Norfolk) sold from the le Strange estate in 1949 and now divided into three self-contained units each separately owned. The le Strange family, who have been associated with the Hunstanton area since Saxon times, continue to own much of the

estate although the acreage has been considerably reduced as
a result of sales to meet death-duty liabilities.

Though listed by Bateman in 1883 as the family seat of Lord
Petre,[9] Thorndon Hall (Essex) was gutted by fire as early as
1878 and was never reoccupied by the family. Ingatestone Hall,
also in Essex, eventually became the principal estate residence.
Thorndon Hall was sold in the mid-1930s but only within recent
years has it been rebuilt and converted for use as flats.

At the time of the survey, Dingley Hall (Northants.), Stopham
House (Sussex) and, for a second attempt, Butleigh Court
(Somerset) were in varying stages of conversion, while plans
had been proposed for Bourne Park (Kent) and part of Downes
(Devon) was to be sold for possible conversion. Dingley Hall is
a Grade I listed building, a house essentially of Elizabethan and
late seventeenth-century origin.[10] It has had a succession of
owners since its sale in 1883 from the Holdich-Hungerford family
to Viscount Downe. In recent years it was derelict, having been
stripped of its contents and gutted. The Victorian extensions
were demolished in 1972. From the late 1970s it has been undergoing conversion into 14 self-contained houses (later reduced
to ten), in a design that retains the historic fabric of the building.[11]

Conversion for multiple occupancy has been for the most part
a post-World War II phenomenon and appears to offer a viable
option for the future use of many country houses, especially
those located adjacent to large urban centres or within reasonable commuting distance; conversion after all is of little value
without a market. At one point in the 1950s Crofton Hall (Cumberland) was to be turned into flats, but no one expressed
interest to live there, it being too remote, and the hall was
subsequently demolished.

Over recent years enterprising schemes have emerged from
the drawing board. The Historic Buildings Housing Association,
for example, has an ambitious plan for the conversion of Toddington Manor (Glos.) involving the house and outbuildings.[12]
However, a number of such schemes have been thwarted by
changes in government policy, notably the curtailment of both
Housing Corporation funding and local authority loans for co-
ownership housing associations.[13] Whether already in existence,
like the Mutual Households Association, or set up to save a
particular house, the failure of non-profit housing associations
to obtain loans and mortgages has led to the collapse of a number
of conversion schemes.[14] Yet conversion to multiple occupancy
offers one solution to the country-house problem. A recommenda-
tion of the Working Party that recently studied alternative uses
for historic buildings stated unequivocally that 'the best use in
most cases is the use for which the building was originally
designed and intended, or a use approximating closely to it'.[15]
In the case of country houses this implies residential use whether
in single or multiple occupancy. Even where a house previously
has been adapted for another purpose, or left derelict, the

Working Party recommended that there should be a presumption in favour of reversion to residential use.[16]

NON-RESIDENTIAL USES OF COUNTRY HOUSES c. 1980

Critical comments have been made from time to time concerning the adaptation of country houses to alternative uses, the severity of criticism often depending on the extent to which a house has been modified internally and externally and its surroundings physically altered and impaired. It cannot be disputed that when a country house ceases to be a home and the contents dispersed, much of its character and atmosphere is immediately lost; a loss which cannot be replaced by any alternative use for the building. Many adapted houses reveal little outward indication of their changed status and for listed buildings there is now a degree of planning control over the extent of permissible alterations. A number of houses, however, have proven of inadequate size for their new use despite the conversion of outbuildings, and have acquired modern appendages which sit uncomfortably in juxta-position to the house or encroach into a former planned land-scape; an often cited case being Stowe (Bucks.) where new buildings have been gradually added to the grounds near the house in its use as a school over the past 50 years.[17] Adaptation, nevertheless, is an alternative to dereliction and demolition and at a minimum can preserve the fabric of a building as evidence of the architecture of the past for the appreciation of present and future generations.

In addition to changes in ownership, not once but perhaps two or three times over the past century, many houses have also progressed through a variety of adapted uses before reaching their present status. By far the highest number of those adapted are now owned by public or institutional owners although a pro-portion are still in private ownership. But it would be true to say that only a few private owners, other than those who open their houses to the public or who use part as a business or estate office, retain the house for an enterprise that they operate themselves. Of note are the country house at Shrublands (Suf-folk) owned by the same family since the late eighteenth century and converted, in 1966, to a private health clinic run by the family as a separate company, and Place House (Cornwall) the heart of a 5,000-acre estate in 1880, now run as a private hotel by the Carlyon family who retain barely a tenth of their former landed property.

The majority of country houses still in private ownership that serve an adapted function are leased. For example, at Woodhall Park (Herts.) the converted stable block about a quarter of a mile from the house is now the family home while the house itself has been leased for use as a school. Part of Knowsley Hall (Lancs.)[18], on the Earl of Derby's estate, is leased to the Mersey-side Police as their Headquarter offices while part has been retained as the Estate Office; the family now living in a new mansion house in an adjacent location.

Whether owned privately, publicly or by an institution there are a number of new uses to which country houses appear to have most commonly lent themselves (Table 9.2). A number in the war years were invaluable as hospitals and convalescent homes and nine sample houses continue to fill such a role today. The seclusion and peacefulness of a country house situated within a park or in extensive grounds has also proven attractive to the needs of a number of religious organisations which have purchased country houses for use as retreats, study centres and bible schools. Nine houses are now used as company head-quarters, research institutes or offices. One such example is Cole Orton in Leicestershire acquired by the National Coal Board in 1947 and now the administrative headquarters for the South Midlands Area. The occupation of Cole Orton by the Coal Board seems pre-ordained both in its name and location. George Dance, who designed the house, built from 1804 to 1808, is reputed to have advised its owner Sir George Beaumont against building on 'rising ground before which coal pits and circumstances belong-ing to such works are principal objects'.[19]

Apart from functions related to recreation and tourism, the pre-dominant adaptive use of country houses has been in the field of education, especially formal education, and it is in this purpose that many large Victorian houses have found a new role. Few would remain in the landscape today but for the English education system and the demand for public schools.

In the total sample as many as 89 original houses, nearly 20 per cent, can be broadly classed in an educational category; 50 are schools, whether administered by a local authority or a pri-vate educational trust, including special schools for the blind, physically and mentally handicapped and borstal institutions; 29 are part of teacher training or technical colleges, colleges of art, agricultural colleges or universities, and a further ten are staff training, conference or field study centres (Figure 9.5). The majority are concentrated in the South East and parts of South West England which tends to reflect the predominant loca-tion of private preparatory schools in Southern England. In the sample group fewer country houses have been put to educa-tional use in the counties of eastern and central England except in the vicinity of certain urban centres such as York and Ipswich.

Among the earliest country houses to become public schools were Bedgebury (Kent), seat of the Beresford-Hope family, sold by them in 1899 and resold for use as a school in 1920; Stowe (Bucks.), seat of the Duke of Buckingham and Chandos which opened as a school in 1922/3, and Bryanston (Dorset), built in 1890 and sold for use as a school in 1931. The majority, however, were acquired after World War II at a time when the expan-sion of education facilities was hindered by government controls over the granting of building permits and licences, controls not lifted until the 1950s. As an outcome local authorities, private educational trusts and foundations were forced to seek existing buildings for conversion, and owners of large country houses found a ready market for their property.

Figure 9.5: Country Houses in Educational Use

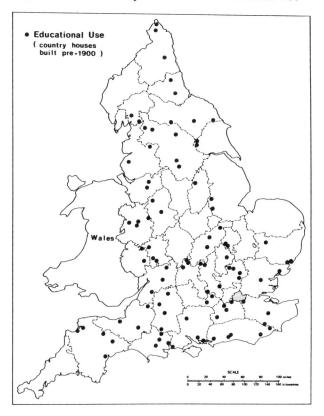

Source: Questionnaire Survey.

University use tended to come later. With the notable exception of Keele Hall (Staffs.) which became the University College of North Staffordshire in 1949,[20] five other country houses, now used as university buildings in one capacity or another were acquired after 1960; Close House (Northld.), Heslington (East Riding), Wivenhoe (Essex), Harlaxton Manor (Lincs.) and Wroxton Abbey (Oxford.), the latter two being overseas campuses of American universities. The four English universities are located within fairly close proximity to the heart of a large city or town and along with the house around 200 acres of estate land was also acquired.

The conversion of country houses for formal education purposes would not appear to have much future. Rather the trend has been that some presently used in this capacity have been threatened with closure, most evident in recent years with teacher training colleges which appear to have over-expanded in the post-war boom of the 1950s and 1960s. The outlook is now brighter for the use of country houses for more informal educational purposes, particularly in relation to their potential within the overall field of recreation and tourism.

THE COUNTRY HOUSE - RECREATION AND TOURISM

The use of country houses for purposes of recreation and tourism is of major and growing importance and a subject that warrants special attention. Country houses open to the public no doubt first spring to mind, but as well as this most obvious role houses have been modified to serve other uses associated with recreation and tourism. A number are now hotels; including Mottram Hall (Cheshire), Place House and Clowance (Cornwall), Coombe House (Devon), Dunkenhalgh (Lancs.), Brandon Lodge (Warwick.), and Broome Park (Kent), a Grade I building that has been adapted for holiday accommodation on a 'time-sharing' basis.[21] Others are golf club-houses and social clubs including in the former case, Thrybergh Park House and part of St. Ives in the West Riding, part of Allestree Hall (Derby.) and Decker Hill (Salop) serving the urban centres of Rotherham, Bingley, Derby and Shifnel, while Close House (Northld.) and Chicksands Priory (Beds.) have found new use as private social clubs respectively owned by the University of Newcastle-Upon-Tyne and the Ministry of Defence (Figure 9.6). Though Swakeleys (Middlesex) was described in 1978 as a private social club owned by the London Postal Region, little use is presently made of the building which is in a rather poor state of repair.[22]

Since it was acquired by the Durham County Council in 1970, Beamish Hall has served in part as an information, exhibition and refreshment centre operated in conjunction with the Open Air Museum located in the adjacent park.[23] With the setting up of Country Parks, following the Countryside Act of 1968, other houses have been given a similar role, Elvaston Castle (Derby.) being a notable early example. Assuredly, there is considerable scope for the future of country houses as administrative offices, information centres, countryside museums and field-study centres in association with Country Parks and other designated protected areas. As a resource for the provision of informal educational opportunities in the countryside the role of the country house is as yet in its infancy.

Also in the formative stage is the use of the country house, and indeed the estate as a whole, for purposes of heritage education. As an outcome of Heritage Education Year in 1977,

Figure 9.6:   Country Houses Open to the Public for Tourism
and Recreation

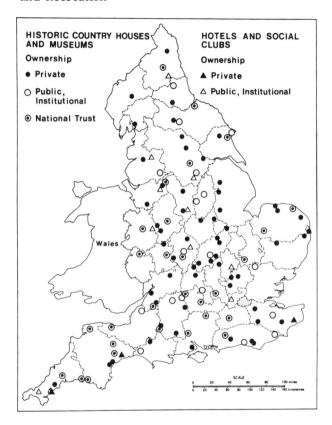

Source: Questionnaire Survey. *Historic Houses, Castles and
Gardens* (ABC Historic Publications, 1979).

organised jointly by the Historic Houses Association, the National
Trust, the Department of the Environment and teachers groups
such as the National Association for Environmental Education,
the Sanford Group was set up to help support and advise
country-house owners, managers and teachers on the development of educational services based on historic properties.[24] In
1980 about 25 country houses in England were listed as offering
educational services of which Beaulieu Abbey (Hants), Belton
House (Lincs.), Doddington Hall (Lincs.) and Harewood House
(West Riding) were amongst the properties in the sample that
received awards for making an outstanding contribution to
heritage education in 1979.[25]

Country-house Tourism: Past and Present
The opening of country houses to the public is by no means a
recent idea but has been the practice of landed society since
before the eighteenth century. Blenheim Palace (Oxford.)
attracted visitors from its inception, and in 1712 the Duke of
Marlborough gave instructions that, 'all persons may see ye
whole Buildings to their Satisfaction'.[26]
  Eighteenth-century upper-class society was noted for an avid
interest in architecture and the visual arts. It was a fashionable
pastime of the period to make tours of country houses and gardens to review the latest architectural and landscape designs.
Improved roads broadened the possibilities of travel and it is
evident from the number of guide books, brochures and pamph-
lets describing various houses, internally and externally, as
well as their parks and gardens, that the popularity of visiting
was at a height towards the end of the century.
  The journals kept by Celia Fiennes of her journeys to different
parts of England in the late seventeenth and early eighteenth
century and the diaries of John Byng (5th Viscount Torrington)
recording his annual forays into the English countryside, provide revealing commentaries on the contemporary country house
scene as well as being invaluable documents on the social and
economic history of the period.[27] Such country-house visitors
as Byng would be accorded the privilege of a conducted tour,
usually by the housekeeper, but the reception varied from place
to place. Of his visit to Raby Castle (Durham) in June 1792
Byng wrote, 'I was obliged to send in my name to Lady D.; and
ask permission of entrance. I am told that many are refused!
Why not a fix'd day, or fix'd hours?'[28] Indeed, the popularity
of some of the larger houses in the eighteenth century led their
owners to set aside specific days of the week as open days for
the public. Woburn Abbey (Beds.) was open on Mondays, while
Holkham Hall (Norfolk) could 'be seen any day of the week,
except Sunday, by noblemen and foreigners, but on Tuesday
only by other people'.[29] The comparative sparsity of documented
evidence in Victorian times seems to imply that the popularity
of casual visiting had declined despite the advent of railway
travel. Country houses, nevertheless, continued to be accessible
to the public. White's Directory of Lincolnshire 1856, notes for
Brocklesby that 'The Hall is about 2 miles from the station, and
it and the Park are open to visitors on Thursdays'.[30] In the
early 1890s a charge was levied to visit Penshurst Place (Kent),
perhaps one of the first instances of an established price for
viewing a country house.[31]
  The phenomenon of public viewing, therefore, is not new.
What is different in the twentieth century has been the growth
of country-house tourism as a recognised estate enterprise.
Casual visitors of the eighteenth and nineteenth centuries, who
voluntarily provided gratuities to the house staff, have been
replaced by the fee-paying public whether as individuals, families or organised tour groups, and planned excursions guided

or directed through the house are now the order of the day. Development began shortly after World War II, especially following the end of petrol rationing. The 6th Marquis of Bath opened the doors of Longleat to the public in April 1949, England's first privately owned stately home to venture into commercial tourism. Over 135,000 visitors were recorded in the first year.[32] Other house owners soon followed suit. In 1955 Woburn Abbey attracted 181,000 in its first year of opening.[33] Relatively few have embraced tourism to the extent of Longleat and Woburn or others in the so-called 'magnificent seven'; Beaulieu, Blenheim, Castle Howard, Harewood House and Warwick Castle, but by 1980 the total number of English country houses regularly open to the public exceeded 800.[34] The vast majority are open for a limited season during the six months from April to September, but a small number are open all year round.

Twenty per cent of sample houses are regularly open to the public (Figure 9.6), while a few others are advertised as being open by appointment only. Concentration appears heaviest in central and southern England, due in part no doubt to the market potential in and around the popular tourist circuit of London, Oxford, Stratford-Upon-Avon and Cambridge. However, houses open to the public are found in all regions and access appears to be associated as much with the Grade of building as location. Examination of the Grade listings for country houses with public access reveals that over 76 per cent are Grade I and a further 7 per cent Grade II*.[35] It is to be expected that houses open to the public would be, for the most part, in the higher-Grade listings since those of outstanding historic and architectural merit, Grades I and II*, more readily qualify for HBCE grants, grants that are tied to a public-access proviso. Undoubtedly such houses would also have greater appeal in the competitive tourist market compared with those of lower graded status.

The tourist industry is currently one of Britain's largest earners of foreign exchange and country houses certainly play an important role as an integral part of the 'heritage package' that attracts overseas visitors. Regional Tourist Board figures indicate that the number of overseas visits to country houses was appreciably higher than from the British public in the mid-1970s, and research undertaken by the BTA has shown that a high proportion of foreign tourists list visits to 'historic properties' as among the most enjoyable things they have done.[36]

The number of tourists, both overseas and British residents, visiting historic properties increased from 4 million in 1965 to nearly 28 million in 1970 and over 55 million by 1978, although figures for 1979 recorded a 5 per cent drop from the previous year with a total of 53 million. These figures released by the BTA, however, include ancient monuments, parks and gardens, as well as country houses. The recorded figures for visitors to country houses in England in 1979 amounted to around 10.5 million, less than one-fifth of the overall total.[37] Furthermore, the distribution of visitor numbers is markedly uneven such that a relatively small group of houses, in private and public ownership, accounted for a disproportionately high share; 20 country houses received over 4.5 million visitors. The popular conception of country-house tourism is generally associated with the large stately homes, most of which annually receive over 100,000 visitors, but for the majority of owners, open for a summer season, the tourist business does not attract such high numbers and the vast majority receive fewer than 50,000 visitors.

Private Ownership. It is widely agreed that private ownership with public access has provided the most satisfactory combination for tourism. Over 50 per cent of country houses open to the public are in private hands, of which, in the sample group, over 90 per cent are still occupied as homes. Even though the 'lived-in' sense may be more of an illusion than a reality, as many families now occupy only a fraction of the entire house, knowledge that a house is still a home and not fossilised as a museum, has particular appeal to the tourist public.

From all accounts there appears to be little financial benefit for the majority of private owners who open their homes. Using visitor numbers to give a broad indication of potential gross revenue, in seven cases sample houses open to the public exceed 100,000, but 31 for which data were available had less than 50,000 and around 20 per cent recorded less than 10,000. Assuming the sum of £1.00 per head generated from entry fees, refreshments, guidebooks and postcards, etc., the majority of houses in private ownership would receive a gross revenue below £50,000, many less than £10,000; in the majority of cases rarely sufficient to support the day-to-day costs of maintaining the country house. Income raised from such sources has to be balanced against the added capital costs incurred with public access, including extra security and insurance, staffing and maintenance as well as the essential paraphernalia of house opening; notices, ropes and druggets to help ensure that visitors tread a desired pathway through the premises and see only what is meant to be seen. In addition, all owners, private and public including the National Trust, are liable for Value Added Tax (VAT) on costs of repairs and maintenance; a tax which was raised from 8 to 15 per cent in 1979.

In the HBCE *Annual Report 1969-70* it was stated that 'it is our impression that entry fees cannot cover the costs of opening them [country houses] to the public, except possibly in the case of a few buildings of exceptional popularity'.[38] Those of 'exceptional popularity' must assuredly include Longleat; however, even in this case, the net revenue after tax set against the cost of daily upkeep and the necessary repairs to the house left an annual overdraft of £20,000 in 1975 and £86,000 in 1978.[39] Recent research on the economics of running a country house indicates that the average annual costs, excluding major repairs, was £40,000 for houses in private ownership regularly open to the public, £31,300 for houses owned by the National Trust and £62,000 for those in public ownership.[40]

For those private owners who qualify under Case 1 of Schedule D for tax purposes, that is, if the country house is run as a business with the intent of making a profit, deductions are allowed for capital expenditures on upkeep and certain losses can be offset, but for owners classed under Case VI of Schedule D deductions are only permitted from pre-tax income for expenses incurred in opening to the public and no relief is given for any loss. Why, one may well ask, do so many, therefore, open their doors? It is apparent at one end of the spectrum that there are owners who enjoy opening their homes to the public and who, over the years, have expanded the estate facilities to embrace a high degree of commercialism. At the other extreme are those who, if given the choice, would possibly opt for privacy but who open their doors because they have received HBCE grants for essential repairs and because the CTT exemptions for country houses of outstanding architectural or historic value, house contents and amenity land, are conditional upon reasonable public access.[41]

Concern over the future of country houses held in private ownership increased notably in the 1970s as repair and maintenance costs continued to escalate and as taxation pressure mounted. In 1973 the Historic Houses Association was formed. Its stated aims and objectives include heritage preservation for the benefit of future generations, but its clear intent is to address specific issues relating to the interests of its membership, for the most part country-house owners.

National Trust Ownership. The National Trust was founded in 1895 to, 'act as a Corporation for the holding of lands of natural beauty and sites and houses of historic interest to be preserved intact for the nation's use and enjoyment'.[42] Under the status of a registered charity the Trust has grown to become the largest conservation society in Britain. It presently owns over 100 country houses.[43] From the outset its mandate included the preservation of houses, but the principal focus until the late 1930s was directed towards the landscape. Barrington Court (Somerset), acquired in 1907, was the only large building owned by the Trust prior to 1914, and few country houses came under its care before World War II. In 1934 in an address to the annual meeting of the National Trust, Lord Lothian drew attention to the need to look to the future of country houses and, due largely to his initiative, the 'Country House Scheme' was launched in 1937. The Scheme enables an owner, 'to endow and transfer to the Trust an historic country house with the contents...while permitting him and his assigns to remain in occupation, subject to public access on specified days'.[44] It followed closely on the heels of the National Trust Act 1937, that contained a clause permitting the Trust to acquire and retain land, buildings, and hereditaments as investments so as to provide from rents and other income for the maintenance and preservation of Trust property.[45] The timing of the Act and the inauguration of the 'Country House Scheme' enabled the Trust to acquire and preserve a number of country houses during the general onslaught of abandonment and demolition that began after the war.

The 1931 Finance Act[46] exempted from death duties land transferred to the National Trust and a series of Finance Acts up to 1951[47] extended exemptions to include land, buildings and securities given as an endowment and to the contents of a building gifted to the Trust. Bequest of property became an increasingly popular tax incentive for private owners, more so as the general costs of upkeep and maintenance increased. More recently in the Finance Act 1972 gifts and bequests to the Trust were exempted from capital gains tax, death duties and aggregation, implying that the Trust can obtain the full value of such acquisitions.[48]

The National Land Fund, established in 1946, was also used to facilitate the transfer of country houses to the National Trust. Under provisions of the Historic Buildings and Ancient Monuments Act 1953 property and chattels accepted by the Treasury in lieu of death-duty could be transferred to the Trust and the Inland Revenue reimbursed through the Land Fund.[49] From the mid-1950s fewer houses and contents were gifted during an owner's lifetime and an increasing number came into the care of the Trust to satisfy a tax obligation.[50]

In the early days of acquisition, country houses of less than first-class standard were accepted,[51] but in recent decades a number have been turned down. In some cases the house was not considered to be an outstanding example of its type. In others there was an insufficient endowment offered with the property to provide for its upkeep, another requirement of the transfer process under the 'Country House Scheme' and one that, since 1977, has become a critical condition for acceptance by the Trust.[52]

Cost of maintenance and repair are high whether a house is held by the National Trust, in private, or in public ownership (see pp. 168-70). Without government support much of the work undertaken by the Trust would not have been possible. As much as any other owner, for example, the Trust qualifies for HBCE grants and has greatly benefited by them, especially regarding houses taken over at the request of the Treasury for which, at present, no endowment is given. In such cases all repairs, costs and maintenance deficits are paid by the HBCE.

Under the National Trust Act 1937 local authorities were empowered to give land and buildings to the Trust or to contribute to the acquisition and maintenance of Trust property.[53] A close relationship has evolved and in some cases a building owned by the Trust is maintained and operated by the local authority. Since it was given to the Trust in 1947 by Lord Newport, Lyme Hall (Cheshire) has been leased to the Stockport Metropolitan Borough Council; Shugborough, acquired in 1966,

is administered by the Staffordshire County Council, and part
of Attingham was leased by the Shropshire County Council for
use as a college of adult education.

State, Local Authority and Other Ownership. It is in government
hands to determine the long-term future not only of houses open
to the public but of all that are to be preserved. Yet, despite
legislation to list important buildings, to protect them by statutory power and to provide grants towards restoration and maintenance, there is a reluctance on the part of the government to
take over the ownership and management of country houses.
Audley End (Essex) is the only large country house in the sample that is owned by the State. It can be put forward that unwillingness stems from legislation in the Ancient Monuments Act
1913 which effectively bars the Ministry responsible, (at present
the Department of the Environment) from becoming the guardian
of any 'structure that appears...to be occupied as a dwelling-
house (otherwise than by a person employed as the caretaker
thereof or his family)'.[54] The Department of the Environment is
responsible for scores of monuments, ruins and empty castles,
but fully preserved country houses, transferred out of private
ownership, have been given to the care of other agencies,
whether the National Trust, other charitable foundations, or
local authorities. Certainly, the government has through the
Land Fund (replaced in 1980 by the National Heritage Memorial
Fund, see p. 173) assisted in the preservation and ownership
transfer of property and not exclusively in lieu of taxation. A
further provision of the Historic Buildings and Ancient Monuments Act enabled the Fund to be used to assist in the purchase
of property by the Ministry of Works and to cover costs of
repair and management while the building was in its care. Thus,
for example, Dyrham Park (Glos.) was purchased by the Ministry
in 1957, repaired and eventually transferred to the National
Trust for over £100,000, and in 1958 Rushton Hall (Northants.)
was acquired and repaired for a sum of over £90,000 and subsequently given to the Royal National Institute for the Blind.

Local authorities have assumed responsibility for a number of
country houses that are open to the public. More especially urban
authorities have realised the multiple-amenity potential of country
houses and have purchased them for such uses as museums,
libraries, art galleries and record offices; the cultural facilities
often being complementary to the house itself. Within the sample
of particular note are Lyme Park (Stockport) and Heaton Hall
(Manchester), both Grade I listed buildings, while of less outstanding architectural merit but performing similar roles are
Ashton Court (Bristol), Sewerby Hall (Bridlington), Bedale
Hall, Lydiard Park (Swindon) and Preston Place (Brighton).

Heaton Hall, purchased by the city of Manchester in 1902, was
one of the first large country houses to be acquired by a local
authority. Most acquisitions have been within the last forty
years or so, and a number have taken advantage of funding

available through the HBCE to help with the cost of repairs. Lydiard Park, for example, was purchased by the Swindon Town Council[55] in 1944 and around £67,000 has been spent on repairs to date of which approximately a third has been provided by the HBCE. The state rooms at Lydiard are used as a museum, and an extension to the Victorian servants' wing built in 1974 is used as a conference centre which is operated as a joint enterprise between a management training company and the Thamesdown Borough Council.

Other country houses open to the public are neither in private family ownership, in the hands of the National Trust nor any government agency but are owned by private charitable trusts and foundations and corporate business enterprises. Leeds Castle (Kent), for example, was bequeathed to the nation in perpetuity following the death of the owner Lady Baillie in 1974. The Castle is administered by the Leeds Castle Foundation, a charitable company registered by the Charity Commissioners and as such qualifies for exemption from capital taxation.

In 1978 Lord Brooke, son and heir of the seventh Earl of Warwick, sold Warwick Castle, its remaining contents and 100 acres of surrounding parkland to Madame Tussauds, part of the S. Pearson group, for £1½ million;[56] possibly heralding the future when other private owners, seeking to avoid the pressures of taxation, divest themselves of their ancestral home and pass the guardianship of England's heritage into the hands of commercial enterprise.

COUNTRY-HOUSE PRESERVATION AND THE FUTURE

Since 1953 grants allocated by the HBCE for the renovation and repair of buildings of historical and architectural significance have been instrumental in the preservation of many country houses, and the operation of the grant system in conjunction with provisions in the Town and Country Planning Act 1968 has without doubt led to a decline in the number of listed buildings demolished.

The annual allocation of grants has increased from a minimum of 87 individual grants in 1954 amounting to £268,054, to 2,524 recommended grants in 1978-9 from an allocation of nearly £9 million.[57] Approximately a third of the total have been to country-house owners; private, National Trust and public.[58] Attaching the availability of funding to a clause of reasonable public access appears politically and morally sound especially when public money is spent to help renovate a privately owned building, but some private owners wish to remain so and are reluctant to apply for support from the HBCE because of the inherent access obligations. In consequence, the physical condition of a number of houses may be in jeopardy. In the long-term interests of future generations it would be as well if preservation could, in all cases, take priority over access. Such a priority is, in

fact, upheld by the National Trust and was well summed up by
John Bailey, Chairman of the Executive Committee in the 1920s,
who said 'Preservation may always permit of access, while without preservation access becomes forever impossible'.[59]

Still other private owners who may be willing to open their
homes to the public, have not sought HBCE support, or have
turned down the offer of a grant as they have been unable to
raise sufficient capital to pay for their share of the repair costs.
Safeguards for the physical upkeep of country houses were
incorporated in the Town and Country Planning Act 1971 which
provided local authorities with the right to serve repair notices
on the owner of a listed building considered to be in disrepair.[60]
Generally, however, authorities have proven reluctant to enforce
this legislation in the fear that an owner in turn may request
the authority to purchase the property. Without additional
government support for purchase through the Land Fund or the
HBCE to cover maintenance costs, few local authorities in the
past were in a position to afford to take over and maintain a
large country house. Under the provisions of the National Heritage Memorial Fund, which replaced the Land Fund in 1980, local
authorities and non-profit making bodies and institutions,
privately or publicly owned, can apply for assistance to purchase
property of importance to the national heritage.[61] Though in
most cases the Fund is intended to assist in acquisition, grants
and loans can be made to help with maintenance and preservation.[62] The Heritage Fund appears to have greater flexibility than
its predecessor and may well prove instrumental in facilitating
the transfer of property into the hands of local authorities and
various trusts concerned with heritage conservation.

It has been suggested that few local authorities are equipped
to undertake the care and maintenance of country houses and
as a general rule they do not offer a realistic ownership alternative, particularly for buildings of outstanding importance as
compared with, say, the National Trust. There does, nevertheless, appear to be some potential for increased public ownership
of Grade II country houses, in association with Country Parks,
amenity and recreational provision.

The National Trust most clearly will continue to play a major
role in the long-term preservation of country houses, but the
Trust cannot, and was never intended to, take over all country
houses that the private sector can no longer support.

In Gower's Report 1950 it was written that 'The owner [private]
of the country house is almost always the best person to preserve
it', and such a resolution is supported by the National Trust
which 'believes that houses are usually best looked after by
private owners, and that something of atmosphere and authenticity is lost when they come into the keeping of even the most
sympathetic organisation'.[63] It is currently government policy
to encourage private ownership not solely because it is in the
best interests of country-house preservation, but because private ownership presently provides the most economical manner,

in terms of income and capital, of sustaining this part of our national heritage. Yet, having issued grants for the repair and maintenance of buildings and having obliged owners to open their homes to the public, the government, in many cases, still does not recognise public access as a business enterprise for tax assessment purposes and makes little allowance for capital costs and no allowance for potential losses incurred. In addition, most private country houses, though some are exempt from CTT, are still part of a landed estate and as such are affected by present capital taxation policies that leave the future of private landownership in serious doubt and the long-term preservation of country houses and their contents in the balance. An interesting interpretation in 1978 from an owner of one of the more popular country houses open to the public ran to the effect that, 'recent changes in capital taxation have radically altered the situation from that which has pertained for most of the period in question. For Russian roulette has been substituted heritage poker'.[64]

Some headway encouraging the establishment of maintenance funds was made in the Finance Act 1980 (see p. 147), but without greater concessions to the private owner it seems inevitable that part of the country-house heritage will be progressively destroyed as families sell out and houses are gradually depleted of their contents, despite the 'safety valve' of the Heritage Fund, in order to pay taxation liabilities, both present and future. The fabric of the building may well survive, but in public or institutional hands and at a cost to the taxpayer in excess of that presently required for country-house preservation.

One alternative, taken up by relatively few country-house owners since the mid 1970s, involves a change in 'ownership personality' (see p. 38). While remaining as tenants under a form of lease-back scheme, similar to agreements between former owners and the National Trust, a private owner can theoretically vest a country house and its contents in a company limited by guarantee and seek charitable-status registration for the company under the 1960 Charities Act.[65] As a private charitable trust the country house and estate land given as an endowment can be exempted from capital taxation. In this manner Burton Agnes Hall (East Riding) since 1977 has been held by the Trustees of the Burton Agnes Hall Preservation Trust, a registered charity. Around 600 acres of agricultural land have been endowed, currently yielding some £10,000 per year. The hall still remains the 'lived in' family home of the Wickham-Boynton family as well as being open to the public for six months every year.[66]

Management control through trusteeship or through ownership, however, are viewed as markedly different situations, especially by owners with direct heirs to succeed them, and it has been suggested that the private charitable trust and the National Trust are seen as second and third alternatives for country-house preservation by private owners.[67] Provisions in the Finance Act 1980, to encourage the establishment of maintenance funds, have assisted the private owner, but go only part of the way to alleviating the long-term problems of funding country houses.

Private charitable trusts still remain a possible option for long-term preservation of outstanding country houses that are part of an ongoing estate, and such houses, managed on a non-profit basis for the national benefit, are not only eligible for assistance from the HBCE but also from the Heritage Fund. If the idea of 'stewardship' or 'social trusteeship' were more widely accepted the creation of a private charitable trust would allow a family to continue to occupy the ancestral home and, as trustees, to retain an element of control in its management. Such an arrangement facilitates not only the preservation of the fabric and content of outstanding country houses, but also the 'atmosphere and authenticity' referred to by the National Trust.

NOTES

1   Ownership data was unobtainable for two houses.
2   F.M.L. Thompson, 'English Landed Society in the Nineteenth Century' (Routledge and Kegan Paul, London, 1963), p. 27.
3   Irrespective of country-house use or whether it has been demolished since date of transfer.
4   Building licensing was not relaxed until 1952-3 and legislation not removed until 1954.
5   Excludes newly built houses.
6   Including the employed household staff.
7   Other than accommodation for household staff.
8   Excludes houses occupied by a caretaker or National Trust staff only.
9   J. Bateman, 'The Great Landowners of Great Britain and Ireland', 4th edn (1883, reprinted Leicester Univ. Press, 1971), p. 358.
10 The Knights Hospitallers built a preceptory at Dingley remains of which may form part of the tower block to the north; M. Binney, The Rescue of Dingley, 'Country Life', 27 Nov. (1980), p. 1992.
11 Ibid., pp. 1990-3.
12 M. Binney, Homes From Historic Houses, 'Country Life', 19 Aug. (1976), pp. 467-8.
13 Ibid., p. 467.
14 Ibid., p. 467.
15 'Britain's Historic Buildings: A Policy for their Future Use' (BTA, London, 1980), p. 81.
16 Ibid., p. 81.
17 J. Cornforth, 'Country Houses in Britain - can they survive?' (Country Life, London, 1974), p. 51.
18 Now in Merseyside.
19 D. Stroud, 'George Dance, Architect 1741-1825' (Faber

and Faber, London, 1971), p. 197.

20　Became the University of Keele in 1962.

21　'Time-sharing' is a recent concept with potential for future development. It involves the division of a house into self-contained residential units for which one or two-week shares can be purchased for a specific time of year. Shares are exchangeable with other tenants for a different week or an apartment elsewhere.

22　I am grateful to M. Binney (Architectural Edit., 'Country Life') for the updated information.

23　Part of the Hall is used as a residential college of Adult Education.

24　P. Neal, 'Heritage Education' (National Association for Environmental Education, Stafford, 1979), Series One, Practical Guide 7, P. 3.

25　'Historic Houses, Castles and Gardens in Great Britain and Ireland' (ABC Historic Publications, Dunstable, 1980), p. 8.

26　Quoted by R. Fedden and J. Kenworthy-Brown, 'The Country House Guide' (Jonathan Cape, London, 1979), p. 71. Original source not given.

27　C. Morris (ed.) 'The Journeys of Celia Fiennes' (Crescent Press, London, 1947); C.B. Andrews and F. Andrews, 'The Torrington Diaries' (Eyre and Spottiswoode, London, 1954).

28　Andrews and Andrews, 'Torrington Diaries', p. 414.

29　Quoted by B. Spraque Allen, 'Tides in English Taste 1619-1800' (2 vols. Pageant Books, New York, 1958), vol. 1, p. 76. Taken from the, 'Norfolk Tour, or Traveller's Pocket Companion'.

30　W. White, 'History, Gazetteer, and Directory of Lincolnshire' (1856, reprinted David and Charles, Newton Abbot, 1969), p. 659.

31　Information from Questionnaire respondent, Viscount De L'Isle, VC, KG, March 1978.

32　D. Burnett, 'Longleat' (Collins, London, 1978), pp. 180-1.

33　Duke of Bedford J., 'A Silver Plated Spoon' (Pan Books, London, 1962), p. 185.

34　English country houses listed in 'Historic Houses, Castles and Gardens in Great Britain and Ireland'. Includes most of the habitable properties open to the public.

35　Per cent of 98 sample houses open to the public for which listed Grade was obtained.

36　BTA, 'Survey of Overseas Visitors' (BTA, London, 1979).

37　Calculated from BTA published list of visitors to historic properties 1979. Excluded, where possible, visits to country house gardens and parks.

38　HBCE, 'Annual Report, 1969-1970' (HBCE, London, 1971).

39　Noted in M. Bence-Jones and H. Montgomery Massingberd, 'The British Aristocracy' (Constable, London, 1979), p. 226.

40   J. Butler, 'The Economics of Historic Country Houses' (Policy Studies Institute, London, 1981), Report No. 591, pp. 47-51. The average annual running cost for all country houses in private ownership was £31,400.
41   Under the Finance Act 1975, Eliz. 2, c. 7., buildings of outstanding historic or architectural interest were given conditional exemption from CTT.
42   R. Fedden, 'The Continuing Purpose' (Longmans, London, 1968), p. 5.
43   'Properties of the National Trust' (National Trust, London, 1978).
44   Fedden, 'The Continuing Purpose', p. 30.
45   National Trust Act 1937, 1 Geo. 6, c. 57, section 4.
46   Finance Act 1931, 21 & 22 Geo. 5, c. 28.
47   Finance Acts of 1937, 1949, and 1951.
48   Finance Act 1972, Eliz. 2, c. 41.
49   Since the Finance Act 1910, the Inland Revenue has had power to accept land and buildings in lieu of taxes.
50   Fedden, 'The Continuing Purpose', p. 56.
51   Arlington Court (Devon) is a notable example in the sample group.
52   Butler, 'The Economics of Historic Country Houses', p. 27.
53   Fedden, 'The Continuing Purpose', p. 65.
54   Ancient Monuments Consolidation and Amendments Act 1913, 3 & 4 Geo. 5, c. 32.
55   Now administered under the Thamesdown Borough Council.
56   'Guardian', 15 Oct. 1978.
57   HBCE, 'Annual Report 1978-79' (HBCE, London, 1980), p. 1.
58   Cornforth, 'Country Houses', p. 24.
59   Fedden, 'The Continuing Purpose', p. 20.
60   Town and Country Planning Act 1971, Eliz. 2, c. 78.
61   National Heritage Act 1980, Eliz. 2, c. 17.
62   'National Heritage Memorial Fund: Guidelines issued to the Trustees' (August 1980), para. 7.
63   Fedden, 'The Continuing Purpose', p. 58.
64   Questionnaire response dated May 1978.
65   Charities Act 1960, 8 & 9, Eliz. 2, c. 58.
66   Correspondence M.W. Wickham-Boynton D.L., 13 Jan. 1978.
67   J. Cornforth, The Chance of a Future, 'Country Life', 26 June (1980), p. 1516.

We are all prone to pay little attention either to objects in
our landscape or to the landscape itself, until it is about
to disappear. D. Stea, 'Landscape Dichotomies', *Landscape*,
Oct. (1975), p. 45.

Whether deriving from the formal era of the seventeenth century
or the more naturalistic styles adopted in the eighteenth or
nineteenth centuries, estate amenity lands were for the most
part man-made, planned and contrived landscapes, the product
of a particular fashion of a particular time. Just as earlier
landowners remodelled and designed their property so also their
twentieth-century counterparts have modified the land according to their tastes and needs. Consequently over the past hundred years there have been considerable changes in land use
and function of estate amenity lands, and while some have been
altered beyond recognition others have undergone change of
ownership and function with minimal loss of landscape integrity.

AMENITY LAND ACREAGE c. 1880 AND c. 1980

One measure of change is obtained by comparing the area of
amenity land still attached by ownership to the country house,
or former house site, *circa* 1980 with that of a century earlier
irrespective of present land use (Table 10.1). At the national
level nearly a quarter of former amenity acreage is no longer
attached to the estate heartland. At the regional level less
change is evident in the North and South West, regions possessing on average smaller acreages in the nineteenth century.
The highest recorded losses are in the South East, Midlands
and North West reflecting, one can surmise, greater pressure
and land-use demands from urban and industrial activities and
the particular impact of metropolitan London on estate heartlands
within its environs.

Amenity acreages still associated with the great-landowner
properties continue to remain well above the national average
though proportional losses marginally exceed the national figure
(Table 10.1).

For 75 per cent of all estates for which comparative data were
available the entire amenity land remains attached by ownership
to the country house or its former site (Table 10.2). Where the
original family still own the country house the figure was as

Table 10.1: Amenity Acreage Loss c. 1880 to c. 1980 - by Region and c. 1880 Landowner Class

Region	Mean acreage c. 1880	Mean acreage c. 1980[a]	Per cent loss c. 1880 to c. 1980
North	163	155	5
North West	349	261	25
East	310	260	16
Midlands	336	248	26
South East	309	206	33
South West	219	175	20
England	287	217	24
c. 1880 Landowner class[b]			
Great landowners	507	378	26
Greater gentry	206	161	22

Notes: a. Area of amenity land still attached by ownership to country house or former site, irrespective of land use. b. Great landowners: $\geqslant 10,000$ acres; Greater gentry: 3,000 to 9,999 acres.

high as 89 per cent, revealing that a house still occupied as a residence rarely stands in isolation but it is usually complemented, at a minimum, by amenity-land acreage.

Of the 74 sample estates where the country house has been demolished and not rebuilt, the site and amenity acreage on over 50 per cent remain intact as an ownership unit. Eight per cent have been greatly reduced in area, but for the remainder it was not possible to obtain accurate ownership and acreage data. None the less, judging from land-use criteria many are now sub-divided, some between a multitude of owners, having been developed in part as private housing estates or industrial parks.

When a country house was sold it was more common than not for a major part if not all of the parkland and home farm, whether inside or outside the park perimeter, to be offered with house and grounds as one lot. Hence many estate heartlands remain, substantially or totally intact, as a unit of ownership. However, country houses have been sold on their own or with only a few acres of grounds or a fraction of the park, the original family or another owner holding the surrounding amenity and farmland or the remainder of the estate having been entirely broken-up. Per cent losses have been marginally greater from amenity areas that were over 300 acres in extent in 1880 (Table 10.2) which in part reflects the divorce of house and its immediate grounds from the remainder of the property on a number of the great-landowner estates, as well as the piecemeal sale or compulsory purchase of parkland for development purposes.

Table 10.2: Estate Distribution According to Amenity Acreage
c. 1980 as a Per Cent of c. 1880

Amenity land area c. 1880 Acres	100% No.	% of total	75-99% No.	50-74% No.	25-49% No.	0-24% No.	Total Estates
> 500	36	64	3	2	5	10	56
401 - 500	15	60	4	–	1	5	25
301 - 400	23	57	2	2	2	11	40
201 - 300	39	70	4	–	2	10	55
101 - 200	63	75	4	5	5	6	83
51 - 100	66	85	–	1	3	7	77
1 - 50	61	88	–	2	3	3	69
Total	303	75	17	12	21	52	405[b]

c. 1980 Area as Per Cent of c. 1880[a] (column span header)

Notes: a. Per cent area of amenity land still attached by ownership to country house or former site, irrespective of land use.
b. For 95 cases either one value for c. 1880 or c. 1980 was not
known.

The abstract trait of ownership may conceivably change without physical alteration of estate character and the sub-division
of amenity land need only imply change of management control.
Thus the 42 acres comprising the country house and grounds
at Sheffield Park (Sussex) since 1972 have been owned by the
Radfords, while 142 acres comprising garden, woodland and
parkland since 1954, has belonged to the National Trust.[1] In
this case, apart from differential public access, there is little
to indicate divided ownership as the composite picture-landscape
has been more or less maintained. More often than not, however,
separation of all or part of the amenity land from the country
house has been accompanied by functional and land-use changes.

AMENITY LAND-USE c. 1980

Examination of the current use of nineteenth-century amenity
areas reveals a number of major changes over the past century
and provides a vehicle for reviewing the more serious threats
to the future of remaining parks, gardens and woodlands. The
collated results of an assessment of major amenity land-uses
in the present day are shown in Table 10.3, subdivided according to ownership of the country house, or its former site, and
by region. As it was not possible in many cases to differentiate
clearly between the use of amenity land still attached to the
country house or former site, and the use of amenity land now
detached by ownership from the estate heartland the entire
range of land-uses have been assigned under the present house

or site owner. Bearing in mind that the house-ownership criterion accounts for a little under 75 per cent of the amenity-land
area, the lack of precise demarcation between ownership and
use somewhat blurs the picture. None the less, it is apparent
that the more traditional land-uses, of agriculture and woodland
within the setting of a private park, continue to dominate on
privately owned estate heartlands while a more diversified range
of uses is evident on land now held by public or institutional
proprietors.

At the regional level the greatest changes are found in the
South East and North West (Table 10.3). The lowest proportion
of land in agricultural use was recorded in counties around
London, but they ranked high in the use of former amenity land
for recreation and development purposes. A similar picture was
evident in the North West though agricultural land-use here was
on a par with the remaining regions. It could be justifiably
inferred from knowledge of late nineteenth century amenity land-
use that the least change is apparent in the East and North of
England, while only in the provision of recreation facilities has
a notable change taken place in the South West.

A pattern of association is also apparent between those estate
heartlands that remain essentially rural in location, which more
often have retained park characteristics in combination with
agriculture and woodland as compared with those now embraced
within urban or urban fringe environments which tend to record
a wider range of present-day uses.

Urban and Industrial Development
Even though landed estates were and are fundamentally rural,
the very term country house implying a location away from large
settlements, over the past century the encroachment of urban
growth into the countryside has resulted in complete and partial
loss of a number of former estate heartlands. Only a fraction of
the sample group have been entirely absorbed within an urban
nucleus and developed as residential, commercial or industrial
land. In a greater number of cases a relatively small proportion
of estate amenity land at the margin of urban expansion has been
sold, compulsorily purchased by a local authority, or developed
by the landowner.

Historically, in the rural-urban fringe legal constraints on
settled or mortgaged estates occasionally prevented land sales,
and some landowners have been reluctant to renounce ties with
ancestral property for the promise of financial gain from residential or industrial development. Consequently, in a number of
cases, urban growth reached a park perimeter but progressed
no further, the park acting as a directional barrier to expansion
so affecting the morphological character of adjacent settlement.

When the 3rd Earl of Bute commissioned 'Capability' Brown,
in 1764, to landscape his park at Luton Hoo (Beds.), he effectively conditioned the spatial development of the town. The
design called for an addition to the existing park of over 900

Table 10.3: Major Present-day Uses of Estate Amenity Land[a]

Country-house or site owner c. 1980	Parkland[b]	Deer park[c]	Agriculture	Woodland	Tourism and recreation[d]	Golf[e]	Housing and industry	Total in sample
Original family	127 (67)[f]	22 (12)	165 (87)	55 (27)	74 (39)	7 (4)	5 (3)	190
Different family	47 (55)	2 (2)	71 (82)	20 (23)	18 (21)	1 (1)	3 (3)	86
Public body	77 (46)	1 (1)	113 (67)	40 (24)	56 (33)	18 (11)	31 (18)	169
National Trust	24 (75)	5 (16)	27 (84)	12 (38)	32(100)	1 (3)	3 (9)	32
Other[g]	6 (26)	–	19 (83)	5 (22)	5 (22)	2 (9)	6 (26)	23
Total	281 (56)	30 (6)	395 (79)	128 (26)	185 (37)	29 (6)	48 (10)	500
Region								
North	21 (38)	4 (7)	40 (71)	11 (20)	15 (27)	3 (5)	3 (5)	56
North West	43 (56)	4 (5)	63 (82)	23 (30)	27 (35)	9 (12)	13 (17)	77
East	50 (68)	2 (3)	61 (84)	21 (29)	20 (27)	3 (4)	4 (5)	73
Midlands	53 (63)	7 (8)	74 (88)	24 (28)	31 (37)	5 (6)	3 (4)	84
South East	73 (58)	4 (3)	86 (69)	25 (20)	56 (45)	7 (6)	19 (15)	125
South West	41 (48)	9 (11)	71 (84)	24 (28)	36 (42)	2 (2)	6 (7)	85
Total	281 (56)	30 (6)	395 (79)	128 (26)	185 (37)	29 (6)	48 (10)	500

Notes: a. Present-day uses of land defined as amenity land c. 1880.
b. All parkland regardless of access.
c. Included in parkland total.

d. Country-house gardens and parks open to the public for tourism and recreation, including safari and wildlife parks, zoos, country parks, field-study areas and nature reserves, caravan parks and permanent camp sites. Excludes: country-house parks and gardens open for special events for only a few days a year; 'semi-public' school playing fields and other institutional grounds.

e. Some parklands used as golf courses are also open for other purposes of tourism and recreation. The two columns are not mutually exclusive.

f. All figures in brackets are per cent values of the 'Total in sample' column.

g. Includes multiple owners and cases where heartland occupies a built-up area. In fifteen cases ownership was not known.

Source: Questionnaire Survey; Ordnance Survey 1:50,000; The Second Land Utilisation Survey; *Historic Houses, Castles and Gardens* (ABC Historic Publications, 1979).

acres of farmland and woodland immediately south of Luton and
the town has subsequently expanded in every direction except
southwards.[2] Despite the sale of 200 acres of estate land on the
edge of Luton in the 1930s,[3] the town morphology continues to be
somewhat lopsided.

In Hertfordshire the town of Watford is still bounded to the
west by the remnants of Cassiobury Park. Since initial sales in
1909 fringes of the park have been developed as residental areas,
though 190 acres, acquired piecemeal by Watford Town Council,
are preserved as open space and public parkland.[4] Further north
the extensive parkland surrounding the Elizabethan palace of
Burghley House (Northants.) similarly appears to have constrained the southward expansion of Stamford, though in this
case the late enclosure of the open fields around the town in the
1870s must also be accredited an important role in its morphological development; a role in which the Marquess of Exeter,
owner of the Burghley Estate, played a substantial part.[5] The
town of Cirencester has for many years been hemmed in by the
estate heartlands of Cirencester Park and the Abbey Estate.
Cirencester House is one of the few large country houses that
was built directly on the edge of a town. From the house an
extensive area of landscape park and woodland, largely the
creation of the Earl of Bathurst in the early eighteenth century,
fans out westwards to occupy over 1,000 acres of Cotswold
countryside. Abbey House to the east, however, was demolished
in 1964 and part of its amenity land is now owned by the local
town council and maintained as public park, while part has been
sold for residential development.

While country-house amenity lands adjacent to large settlements may have deterred urban expansion in the past, today
such areas are valued as open space and their future not only
viewed as potential development land but as amenity resources
to provide the essential lungs for urban areas. In the four
examples discussed above, the estates at Cirencester, Burghley
and Luton Hoo are in private ownership, but in each case benefit of part of the amenity land is already extended to the public.

Amenity lands engulfed by or in proximity to urban centres
more often than not have been retained, at least in part, as
public parks or gardens or converted to a particular recreational
use, but in a small number of cases only a suburb name or
perhaps isolated relics remain, the land area having been submerged by urban or industrial development.

Montreal Park (Kent), until 1925, was the seat of the Earl of
Amherst and until 1933 the property of Mr J.J. Runge, who had
purchased the estate intact with a view towards keeping it clear
of commercial development. In the late 1930s the country house
was demolished and part of the park opened for building. Montreal Park now lends its name to a suburb of Sevenoaks. Similarly,
Wheatley Hall (West Riding), the seat of Sir W.C. Cooke, was
demolished in 1938 and the amenity land, now built over, forms
a district of north-east Doncaster, while Cleve Hill (Glos.), sold

up in the 1920s by the Cave family, is now part of Bristol subur-
bia. Five hundred acres of the former Dagnam Estate (Essex),
including the park and house were sold in 1948 to the London
County Council for the building of the Harold Hill housing estate
at Romford.[6] Dagnam House was demolished in 1948. North Seaton
(Northld.), Brookman's Park (Herts.) and Preston Hall (Kent)
comprise other sample estate amenity lands now partly or entirely
built over, the latter site occupied since 1925 by the British
Legion Village, an integrated community of hostels, houses and
factories.

A number of estate heartlands are now sites of industrial
activity; two lend their names to industrial parks, the complete
antithesis of their former landscape. It is hard to believe that
Trafford Park (Lancs.) situated less than four miles from the
centre of Manchester was once a well-wooded parkland. By the
late nineteenth century the relentless growth of Manchester,
the spread of industry, trade and commerce had encroached to
the very park gates. The park itself was virtually an island;
the course of the Manchester Ship Canal, opened in 1894, took a
wide bend for over three miles around the northern perimeter
and to it was connected the old Bridgewater Canal that had,
since 1761, skirted the southern edge of the park for over three
miles. Trafford Park and its country house by the mid-1890s
were no longer considered suitable as a country residence and
Sir Humphrey de Trafford obtained the permission of Parliament
to break his family entail in order to dispose of the property.[7]
A proposal that the city of Manchester should purchase the
park, to preserve at least its central core as public open space,
did not come to fruition. Instead, the Trafford Park Estate of
1,183 acres, which included four farms as well as the park,
was acquired by private treaty on 14 April 1897 by Trafford
Park Estates Ltd, a public company formed in 1896 to develop
the estate as an industrial park.[8] Trafford Park became the first
and for many years the largest industrial estate in the world.[9]
The house was converted to a hotel in the 1890s but had been
resold and abandoned by the 1930s and was demolished in an air
raid in 1940. A dense network of roads now cross the park and
over 250 firms occupy the site, part of which is still owned and
leased out by Trafford Park Estates Ltd, while other plots have
been sold and resold over the years. Only the name essentially
records the historic link between the former and the present-day
estate and the family that for many centuries held the land.[10]
Park relics are few. When the Manchester Ship Canal was completed, Sir Humphrey de Trafford constructed a seven-foot high
wall along the northern boundary to screen the park from the
canal. A short length of the sandstone walling remains. Most
prominent, however, are the main entrance gates and lodges
which are preserved in the local landscape but on a new site.
They were moved from Throstles Nest on the Chester Road in
1922 and re-erected on the other side of the road at the entrance
to Broadstone Park, a local authority recreation area.[11]

The amenity land surrounding Osmaston Hall on the outskirts of Derby has had a somewhat chequered history since the sale of the estate heartland by the Wilmot-Horton family to the Midland Railway Company in 1889, but in more recent times, shortly after World War II, Derby Corporation purchased 88 acres for a site to serve the needs of light industry, now known as the Osmaston Park Industrial Estate.[12] The hall was demolished in 1938.

Factors other than proximity to large urban centres have led to the industrial use of a number of estate heartlands. The Drakelow Estate, advantageously situated on the banks of the River Trent a few miles south of Burton-Upon-Trent, was one of the oldest landed properties in Derbyshire having been retained in the Gresley family for 28 generations, nearly 850 years, until its sale in the 1930s. In 1935 Drakelow Hall was demolished, and in 1948 750 acres of land including Drakelow Park and Warren Farm were compulsorily acquired by the Electricity Generating Board for the construction of three generating stations,[13] accessibility to water from the River Trent being an important site determinant. Similarly, the heartland of the Hams Hall Estate (Warwicks.), former seat of Lord Norton and adjacent to the River Tame, is now occupied by a power-station complex which takes its name from the Georgian mansion that once occupied the site.

A notable loss in Hampshire has been the country house and amenity land at Cadlands, an estate located on the banks of the Solent at Fawley. Both the house and its landscaped setting were the work of 'Capability' Brown.[14] In 1947 1,000 acres of the Cadlands Estate, including the house and park, were acquired by the Esso Petroleum Company Ltd. The house was demolished in the same year and the land area adjacent to the Solent estuary has been extensively developed as the Fawley Refinery.[15]

Commercial exploitation of sand and gravel, of coal and other minerals has resulted in the loss of a number of estate parklands. One notable example is that of the relatively short-lived Carew-Gibson Estate at Sandgate (Sussex). The 4,000-acre estate assembled by the family in the period 1850 to 1870 was broken up by sale as early as 1887. The house and park underwent several changes of use until they were acquired by a sand-extraction company after World War II at which point the house was demolished. Some 18 acres of park were purchased in 1978 by the local authority as an amenity area and part of the north-ern section of the park has been sold for residential development. As to the remaining land, in 1974 the 'Sandgate Preservation Society' was formed to advocate a scheme for the reinstatement and conservation of the parkland when the sand has been worked out.[16] The potential for recreational and amenity use of worked-out quarry and mineral extraction sites has already been well demonstrated at Holme Pierrepoint near Nottingham and Irchester near Wellingborough, both now established as Country Parks created from restored sand and gravel pits. Perhaps this will be the ultimate fate of land on the Withington Estate (Cheshire) now in process of being quarried for silica sand. Just recently in 1979 the heartland of the Mells Park Estate (Somerset) was sold to the Amey Roadstone Corporation who plan to quarry stone from a large area of the estate.[17] The long-term future of the house, rebuilt in 1922 by Sir Edward Lutyens, and the parkland of approximately 300 acres remains uncertain.

Transport and Communications
In the nineteenth century the integrity of landscape parks was endangered by railway construction, but landed society was politically strong and large-estate owners were often able to reroute unwanted lines to prevent interference with their property. Not so in the present day. The individual landowner now has little voice or power, without considerable support from other community members, to override government policy decisions and powers of compulsory purchase that can be applied to expropriate privately owned land for public use.

In the twentieth century road construction has come to the fore as a major threat to estate amenity land. The building of town bypasses and, since 1955, the development of the national motorway system have already had a significant impact on a number of landscape parks and the future of others continues to hang in the balance.

Views of the countryside are most often seen from the road,[18] thus it could be put forward that adopting a course through or alongside a scenic park provides an attractive panorama which can be enjoyed by a great number of people – possibly for a minor road, but for motorway development it is to be doubted that much landscape appreciation can take place at speeds of seventy miles per hour! Such rationale, fortunately, holds little weight in the decision-making process for proposed routeways, but unfortunately for the proponents of parkland preservation, neither do arguments based on loss of aesthetic or heritage value. Aesthetic concepts and cultural ideals are unquantifiable, and as such are not included in any cost/benefit analysis assembled to evaluate proposals for a major routeway.[19] A large area of privately owned park in fact presents an almost ideal target for compulsory purchase, particularly if located adjacent to an urban area seeking to relieve a traffic-congestion problem. Being in single ownership potentially fewer objections will be raised at expropriation, while the complexity of multiple real-estate assessments, sale negotiations and compensation payments are minimised. In addition, the fact that many parks occupy poorer-quality land could no doubt provide further justification for their use which would appeal to those alarmed at the apparent rate of loss of first-class agricultural land.

Parks disfigured and endangered by road building formed the basis of a number of articles in *Country Life* in the mid-1970s.[20] Already at that time work was well underway on the Tring

bypass (Herts.), a road of motorway standard which, now
complete, bisects Tring Park and has spoilt the park as a landscape unit. The A38 Plympton bypass has shaved off a corner
of Saltram Park (Devon), a motorway standard bypass has been
constructed through Panshanger Park (Herts.) and 50 acres of
Hall Barn Park (Bucks.) were expropriated for the construction
of the M40 near Beaconsfield.

Petworth Park (Sussex), recognised as one of 'Capability'
Brown's masterpieces, has been threatened by the construction
of a bypass, either as a road through the park or as a cut-and-
cover tunnel near the house and since the early 1970s the route
of the M20 from Maidstone to Folkestone has been projected to
cut across Chilston Park (Kent) and that of the M54 to cut a
corner from the landscape park at Chillington (Staffs.), another
major work of 'Capability' Brown.[21] Up to 1980 all three parks
remained intact but more for financial reasons, based on current
economic cutbacks, than conservation concerns. In June 1980
the government of the day announced that the construction of
the M20 between Maidstone and Ashford, that is, the section
incorporating part of Chilston Park, would be deferred until
later in the decade.[22] Large sections of the motorway are, however, already complete and in view of the routeway's function
as a main link-road to the continent it is likely to be completed
in the not-too-distant future. Meanwhile, Chilston Park has a
temporary reprieve. Similarly, plans for Petworth are in abey-
ance. The fate of Chillington, however, is sealed. Formal compulsory purchase orders were issued in 1980 for part of the
park land and the Midland Road Construction Unit has put
contracts out for tender.[23] The holistic conception of the landscape park at Chillington is to be forever destroyed as the
motorway will penetrate at the very point where the ornamental
temples and bridges are clustered.[24]

A variety of landscapes were incorporated in the design of
estate amenity lands. Links were created between house, garden
and park and the entire layout formed a planned harmony of
visual effects. Some parks turned in on themselves enclosed in
a belt of woodland that obstructed the view beyond their boundaries, while others merged into the surrounding countryside
incorporating a farm landscape of hedges and fields as an integral part of their overall plan. Eyecatchers placed outside park
boundaries added interest to a prospect, and picturesque farm
buildings and cottages were sometimes sited for visual effect.
In the present day urban and industrial development, major
roads, overhead power lines and even the poor siting of new
farm buildings, especially industrialised and prefabricated
structures, in the surrounding landscape can destroy a planned
vista as much as land-use changes within the estate heartland
itself.[25]

At Saltram Park (Devon) the National Trust have planted a
new woodland along a previously open perimeter in order to
screen out housing developments taking place on the outskirts

of Plympton. It is debatable whether turning a previously open landscape in on itself is preserving or redesigning the park, yet such touch-ups are perhaps necessary to maintain a picture-landscape free from external interference. Such modifications are not always possible. For example, the view over Radley to Oxford was an important factor in the siting of a new house at Nuneham in 1755 for the 1st Earl of Harcourt. The house was built on the crest of a hill and the park landscape, designed in 1777 by 'Capability' Brown, maintained and emphasised the open vista. Today a line of electricity pylons disfigures the scene.[26] The Council for the Protection of Rural England in 1971 strongly recommended that all sectors of the electrical supply industry should have a stronger obligation towards the landscape especially in the siting of overhead power lines and substations.[27]

Rural Land-use
Land-use changes affecting estate amenity areas have been brought about not only from urban, industrial or communication sources but also from developments within the rural ambient. Changes in agricultural production in response to demands of technologically efficient farming of the 1960s and 1970s have had notable impact on amenity land and the surrounding farm landscape.

Agriculture. The most notable change has been the increased arable use of former park pasture. In the sample survey over 100 estate owners, public and institutional as well as private, whose 1880 park acreage remained intact classified land as 'agricultural' rather than 'park', though 37 added the corollary that 'agricultural' use was purely pastoral. Many indicated both 'park' and 'agricultural' use and judging from the number still identified as 'parks and ornamental ground' on the 1:50,000 Ordnance Survey, possibly far more come under the pastoral category than their owners chose to indicate. The greater number are apparently divided between arable and pastoral use. In either use, however, the planned layout of trees and woodlands can remain intact so retaining the essential landscape character of a park. Such is the case at Sandbeck Park (West Riding) where the land has been in arable use since 1950, but the parkland trees and avenues remain.[28] The effect of crop rotation too can change the character of parkland from year to year. At Hall Barn Estate (Bucks.), for example, the park is no longer under permanent pasture, but grass is rotated with cereal crops so that for say three years out of seven the land resumes the appearance of a landscape park,[29] a pattern no doubt repeated elsewhere.

It has been noted that parks were often located on the poorest estate land, though extensions in the eighteenth and nineteenth centuries were sometimes at the expense of better-quality arable land. Many originated from enclosed areas of scrub, heath or woodland such as Rufford Park (Notts.) carved out of the extensive lands of Sherwood Forest, its very name thought to refer to the poor quality of the local terrain. Many remain under permanent, semi-permanent pasture or woodland simply because their soils are best suited to such land uses. The meagre results of the wartime plough-up campaign was testimony to the general low arable productivity of many estate parklands.[30]

Woodland and Ornamental Trees. Not only on estate amenity lands but throughout the entire countryside woodland has been fast disappearing in the twentieth century. Substantial quantities of timber were felled to meet the unexpected demands of two World Wars and led to the establishment of the Forestry Commission in 1919. In recent decades the grubbing up of hedgerows, removal of coppices and old woodlands to create large fields and farm units has led to significant landscape changes over much of England, particularly in the intensively farmed lowlands. It has been calculated on average that 4,500 miles of hedgerows have disappeared every year between 1945 and 1970.[31] In terms of tree-cover some of the species most common to the English countryside have been depleted; ash, beech, elm and oak. The actions of man in the destruction of estate parklands and other rural landscapes have been compounded by the vicissitudes of nature and the natural mortality of organic material, aptly described in a passage by Evelyn Waugh concerning the park at the fictitious Boot Magna.

> The immense trees which encircled Boot Magna Hall, shaded its drives and rides, and stood, singly and in groups about the park, had suffered, some from ivy, some from lightening, some from the various malignant disorders that vegetation is heir to, but all principally from old age.[32]

Disease, for example has accounted for the loss of some native trees. Early in the century oak mildew and an unprecedented plague of caterpillars decimated oak woodlands in parts of England, while the ravages of Dutch Elm disease in the 1930s and in the more recent outbreak beginning in 1969 has particularly affected the English elm.[33]

In 1962 a disastrous gale damaged a number of notable park woodlands. Over 20,000 trees were destroyed at Harewood (West Riding), a park landscaped by 'Capability' Brown, and a similar tragedy occured at Bramham Park less than ten miles away. On both estates replanting has done much to repair the damage and reinstate former landscapes though, 'it will be many years before we see the full glory of Harewood again'.[34]

Present generations are witnessing the maturity and overmaturity of ornamental trees and amenity woodlands planted in the late eighteenth and nineteenth centuries, on average, over two hundred years ago. Such organic landscapes cannot endure forever and there is a growing need in many parks to replace individual trees and woodlands that are past their prime and beyond economic maturity.

In the past estate owners maintained park woodlands and trees as much for aesthetic value as for their timber, though on many estates timber production was also an economic enterprise. After World War II, particularly in upland and marginal farm areas, forestry became a major estate enterprise induced by favourable tax incentives and grant provisions associated with the establishment of private woodlands under Dedication and Approved Woodland Schemes.[35] But forestry has not developed as a major enterprise in lowland England and many park woodlands, in recent years, have not been restocked. As of 1977 the Forestry Commission have provided grant aid for planting small woods, a scheme that may conceivably renew activity in previously neglected areas.[36]

The replanting and care of new trees for non-commercial purposes on private estates is an investment with no benefit other than the intangible value of visual pleasure to present and to future generations. The decision to refurbish and maintain privately owned amenity woodland is fundamentally a voluntary act of conservation. Today the cost of amenity planting need not be borne entirely by the landowner. Since the National Parks and Access to the Countryside Act 1949, grants have been available to local authorities to plant trees in order to preserve or to enhance the natural beauty of the countryside.[37] The Countryside Commission, established in 1968,[38] is empowered to administer grants or loans to local authorities, other public bodies and private landowners for purposes of amenity tree-planting and management, in accordance with the 1949 Act, the Countryside Act 1968 and Section 9 of the Local Government Act 1974.[39] For the most part private landowners are encouraged to work through a local authority in seeking financial assistance.

Renewal and maintenance of park trees and woodland has been built into a number of private and public estate-management plans, one of the most notable being the policy of the National Trust which has established a replanting plan for all of its 80 or so landscape parks. In pursuing its woodland policy one of the aims of the Trust is to preserve the traditional appearance of the landscape. Felling and replanting is therefore undertaken so as to cause minimal disturbance, particularly in landscape parkland.[40]

Deer Parks. Of the 129 sample estates (26 per cent) that possessed parks stocked with deer in the late nineteenth century only 30 (6 per cent) retain deer in the present day.[41] Major losses began around World War I when many herds were removed from parks. The cost of maintaining fences and walls and of guards to protect young trees from browsing deer, plus the fact that venison simply went out of fashion, are major reasons given for the decline. More recently with Britain's entry into the EEC, the production of venison has risen in response to demands from the German market. It is likely that deer herds may well be reintroduced on a number of estates as a revenue earning enterprise in addition to their aesthetic attraction. In a healthy herd as high as 25 to 35 per cent can be culled annually, and recent studies have indicated at least in the Scottish Highlands that deer can be more profitable than sheep.[42]

Gardens. 'No authentic Tudor, Elizabethan or Jacobean garden apparently survives today – those thought to be of this date are all transpiring to be in large part 19th-century recreations'.[43] Despite this fact the value of country-house gardens in their own right and as settings for the house are of no less importance in the present day. Over the past century, however, there have been considerable changes in the design and layout of many historic gardens principally due to the two interrelated factors of increased cost of maintenance and availability of staff.

The garden at Shrublands (Suffolk) was tended by 52 staff in 1848 and even in 1900 there were between 25 and 30 gardeners compared with a number of less than five in recent decades.[44] Similarly at Weston Park (Salop) numbers fell from 23 in 1903 to four in 1979.[45] Certainly, as with the country house, modern machinery has facilitated a reduction in staff requirements, but great economy has been made by eliminating the labour-intensive layout of flowers and shrubs in formal beds with lawn and herbaceous borders. How much the dictates of fashion have led to such changes and how much is due to economy is a matter of conjecture. Economy undoubtedly plays a significant role as can be appreciated by a cursory examination of present gardens. Private owners are no less concerned with upkeep as the National Trust and public bodies, but the latter both tend to exhibit more elaborate gardens having greater access to centralised services for their upkeep.[46]

Under section 4 of the Historic Buildings and Ancient Monuments Act 1953, the HBCs can make grants available for the 'upkeep of any land comprising, or contiguous or adjacent to' a building of outstanding historic or architectural interest,[47] conceivably embracing all manner of replanting and renovation schemes for country-house gardens and parks, and in 1974 the mandate was extended to cover outstanding gardens in their own right. Notwithstanding such provisions relatively few grant applications have been made to date and, because of limited funds the HBCs have given greater attention to buildings. It has been put forward that 'what is needed is a special allocation for gardens, parks and historic landscape'.[48]

Recreational Use of Estate Land
When Gower's report was written in the early 1950s the future of country houses and associated amenity land was framed in a perspective of tourism based primarily on the historic and architectural significance of the country house and the aesthetic qualities of the park and gardens.[49] In the decade or so following

World War II many country houses and parks were open to the
public on this premise as indeed the majority are today. However,
in more recent years an unprecedented increase in leisure activities and demand for recreation in the countryside has considerably broadened the potential uses for both the country house
and its amenity land, and an increasing number of estates both
privately and publicly owned now offer a wide range of facilities
for informal, passive and active recreational pursuits.

Country Parks. The value of parkland as part of present and
future recreational resources in the countryside was officially
recognised in the Government White Paper *Leisure in the
Countryside* (1966) in which the concept of a Country Park was
formulated.[50] Legislation for the establishment of Country Parks
followed in the Countryside Act 1968 when the Countryside
Commission was empowered to assist financially local authorities
and private landowners to set up Country Parks.[51] In the early
years exchequer grants could be allocated to a maximum of 75
per cent of approved expenditure on land acquisition and management, a ceiling that was lifted in 1974.[52]

A Country Park as defined by the Countryside Commission is
'an area of land, or land and water, normally not less than 25
acres in extent, designed to offer to the public, with or without
charge, opportunity for recreational pursuits in the countryside'.[53] The definition is broad in scope and recreational pursuits
have to date embraced all manner of activities including water-
based sports, sailing, canoeing, rowing and fishing, to golf,
and horseback riding. Playgrounds for children, refreshment
facilities, camping and caravan sites have also been set up.
Other design elements have catered for the quiet and passive
enjoyment of the countryside in the provision of footpaths and
bridleways. Country Parks have been established in open land,
in woodlands, on barren moorlands, in reclaimed gravel workings
and along disused railway lines, on the coast and inland, some
in conjunction with access to historic sites and monuments and
others with access to landscape parks and gardens. Policy is
directed towards potential as well as present park sites, it is not
exclusively aimed at estate amenity lands although the concept
was to an extent modelled on existent amenity areas, both public
and private, in which landed estate parks and gardens were
prominent. Estate parklands, therefore, as would be expected,
have proven well suited for the requirements of Country Parks.
As of March 1980, 142 Country Parks in England have been
recognised by the Countryside Commission; 116 are administered
by a local authority and only 26 are under the management of
the National Trust or other private ownership.[54] Of the total
approximately a fifth are based on the amenity lands of former
or continuing landed estates; of which nine are in the sample
(Table 10.4). One of the first Country Parks to be accorded
recognition by the Countryside Commission was Elvaston Castle
(Derby.). Grant aid for acquiring land and setting up the

Table 10.4:　Country Parks Associated with Former and Ongoing Landed Estates

Country Park name[a]	Administrator	Land area (acres)
Bretton (West Riding)	Wakefield Metropolitan District Council	96
Cusworth (West Riding)	Doncaster Metropolitan Borough Council	54
Knebworth (Herts.)	The Hon. D. Lytton-Cobbold	190
Langley Park (Bucks.)	Buckinghamshire County Council	136
Lyme Park (Cheshire)	Stockport Metropolitan Borough Council	1,323
Marbury Park (Cheshire)	Cheshire County Council	190
Rufford (Notts.)	Nottinghamshire County Council	151
Thorndon (Essex)	Essex County Council	353
Weald and Downland Open Air Museum (Sussex)	Weald and Downland Open Air Museum	36

Note:　a. With the exception of the Weald and Downland Open Air Museum, each Country Park has the same name as the estate. In the latter case the park has been established on part of the West Dean Park Estate.
Source:　Countryside Commission: List of Country Parks as of 24 March 1980.

park was approved in December 1968, and in June 1969 Derbyshire County Council purchased 390 acres of the Elvaston Estate heartland, formerly the seat of the Earl of Harrington. Elvaston Castle, situated less than six miles from Derby, was opened to the public in 1970 as a contribution towards European Conservation Year. The house is now a countryside museum and field-studies centre operated in conjunction with the park.[55] Other Country Parks are also run in association with the country house. Such is the case for five of the nine sample estates; Cusworth, Knebworth, Langley Park, Lyme Park and Rufford. By no means all Country Parks that have been developed on landed estates have been established in close proximity to the house. A number in fact have been deliberately sited some distance away as at Goodwood (Sussex), Hardwick Hall (Derby.) and most recently at Wellington (Stratfield Saye House, Hants). In the two former cases the provision of park facilities were intended to alleviate the pressure of visitors to the country house. In the latter the country house and Country Park were opened almost simultaneously, and it has been found in fact that the two enterprises attract a different public.[56] On some estates the country house has been demolished as at Marbury (Cheshire) and at Clumber Park (Notts.) or is under different ownership or administration from the Country Park. West Dean Park (Sussex), now known as West Dean College, established by the Edward James Foundation, is administered separately from the Weald and Downland Open Air Museum that occupies part of the estate heartland. Thorndon (Essex) was designated a Country Park in 1971. It is located in the greater London Green Belt and is administered by Essex County Council. The land was acquired in 1938 under the Green Belt Act that facilitated local authority compulsory purchase of urban fringe land for the purposes of controlling industrial or building development. Thorndon Country Park is completely detached from Thorndon Hall. Much of the park originated as a medieval deer enclosure located on poor, sandy and gravelly soils. In the eighteenth century it was extended and the newly enclosed grounds, landscaped by 'Capability' Brown, formed the site for a new Thorndon Hall.[57] The landscaped area adjacent to the hall is now a golf course while part of the original deer park, at some distance away, is contained within the boundaries of the Country Park. Part of the deer park on the Bretton Hall Estate (West Riding) was set up in 1978 by the Wakefield Metropolitan District Council as Bretton Country Park.[58] Bretton Hall, adjacent to the park, has been used for a number of years as a college of higher education.

Proportionally, the number of private landowners who have applied for grants to date is small. In the sample group only Knebworth and the Weald and Downland Open Air Museum are under private administration. Undoubtedly some owners are reluctant to undertake an enterprise that is essentially commercial, while for others the question of time and the process of application, involving the necessity for an approved comprehensive design and long-term administrative proposal, are possible deterrents. The period between application and acceptance has sometimes been long. In the case of the Wellington Country Park it took from 1969 to 1973 to obtain final sanction.[59]

The creation of a privately owned and administered Country Park can be considerably cheaper for the public purse since no land acquisition costs are necessitated in the grant provision and, in view of the fact that such an enterprise can offer revenue earning potential for poorer-quality estate land, it is surprising that so few private landowners have, as yet, taken advantage of the scheme. As with all innovations, some are prepared to experiment while others prefer to wait on the side lines before undertaking the risk of such a new venture. Country Parks are, after all, a relatively recent development and reflect a small but increasingly significant aspect of the changes taking place on estate lands in the area of recreation provision.

Other Recreation Developments. Since the 1950s a number of country-house owners, private and public, have experimented with additional commercial facilities to attract visitors. Research undertaken in 1968 by the BTA and the Countryside Commission on three popular country houses and the range of facilities offered by each, revealed that specific attractions within the house 'are relatively unimportant compared with the overall appeal of the house and grounds as a destination for a day trip'.[60] On such a premise, and in recognition that a wider income and class-range of the general public now have greater mobility and seek access to the countryside, an increasing number of country-house owners are offering a variety of

informal recreational facilities as a complementary attraction to
the country house. In some cases, where the country house has
been demolished, the park and grounds have been developed
as a commercial recreation enterprise. Looking at the sample
properties, for example, a number have introduced animals as
attractions whether in zoos, wildlife or safari parks as at Arlington Court (Devon), Cricket St. Thomas (Somerset), Drayton
Manor (Staffs.), Knowsley (Lancs.), Longleat (Wilts.) and
Sewerby Park (East Riding). A large number provide play areas
and special facilities for children. Some are attracting overnight
visitors and more permanent holiday makers by providing camp-
sites as at Ashburnham (Sussex) and Birch Hall (Essex), or
caravan parks as at Blackmore Park (Worcester.), Constable
Burton (North Riding) and Nostell Priory (West Riding), while
holiday bungalows have been erected on part of the amenity land
surrounding Hengar House in Cornwall, the house itself having
been converted to self-catering flats as part of a tourism enterprise.

Estate Land as an Education Resource
Country houses have for many years been adapted for formal
education purposes and their surrounding grounds utilised for
sport and other recreational activity. Parallel with the introduction of informal educational services in association with country
houses (see pp. 164-5), estate owners have also perceived a wider
educational role for amenity areas and the estate in general. At
Beaulieu (Hants), for example, the position of education officer
was created in 1971 with responsibility for co-ordinating activities involving the house and estate. Nature trails and a nature
reserve, farm visits and the use of the estate for the study of
history and architecture provide attractive resources for schools
in the Southampton area. A non-profit-making trust has been
established at Beaulieu for the education programme.[61]
 Other estate lands are now utilised, independently or in conjunction with the country house, as field-study centres and
open-air museums, another recent development that has considerable potential for future expansion. In the sample group
Beamish (Durham), Norton Priory (Cheshire), Chillington
(Staffs.) and the Weald and Downland Country Park (Sussex)
are open-air museums while Malham (West Riding) and Drakelow
(Derby.) are just two examples of the use of former estate
heartlands as field-study centres. Malham is one of nine centres
operated by the Field Studies Council. Eight hundred acres of
the former Morrison estate including Tarn House, were presented
to the National Trust in 1946[62] and later acquisitions have
brought a total of 3,406 acres into the ownership of the Trust.[63]
The house, tarn and 184 acres are leased to the Field Studies
Council. Site facilities at the Drakelow power station complex
(see p. 186) have been developed as an educational resource.
Despite its intensive industrial use, areas of park woodland on
the site perimeter were retained to help screen the three

generating stations and the Central Electricity Generating Board
has actively pursued a conservation programme to preserve as
much of the former park landscape as possible. A field-study
centre was opened in 1967 with the help of the Nature Conser-
vancy and local education authorities. It is believed to be the
first such centre inaugurated on an operational industrial site
anywhere in Europe.[64] In 1970 a wildfowl nature reserve was also
opened utilising an area of lagoons, remnants of gravel workings,
along the bank of the River Trent.[65]

Interpretive walks and nature trails have been developed as
part of a number of park facilities, especially in Country Parks.
A few also contain areas designated as Sites of Special Scientific
Interest, particularly those with surviving ancient woodlands
and early deer enclosures where the natural flora and fauna have
been less disturbed by man. Part of the deer park of the Bretton
Hall Estate (West Riding) is a Site of Special Scientific Interest,
now known as the Bretton Lakes Nature Reserve, managed
jointly by the Yorkshire Naturalist Trust Ltd and Bretton Hall
College.[66]

Recreation and Location
Over the past century increasing pressure has been placed on
amenity areas in close proximity to built-up areas in the growing
need for urban access to open space. It has already been shown
that estate heartlands encompassed by urban growth or in the
rural-urban fringe have been adapted to serve a variety of
uses. A small proportion have been developed as residential or
industrial areas, but a larger group have been maintained as
parks and gardens or recreational space for public use.

As early as the 1880s estate gardens and parks began to be
acquired by local authorities for public use. Among some of the
early purchases were Preston Place (Sussex), Heaton Park
(Lancs.) and Cassiobury (Herts.). Preston Place (Sussex),
located in Brighton, was sold by the Fane-Bennett-Sanfords to
the Corporation in 1883 for the sum of £50,000, but it was not
until 1933 that the latter was able to take over a remaining four
acres of gardens and grounds that included Preston House. The
entire area of approximately 62 acres is now public park, gardens and recreational space.[67] Heaton Park, a recreational area
of one square mile lying six miles north of Manchester city centre,
was purchased by the Corporation in 1902 and Cassiobury Park,
adjacent to the town of Watford, was purchased piecemeal by the
Town Council beginning in 1909. Regarding the latter, it is
interesting to record the attitude of the local residents at the
beginning of the century toward the need for a public park.[68]
Early in 1908 a syndicate bought 185 acres of Cassiobury Park,
former property of the Earl of Essex, for building development
and offered 65 acres to Watford Town Council.[69] Even though
for many years the inhabitants of Watford had enjoyed access to
the park, the pressure of local opinion was against land purchase for this use, largely on the basis of cost to the rate-

payers, but also in the belief that there was plenty of alternative open space and beautiful countryside around Watford.[70] A
poll of townspeople in September 1908 overwhelmingly opposed
the purchase with only 607 votes for and 3,644 against,[71] yet
despite the result the Town Council in January 1909 borrowed
£16,500 and purchased 50 acres of the offered land[72] - public
opinion, then as now, seems to have held little weight! In a local
newspaper article it was stated that,

> we hope that everybody will bring themselves to feel that the
> best has been done for the present and the future and ulti-
> mately rejoice in the acquisition of an open space which, if
> all cannot see the want of it now, would have made its neces-
> sity felt in the years to come.[73]

Subsequent purchases in 1913, 1923 and 1930 brought the extent
of the park to 190 acres which, added to the 162 acres of Whip-
pendell Wood and a golf course of 261 acres, has provided the
residents of Watford with a valuable area of recreational space.[74]
   In 1928 the Horsham District Council purchased Horsham
House (Sussex) and 56 acres of amenity land that has been
maintained for public walks and pleasure grounds. Bristol Corporation have owned part of the Kings-Weston Estate (Glos.[75])
as public park since 1937. Allestree Hall (Derby.) and 325 acres
of park were bought by Derby City Corporation in 1944 and the
land is now used as a public recreational area and golf course.
As many as 29 sample estate parklands, the majority located on
the fringe of a large urban centre, have been converted to golf
courses, some developed by a local authority, others under
institutional ownership and a few retained by private landowners
(Table 10.3).
   The need for open space in and around built-up areas is now
widely recognised. The Green Belt Act 1938 first acknowledged
the need in London and the Home Counties, and the Town and
Country Planning Act 1947 included parks, pleasure grounds,
nature reserves and other open spaces as part of local authority
development plans.[76] Since the Countryside Act 1968 a number
of local authority recreation and amenity areas have been enhanced by the provision of grant aid and converted into Country
Parks. Broad guidelines for the creation of a Country Park infer
that a park can be set up in any area of the countryside within
reasonable distance of a built-up area and especially where existing informal recreational facilities are inadequate.[77] Recent
studies have shown that in terms of access to recreational facilities the urban public is prepared to travel within the range of
from 15 to 40 miles (one way) for a day or half-day excursion.[78]
There are estate amenity lands, as yet undeveloped, or under-
developed, for recreational and educational use, well within a
20 mile radius of urban centres let alone 40. Such amenity areas
provide potential and valuable resources for future development.
The often conflicting pressures of present-day land use pose

serious threats to the survival of estate parkland, yet opportunities for development in the field of informal recreation, undertaken with due care for the natural environment, can offer one means of long-term preservation.

PUBLIC ACCESS: THE SAMPLE

A problem is presented in analysing access to estate amenity lands in that only part may be open to the public while the remainder may still be private and, in a number of cases, the land area has been sub-divided for different recreational purposes, part public park, part golf course for example. Nevertheless, an approximation of property numbers with single or multiple-use public access was obtained from the sample responses and from additional secondary sources (Table 10.3). On a total of at least 185 estate heartlands public access is permitted for purposes of tourism and recreation, irrespective of whether or not a charge is levied. For approximately three-quarters of the total access is on a seasonal basis, usually in the summer months from April through to September, while the remainder have access year round. As many as 60 per cent are open in conjunction with the country house. In a few cases only the gardens or parkland are open to the public even though they are still attached by ownership to the country house, the latter remaining a private residence or used for an adapted function. Thus, for example, at the National Trust properties of Scotney Castle (Kent), Trelissick (Cornwall), and on the privately owned estates of Pusey (Berks.) and Thorpe Perrow (North Riding) there is seasonal access to the gardens and, in the latter case, to the arboretum only. The pinetum at Bedgebury (Kent) is open on a seasonal basis. Here the house is under different ownership. In other cases the country house is used as a school, but access is permitted to the gardens as at Stowe (Bucks.) and Duncombe Park (North Riding). Amenity lands open all year round are for the most part in public or institutional ownership; at least 29 publicly owned parks were recorded. Part of a few extensive parklands still in private hands and adjacent to urban communities have been set aside for year-round public recreational use. Such is the case at Petworth (Sussex), Luton Hoo (Beds.) and Cirencester (Glos.). At Cirencester 300 acres now form the Cirencester Park Leisure Area, similar in function to a Country Park though not formally recognised as such.[79]

On 89 properties the former estate amenity area can be classed as semi-public, referring to parks and ornamental grounds attached to an institution such as a school, college or university, or hospital, or even the grounds of an hotel which still serve as recreational space but are not advertised as being open to the public.

Over 100 privately owned estates continue to retain an area of ornamental ground or parkland that is strictly for private use.

In some cases this may entail a relatively small plot of wooded pasture, a paddock or a large garden in the vicinity of the country house. On some estates part of the amenity land may have public access while another area is reserved for family use. Even among the landowners who classed their entire amenity land as private, limited public access is usually permitted for short-duration recreational activities. Such is the case at Henham Park (Suffolk) for which it is estimated that several thousand people enjoy the park every year for particular events free of charge.[80] The large landscape parks well exemplified by Henham and Burghley (Northants.) have proven ideal settings for equestrian meets, three-day events, horse trials, gymkhanas, agricultural shows, scout and youth-group camping and activities sponsored by similar organisations. Landowners have also provided small areas for local community field sports.

In the provision of space for local community events and recreational activities many landowners still retain part of the spirit of *noblesse oblige*. In a similar vein a number open their gardens to the public in aid of charity for a few days a year whether for a local benefit or through the National Gardens Scheme. The latter was initially set up as a memorial fund for the District Nursing Service, but is now a registered charity linked in its support with the National Trust and other charities. Nearly 1,500 gardens were involved in the scheme in 1980, over 1,250 of which are private gardens not normally open to the public.[81] By no means all are attached to landed estates. Of the total sample group 77 gardens were listed in the 1980 catalogue, of which just over half are open at other times of the year, while the remainder permit access only in support of the National Gardens Scheme.

PRESERVATION OF AMENITY LAND AND OTHER ESTATE FEATURES

As an integral part of England's countryside heritage the future of surviving amenity lands and other estate features is embraced within the broad issue of historic landscape preservation, a topic of growing concern in the present day.

In recent decades the greatest force for change in the countryside has come from the agricultural sector. Since World War II the technological revolution in farming has created new farm landscapes over much of England, especially in lowland areas where loss of cover, trees and woodland have been most notable (see p. 190). Landowners and farmers have been encouraged through government grants and advice to drain wetlands, enlarge fields by removing hedges, to clear woodlands and plough up permanent pasture and heath land in the pursuit of increased agricultural production, a policy goal reinforced in the recent Government White Papers, *Food from Our Own Resources* (1975) and *Farming and the Nation* (1979).[82] However, it was

written in the latter that, 'a sustained increase in agricultural
net product is in the national interest and can be achieved,
without due impact on the environment' and moreover that 'policies will be framed with due regard to the claims of conservation
and other uses of the countryside'.[83] Emphasis is now on expanding production from existing resources rather than the enlargement of productive area which may partly curb the rate of loss
and conversion of traditional landscape features, but continuing
changes in the technology of farming, the increased use of pesti-
cides, herbicides and the automation and mechanisation of production processes will continue to bring about notable changes
in the rural landscape. It must be remembered, however, that
what has come to be regarded by the present generation as the
'traditional English landscape' is in fact the product of an earlier
agricultural system reflecting man-made decisions and values of
a former time-period. Landscape change is an inevitable and
continuous process. It is the rate of change in recent decades
that is somewhat alarming, especially to those with concern for
preserving the rural environment and landscape heritage. Old
landscapes, whether from the nineteenth century or earlier,
are being rapidly eradicated. Yet new or increased intensity of
existing land-uses need not completely eliminate former landscape patterns. Progress and conservation are not incompatible.
With regard to historic features, conservationists do not seek
to fossilise existing structures to create museums of the landscape, but are concerned to ensure that all is not lost in the
process of change and that certain landscapes are maintained as
representatives of their type for present and future generations.
In a rural environment principally devoted to agricultural production historic estate features need particular recognition and protection if they are to be preserved. This includes not only
features designed as pleasurable amenities for visual effect,
associated with parks and gardens, but broader scenic landscapes and other structures such as farm houses, cottages and
other estate buildings; structures that nowadays may present
obstacles to efficient farming, be unsuited to present needs and
have value only as intangible assets of England's heritage.

Identification
Protection, preservation and restoration of historic landscapes
and their individual heritage features are vital issues, but as a
primary step it is first necessary to identify and document what
remains to be protected.[84] This implies the need for a recognised
list of what constitutes an asset of value and what is worth
preserving and possibly restoring. The values and tastes of
the present generation must be used to select for future generations at least a representative cross-section of the countryside
heritage before changes now in progress completely obliterate
former landscapes. However, for the intangible factor of aesthetic and visual quality much remains to be resolved. Certainly
the interpretation of landscape is receiving more attention. Of

particular interest has been the recent work of Appleton who has devised a means of landscape assessment based on the ideas of 'prospect' and 'refuge', but he admits, in his description of the picturesque park landscape at Hawkstone (Salop), that 'we are still far from conceiving a quantitative technique which can reduce the aesthetic properties of a landscape like this to terms which can meaningfully be measured'.[85] No commonly accepted criteria as yet have been assembled to generate a quantitative value for landscape although research has been undertaken and is underway on the use of statistical techniques for assessing visual quality.[86]

Amenity Landscapes. That the need for documenting surviving landscapes has been little perceived in the past is evident for example, in the lack of present-day knowledge on the general state of landscape parks and gardens in England. Despite the importance attributed to the work of the more famous landscape gardeners, no comprehensive catalogue exists that records the present-day condition of their work. Certainly, this is not to discredit the admirable research of Stroud and Hyams who both note some of the important losses of the works of Brown and Repton.[87] Other writers have made passing remarks about the situation pertaining to a particular county. White, for example, noted for Kent that 13 parks were attributed to Brown or Repton and none remains intact.[88] Within the sample group of the 100 amenity areas to come under the influence of either Bridgeman, Kent, Brown or Repton, 80 still possess land classed as 'park or ornamental ground' on the 1:50,000 Ordnance Survey. For some this undoubtedly represents only a remnant of their former extent, but for the majority at least part of the designed landscape potentially survives. Even if in a dilapidated state with trees in need of replacement, ornaments in varying stages of deterioration and bodies of water choked with weeds and in need of dredging, the renovation and restoration of such land is possible, but not so for the 20 amenity areas that have disappeared under urban, industrial or intensive agricultural use.[89]

Even less is known about parks and gardens laid out by amateurs or local designers. Without doubt areas of parkland and ornamental ground are still a pervasive feature of many county landscapes and a number of local authorities have compiled lists of gardens and parks in their area.[90] In 1973 Northamptonshire County Council identified 73 parkland areas totalling 11,998 acres, ranging from 15 to 832 acres, as part of the data collection for the County Structure Plan.[91] Identification of parks and ornamental land from the two and a half-inch Ordnance Survey as used by Northamptonshire would be a relatively straightforward process for all English counties and at a minimum would provide an essential take-off point from which to begin more intensive groundwork embodying some form of visual quality classification and recording of tangible historic assets. Since 1977 ICOMOS[92], with the assistance of the National Trust and

the Garden History Society, has compiled a list of 180 parks
and gardens in England considered of 'outstanding' importance
and the HBCE has recently drawn up a draft list of 233 classed
as Grade I and Grade II*.[93] The condition of these listed properties varies considerably, but a start has been made with identification from which can follow more specific proposals for protection and renovation.

Estate Buildings.   For tangible items the process of identification
and recording is straightforward yet much remains to be done.
Undoubtedly there has been a growing interest in the past
decade over the conservation of old buildings both in urban and
rural areas. The range of buildings on an historic estate property is considerable and embraces not only the country house,
its associated outbuildings and ornamental features in the park
landscape, but also property in estate villages and farm buildings scattered throughout the countryside. Some estate buildings,
in addition to country houses, are already listed in the National
Monuments and National Buildings Records, not as an integral
part of an historic estate property, but perhaps as an example
of local vernacular architecture or an item of special historic
or architectural significance. Thus a few outstanding follies,
park ornaments and 'eyecatchers' have been given listed building
status though most remain unlisted and therefore unprotected
and often in a ruinous, dilapidated and deteriorating state.
Individual buildings in an estate village may have listed status
but not the village as a unit.
   Concerning farm buildings it was written in 1972 that, 'At
present no organisation has made any assessment of our stock
of farm buildings, nobody accepts responsibility for them and
nobody has started to assess which are worth keeping.'[94] Historic
farm buildings are as important a part of our cultural heritage
as any other feature, yet they are being swept away so fast that
it has been estimated that, 'within 25 years about 90 per cent of
the working farm buildings in Britain will have been built since
1960'.[95] Essex County Council published a report on historic
barns in the county in 1979, but this is one of the few examples
of local authority initiative in this area and as of 1980 it was
still noted that for Britain as a whole 'the vast majority of architecturally or historically interesting farm buildings remain
unidentified and unprotected'.[96]

Protection and Preservation
Control over the destruction of listed buildings has significantly
reduced the rate of country-house loss since the 1960s, but
there is a lack of legislation to protect the amenity lands in
which they are set and virtually nothing to prevent the destruction of estate features in agricultural areas outside the estate
heartland. Estate properties fortuitously located in a Conservation Area or National Park are subject to some planning control,
but outside such designated areas protection of notable land-

scapes and landscape features has yet to be sanctioned. Legislative controls presently available are few. Since the Town and
Country Planning Act 1947 local authorities have had the power
to prevent the unnecessary removal of trees and woodland of
amenity value from the landscape through the use of tree preservation orders,[97] and following the Town and Country Planning
Act 1971, it has been necessary for landowners to obtain permission for the siting of farm buildings that exceed a dimension
of 5,000 square feet.[98] The latter is the only farming operation
presently regulated by planning control. In 1975 the Council
for the Protection of Rural England (CPRE) suggested that
building legislation did not go far enough and that *all* farm
buildings should be subject to control both in their construction
and demolition.[99] Bringing the demolition of farm buildings within
the scope of planning control could help to preserve those of
particular historic or amenity value, which if no longer functional for the purpose for which they were built, potentially,
could be adapted for an alternative use.[100] Already the growth
of recreation and tourism has given a new lease of life to some
estate buildings. For example, barns have been restored and
modified to provide refreshment facilities at Treslissick (Cornwall) and Knebworth (Herts.) and a scheme has been prepared
to convert three barns on the Chatsworth Estate (Derby.) for
simple overnight accommodation for hill walkers and similar
groups. There is also considerable potential for the use of
cottages and other farm buildings for holiday accommodation in
remote and marginal agricultural areas.[101]

Estate buildings have been modified to accommodate small
businesses and light industries as on the Lockinge Estate
(Berks.[102]) in the villages of Ardington and Lockinge where
some 55 jobs have been created since 1975.[103] In a countryside
characterised by a decline in the numbers employed in farming
such an estate policy involving the new use of existing buildings
can play an important role in sustaining village communities.

In 1979 it was announced that the CPRE jointly with the CLA
plan to introduce a farm buildings award scheme to cover both
the restoration of agricultural buildings and their conversion
to appropriate new uses, and in 1981 the Countryside Commission
intend to publish a design handbook for the alternative use of
barns.[104]

Regarding landscape preservation, it was suggested by the
CPRE in 1975 that landowners and farmers could be required to
notify their local planning authority of any major physical change
that would substantially alter the landscape, although it was
stated that,

> we reject the bringing under planning control of the removal
> of landscape features. We look rather towards a warning
> system coupled with (in exceptional cases) a last resort power
> of control and - most important - the provision of financial
> compensation and inducement for the farmer who conserves

landscape features.[105]

A move towards control that embodies part of the latter concept is the idea of a 'Management Agreement' or 'Landscape
Agreement', the most practical notion to emerge over the last
decade[106] and one that appears to have considerable scope for
development in a wide variety of forms. The Countryside Commission recommended in 1972 the need for 'Landscape Agreements', similar to the Forestry Commission dedication or approved
woodland schemes or present 'access agreements', whereby a
private owner would agree to manage land in a specified manner
to satisfy the particular public need, in return for some form of
consideration, be it grant aid or tax concessions.[107] Agreements
could conceivably cover, for example, the expense of replanting
amenity woodlands and ornamental trees as well as a wider range
of tasks to enhance and maintain a landscape and to conserve
an area of recognised historic value. Davidson and Wibberley
have suggested that the notion of a 'Landscape Agreement' is
too narrowly framed unless it can 'incorporate measures designed
to safeguard and improve other aspects of the rural environment
for which there are at present, few encouragements'.[108] For
example, with reference to the recreational use of an amenity
area, a co-ordinated programme of tasks can be agreed upon to
enhance and preserve the landscape while at the same time providing additional recreational resources. Farm trails, parking
and picnic areas could be embraced in a more widely defined
'countryside agreement'.[109]

There is a danger that the present piecemeal legislation may
protect only selected historic features without due regard for
the setting in which they are located. Buildings in an estate
village, for example, may achieve listed status, but the visual
unity of the village may be spoilt by a lack of planning control
that allows poor siting of modern housing. The character of
many rural settlements already has been drastically changed by
the housing development and infilling in the interwar and post-war
era. A number of villages and hamlets remain part of an ongoing
estate, their development still under the control of a single
landowner. Many such settlements have seen little external change
over the past century, but few are guaranteed long-term survival in their present form. The future preservation of Blaise
Hamlet (Glos.) as a model picturesque settlement has been
assured since it was placed in the care of the National Trust in
1943.[110] This is not, however, to advocate that other estate
villages and rural settlements be fossilised, but to express concern that in an area identified and listed as of historic interest,
any growth should be planned in recognition of this fact.

Local authority use of tree-preservation orders occasionally
has proved detrimental to the wider goals of landscape preservation. Two examples relating to estate parklands were cited in
Country Life in the mid-1970s and are worth repeating. On the
Mapledurham Estate (Oxford.) the owner was required to replant

an avenue of elms before felling the existing trees badly in need of replacement. The original avenue had been aligned to the centre of the country house, but the configuration was impossible to replicate under the replanting stipulations imposed. The long-term outcome has been no avenue at all; when the original trees were cut a number fell on those newly planted and a fire eliminated the remainder.[111] The second example concerns the M20 routeway across Chilston Park (Kent). In their regard for the preservation of individual trees and a small pond the Kent County Council gave support to a route which would cut further into the park; a clear case of not being able to see the wood, in this instance the park, for the trees![112]

Already for some former estates isolated remnants remain as the only indicators of past history: a mark of ownership on a cottage or farm house, an obelisk on a distant hill top, a park entrance complete with gate piers and lodges leading only to a pastured field perhaps dotted with an exotic tree or two, or clumps of trees deliberately placed for visual effect over two hundred years ago. Already enough is protected to ensure that such scattered vestiges will never be the only indicators of former landed estates. But are we preserving enough? Is there already a representative sample of estate parks and gardens and other features in the protective care of the National Trust, private trusts or public ownership to disregard that which remains presently unprotected? In some aspects all is unique, in location, date of origin, composition or historic association, but choices have to be made and legislation enacted to ensure that preservation and maintenance are achieved in a manner that makes the most appropriate use of such heritage resources whether aligned with agricultural, recreational or multiple land-use options.

NOTES

1   'Properties of the National Trust' (National Trust, London, 1978), p. 75.
2   D. Stroud, 'Capability Brown', 2nd edn (Country Life, London, 1957), pp. 133-4.
3   Questionnaire respondent; N.H. Phillips, Luton Hoo, Beds., March 1978.
4   L. Ellis, 'Future Proposals for Cassiobury Park' (Parks and Recreation Department, Borough of Watford, c. 1972), sec. 2, para. 2.2.
5   S. Elliott, The Cecil Family and the Development of 19th Century Stamford, 'Lincolnshire History and Archaeology', no. 4 (1969), pp. 23-31.
6   Part of Dagnam Park still survives.
7   T.H.G. Stevens, 'Stevens of Manchester' (1962), p. 6; documentation received in correspondence from R. Winsby, Estate Office, Trafford Park Estates Ltd.

8   The estate was first purchased by E.T. Hooley, a financier, and subsequently transferred to the Estate Company. Date of sale provided in correspondence from R. Winsby (ibid.).

9   T.H.G. Stevens, 'Some Notes on the Development of Trafford Park, 1897-1947' (1948), Source, R. Winsby (ibid.).

10   Ancestors of the Trafford family are said to have been established in the parish of Eccles even before the Norman Conquest. E.P. Shirley, 'The Noble and Gentle Men of England' (John Bowyer Nichols, Westminster, 1859), p. 109.

11   Source, R. Winsby, Estate Office, Trafford Park Estates Ltd.

12   'The County Magazine', vol. 25, no. 3 (1960), p. 22; 'Derby Evening Telegraph', Feb. 1962.

13   H.J. Wain, 'The Story of Drakelow' (Midlands Region Central Electricity Generating Board, Birmingham, n.d.), p. 16; Information from CEGB, October 1977.

14   Stroud, 'Capability Brown', p. 177.

15   Questionnaire respondent; M.A.C. Drummond DL, JP, Manor of Cadland, Fawley, March 1978.

16   Sandgate Preservation Society, Newsletter No. 5, Autumn 1977, p. 1; Questionnaire respondent: J.R. Armstrong, Storrington, West Sussex.

17   Questionnaire respondent, C.J.R. Trotter, Mells Park Estate, Somerset, Nov. 1978.

18   S. Crowe, 'The Landscape of Roads' (Architectural Press, London, 1960), p. 12.

19   CPRE, 'Roads and the Landscape' (CPRE, London, 1971), p. 27.

20   Conservation in Action: Motorway Madness, 'Country Life', 13 Sept. 1973, pp. 727-8; Conservation in Action: A Doomed Landscape Park, 'Country Life', 27 June 1974, p. 1680; M. Binney and P. Burman, Landscape Parks in Danger - 1, Assault by Motorway, 'Country Life', 15 Aug. 1974, pp. 418-20.

21   Binney and Burman, Landscape Parks in Danger, pp. 418-20.

22   Dept. of Transport, 'Policy for Roads: England 1980' (HMSO, London, 1980), Cmnd. 7908, p. 31.

23   Correspondence, P. Giffard, Chillington Hall, Staffs., Sept. 1980.

24   Binney and Burman, Landscape Parks in Danger, p. 420.

25   For discussion on package buildings and the landscape see, CPRE, 'Development Control: Package Buildings' (CPRE, London, 1974).

26   Stroud, 'Capability Brown', pp. 189-93; J. St. Bodfan Gruffydd, 'Protecting Historic Landscapes' (J. St. Bodfan Gruffydd, Gloucestershire College of Art and Design, Cheltenham, 1977), p. 7.

27   CPRE, 'Electricity Installation and the Landscape'
      (CPRE, London, 1971), p. 18.
28   Questionnaire respondent; the Earl of Scarbrough,
      Sandbeck Park, Rotherham, South Yorkshire, Nov. 1977.
29   Questionnaire respondent, Lt. Col. the Lord Burnham,
      Hall Barn, Bucks., Dec. 1977.
30   H. Prince drew attention to the unsuitability of parklands
      in the Chilterns for arable farming, as demonstrated in
      the war years. H. Prince, Parkland in the Chilterns,
      'Geographical Review', vol. 49 (1959), p. 31.
31   CPRE, 'Landscape – The Need for a Public Voice' (CPRE,
      London, 1975), p. 9.
32   E. Waugh, 'Scoop', (1938, reprinted Penguin, Harmonds-
      worth, 1977), p. 17.
33   O. Rackham, 'Trees and Woodlands in the British Land-
      scape' (J.M. Dent, London, 1976), p. 36 and pp. 105-6.
34   A. Mee, 'Yorkshire – West Riding', 2nd edn (Hodder and
      Stoughton, London, 1969), p. 114.
35   Forestry dedication schemes were introduced in the
      Forestry Act 1967, Eliz. 2, c. 10, sec. 5.
36   Forestry Commission, 'Managing Small Woodlands' (HMSO,
      London, 1978), Booklet 46, p. 36.
37   National Parks and Access to the Countryside Act 1949,
      12, 13, & 14, Geo. 6, c. 97, sec. 89.
38   The Countryside Commission was established in place of
      the National Parks Commission in The Countryside Act
      1968.
39   Countryside Commission, 'Grants for Amenity Tree Plant-
      ing and Management' (Countryside Commission, Cheltenham,
      Aug. 1977), CCP 103, p. 1: Local Government Act 1974,
      Eliz. 2, c. 7. In 1979-80 £1.2m was spent by the Commis-
      sion on grants for amenity tree planting.
40   'The National Trust and Woodlands (The National Trust,
      London, Jan. 1979).
41   A further 3 properties possessed deer, but as part of a
      wildlife park or zoo and not in an historic deer enclosure.
42   M. Binney and P. Burman, Landscape Parks in Danger
      – II, Recreation and Recycling, 'Country Life', 22 Aug.
      (1974), p. 515.
43   M. Binney and A. Hills, 'Elysian Gardens' (Save Britain's
      Heritage, London, 1979), p. 6.
44   Ibid., p. 6.
45   Ibid., p. 7.
46   J. Butler, 'The Economics of Historic Country Houses'
      (Policy Studies Institute, London, 1981), p. 55.
47   Historic Buildings and Ancient Monuments Act 1953, 1 & 2
      Eliz. 2, c. 49, sec. 4.
48   Binney and Hills, 'Elysian Gardens', p. 52.
49   'Report of the Committee on Houses of Outstanding Historic
      or Architectural Interest', Chairman Sir E. Gower, (HMSO,
      London, 1950).

50   'Leisure in the Countryside' (HMSO, London, 1966),
      Cmnd. 2928.
51   Countryside Act 1968, Eliz. 2, c. 41, sec. 6, 7, 8.
52   Local Government Act 1974, Eliz. 2, c. 7, sec. 9.
53   CRRAG, 'Countryside Recreation Glossary' (Countryside
      Commission, 1970), sec. 2.8, Country Park, p. 13.
54   List received from Countryside Commission (Chelten-
      ham, Gloucestershire), dated 24 March 1980.
55   H. Cowley, Elvaston Castle Country Park: Its conception
      and development, County Planning Office, Derbyshire
      County Council, Jan. 1975.
56   C. Scott, Stratfield Saye and Wellington Country Park
      (CRRAG Conference, Durham Univ., Sept. 1976), p. 116.
      The Country Park is located on the eastern edge of the
      estate separate from Stratfield Saye House.
57   A. Duchars, 'Thorndon Country Park' (Essex County
      Council, n.d.), p. 10.
58   Bretton Country Park (flier) (City of Wakefield Metropolitan
      District Council, n.d.).
59   Scott, Stratfield Saye and Wellington Country Park; local
      opposition over a wide area delayed official planning con-
      sent, p. 114.
60   'Historic Houses Survey' (BTA and Countryside Commission,
      c. 1969/70), p. 9.
61   J. Cornforth, 'Country Houses in Britain – can they
      survive?' (Country Life, London, 1974), p. 62.
62   'Estates Gazette', 24 Aug. 1946, p. 168.
63   'Properties of the National Trust', p. 123.
64   'A Natural Concern' (CEGB, Midlands Region, Warwick-
      shire, n.d.), p. 9.
65   Ibid., p. 10.
66   The nature reserve is adjacent to the Country Park but is
      under separate management.
67   Information received from M. Waller, the Royal Pavilion,
      Art Gallery and Museums (Preston Manor), Brighton,
      Jan. 1978.
68   Information relating to Cassiobury received from
      A.G. Davies, Museum Curator, Hertford Museum.
69   'The Advertiser', 20 June 1908.
70   'Mercury', 28 Nov. 1908.
71   'Mercury', 19 Sept. 1908.
72   'Mercury', 9 Jan. 1909.
73   'West Hertfordshire and Watford Observer', 30 Jan. 1909.
74   Ellis, 'Future Proposals for Cassiobury Park', sec. 2,
      para. 2.2.
75   Now Avon County.
76   Town and Country Planning Act 1947, 10 & 11 Geo. 6,
      c. 51, sec. 5.
77   Countryside Act 1968, Eliz. 2, c. 41, sec. 6.
78   J.A. Zetter, 'The Evolution of Country Park Policy'
      (Countryside Commission, Cheltenham, 1971), comments

that distances travelled to a country-park-type facility are usually in the range 15 to 30 miles, p. 2; M.J. Elson, Some Factors Affecting the Incidence and Distribution of Weekend Recreation Motoring Trips, 'Oxford Agrarian Abstracts', vol. II, no. 2 (1973), observed that 'attractiveness of destination is of more importance than distance travelled and time used provided the journey is less than 40 miles', p. 168. The average distance travelled to the three country houses in the BTA/Countryside Commission, 'Historic Houses Survey' was 27, 30 and 39 miles for Tatton Park, Ragley Hall and Castle Howard respectively, p. 10.

79   Cornforth, 'Country Houses', p. 59 and 61. The Cirencester Park Leisure Area received no grant from the Countryside Commission for its establishment.

80   Correspondence, Earl of Stradbroke, Henham, Suffolk, June 1978.

81   'Gardens Open to the Public in England and Wales' (The National Gardens Scheme, London, March 1980).

82   'Food From Our Own Resources' (HMSO, London, 1975), Cmnd. 6020; 'Farming and the Nation' (HMSO, London, 1979), Cmnd. 7458.

83   'Farming and the Nation', p. 6, sec. 24.

84   The proceedings of the conference held at the Polytechnic of North London in 1978, 'Historic Landscapes: Identification, Recording and Management' (Dept. of Geography, Polytechnic of North London, March 1978), and the work of B. Gruffydd, 'Protecting Historic Landscapes', both emphasise identification and recording as a priority concern.

85   J. Appleton, 'The Experience of Landscape' (John Wiley, Chichester, 1975), p. 247.

86   Some of the more recent studies are listed in P. Dearden, Aesthetic Encounters of the Statistical Kind, 'Area', vol. 12, no. 2 (1980), pp. 172-3.

87   Stroud, 'Capability Brown'; D. Stroud, 'Humphry Repton' (Country Life, London, 1962); E. Hyams, 'Capability Brown and Humphry Repton' (Charles Scribner, New York, 1971).

88   J.T. White, 'Parklands of Kent' (Arthur J. Cassell, Sheerness, 1975), p. 22.

89   Detailed field work is necessary to obtain knowledge of the exact condition of each amenity area. Even those presently under intensive agricultural use can be restored if the planned layout of ornamental trees and woodlands remain intact.

90   Binney and Hills, 'Elysian Gardens', p. 48.

91   Northamptonshire County Planning Office, Historic Houses and Gardens Open to the Public, Survey (1973).

92   The United Kingdom National Committee for the International Council on Monuments and Sites (ICOMOS).

93   Binney and Hills, 'Elysian Gardens', p. 48 and pp. 52-3.
94   The Countryside: A Landscape in Decline, 'Design',
     no. 287 (1972), p. 45.
95   Ibid., p. 45.
96   'Historic Barns: A Planning Appraisal' (Essex County
     Council, 1979); 'Britain's Historic Buildings: A Policy
     for their Future Use' (BTA, London, 1980), p. 25.
97   Town and Country Planning Act 1947, 10 & 11 Geo. 6,
     c. 51, Pt. III, sec. 28.
98   Town and Country Planning Act 1971, Eliz. 2, c. 78.
99   CPRE, 'Landscape', p. 21.
100 Ibid., p. 21.
101 'Britain's Historic Buildings', p. 27.
102 Now Oxfordshire.
103 Alterations to buildings are zero rated for VAT, while
     repair and maintenance costs are subject to VAT at 15%.
104 CPRE, 'Annual Report, 1979' (CPRE, London, 1980),
     p. 16; 'Britain's Historic Buildings', p. 24.
105 CPRE, 'Landscape', p. 14.
106 Management Agreements were first suggested by
     R.J.S. Hookway in 1967 in, 'The Management of Britain's
     Rural Land' (Proceedings of the Town Planning Institute,
     Summer 1967).
107 Countryside Commission, 'Landscape Agreements',
     (Countryside Commission, Cheltenham, 1973), CCP.-61,
     p. 1. The most comprehensive study in the use of
     Management Agreements to date is M.J. Feist, 'A Study
     of Management Agreements' (Countryside Commission,
     Cheltenham, 1978).
108 J. Davidson and G. Wibberley, 'Planning and the Rural
     Environment' (Pergamon Press, Oxford, 1977), p. 199.
109 Ibid., p. 199.
110 'Properties of the National Trust', p. 1.
111 Binney and Burman, Landscape Parks in Danger - II,
     Recreation and Recycling, p. 514.
112 Conservation in Action: A Doomed Landscape Park,
     p. 1680.

11 CONCLUSIONS - THE FUTURE

> no nation, any more than a single individual has the right
> to dispose at will of property that may concern men of
> tomorrow as well as those of today. *Pictures from a Living
> Past* (UNESCO, 1978).

Over the past century the position of the large, privately owned
landed estate has undergone radical adjustment from being the
hub of local influence and the focal point of an established
hierarchical order of rural society to an ownership unit facing
constant threats of break-up from economic and political forces
largely external to its control. For a number of decades after
1880 a facade of stability was maintained, but following
World War I the decline of large-scale, private landownership
began to have effects not only in terms of the subdivision of
estate property but also on the landscape. The future of private
landownership and the long-term survival of remaining landed
estates are complex interrelated issues. The traditional estate is
the very product of a land system dominated by private ownership, but the continuity of the association in the twentieth
century has been a principal factor in the break-up of property.
Policy makers have failed to distinguish between the two such
that an inevitable consequence of pressure on private ownership
has been the concomitant loss of estate heritage features. In the
present day an historic estate as a physical unit of management
can be maintained outside the control of the private sector, but
the long-term fate of the majority remains inexorably linked with
the future of private landownership.

THE FUTURE OF LARGE-SCALE PRIVATE LANDOWNERSHIP

The pattern of landownership in England has been constantly
changing since the first individual claimed territorial rights to
land. What we are witnessing in the second half of the twentieth
century is the beginning of a trend that, taken to extremes,
can be viewed as the reversal of the historic process that began
with the dissolution of the monasteries and the sale and transfer
of Church and Crown land to private owners. For the following
three hundred or so years large-scale private landownership
was omnipotent. By the late nineteenth century 43 per cent of
land in England was concentrated in the hands of fewer than
1,500 families and 95 per cent of all land was in private owner-

ship (see p. 20). Landownership and occupation were, for the
most part, separate, and the landlord-tenant system prevailed
over the greater part of the country. In the present century the
process of private accumulation of large landed estates has
generally reversed, while a trend towards an increase in the
ownership of land by public, semi-public and institutional owners
has slowly emerged. As custodians of large estates the traditional
landowning bodies, the Church, Crown and Universities, have
been joined by insurance companies, pension funds, unit-trusts
and other financial intermediaries, a reflection of the new economic order of twentieth-century capitalism. Public ownership of
land is also increasing whether held by central or local government, be it through a statutory agency such as the National Coal
Board or Central Electricity Generating Board, a local or district
authority, a county council, the Forestry Commission or the
Department of the Environment.

Gibbs and Harrison estimated that in 1971 approximately 15 per
cent of land in Britain, 8 per cent of farm and forest land, was
owned by public and semi-public institutions.[1] In 1976 a further
study indicated that farmland holdings by public and semi-public
institutions in Britain was 11 per cent, while for England alone
the figure was 10.2 per cent.[2] Over the five-year period the
area owned by financial institutions had notably increased as
also, but to a lesser extent, had the holdings of conservation
authorities.[3] As it is estimated that only 1 to 1.5 per cent of
land changes hands per year,[4] the proportion held by the non-
private sector in 1980 will still be relatively small and even by
the year 2020 it has been predicted that 'Agricultural land will
remain predominantly privately owned, although the public sector
and the traditional and financial institutions could between them
own something over 15% of the agricultural area.'[5]

Private landownership is expected to remain dominant for some
time to come, especially in the countryside and more particularly
within the agricultural sector. However, the structure of private
ownership is changing and threatens to alter more dramatically
in the near future. Many factors, dealt with at length in Chapter
7, have steadily eroded and continue to undermine the foundations
of large-scale private landownership. Fiscal policies, overtly
aimed at reducing private wealth; death duties, estate duties,
and more recently the imposition of capital gains tax, CTT and
the possibility of a wealth tax following a future change of
government, have forced a number of families to sell their ancestral property and led to the fragmentation and disintegration of
many historic estates.

Under present taxation it is not difficult to foresee the elimination of the large privately owned estate, some would even predict
within the next generation.[6] In a discussion paper *The Future
of Landownership* it was concluded by the CLA that the present
rates of capital taxation will increase the pressure to sell land
especially on estates of 1,000 acres or more, the ultimate result
being the break-up of remaining traditional landed estates and

a reduction in the average size of ownership unit, at least in private hands.[7] Such predictions have been made in the past. The *Estates Gazette* in 1921 reported, 'Nearly every week the country obtains some fresh indication of the gravity of the position which has been created for landowners, great and small, by the existing abnormal taxation.'[8] Yet, despite dire and pessimistic forecasts throughout the twentieth century, large-scale private landownership has persisted to date with remarkable tenacity in the face of seemingly impossible odds. Perhaps this time the private sector has cried wolf with justification. Only time will tell.

The results of the sample survey revealed that over 50 per cent of the original families still own at least part of their nineteenth-century estate, the continuity of family association being much higher from those with over 10,000 acres in 1880 compared with the former 3,000 to 10,000-acre landowners. From the total sample 30 families are known to own properties in excess of 10,000 acres and 110 retain from 3,000 to 10,000 acres (see pp. 119-22). For the majority of these landowners the sample property was, and continues to be, the principal estate. Few now retain more than one large country house, though there are exceptions. Sales of secondary estates and peripheral land account for a high proportion of the reduced family acreages. For the majority, the principal seat, country house and amenity land, represents the last bastion of family loyalty and responsibility and the final link with the land to be relinquished. Entrenchment around the estate heartland, consolidation and rationalisation of estate holdings have been dominant trends throughout the present century. Increases in agricultural productivity have offset reductions in acreage such that a more compact estate has not necessarily seen a decline in output or revenue, especially in cases where land sales have involved outlying marginal and poorer-quality land.

Changes in ownership structure have brought a decline in the traditional landlord-tenant system. Many large private estates, however, still let land, whether through choice or inertia being locked in a system which, from 1948, has provided greater statutory security for a tenant and since 1976 has extended security of tenure to the next generation.[9] Pressure on landowners to take land in-hand as occupation falls vacant is now more intense both from the strengthened position of the tenant and current fiscal policy which provides for a reduced incidence of capital taxation on owner-occupied land. There also remains a persistent refusal by the government to treat ownership of let land as a business for taxation purposes. Certainly on smaller estates former landlords have become active farmers, but it would be far from true to generalise on the change of role from 'aristocrat' or 'gentleman' to farmer or agri-businessman for all remaining large landowners. In a recent study Perrott reported that of 50 landed lords and gentry he met only one could simply be described as a farmer.[10]

Though the trend has been to increase the size of the home farm, many owners of large estates continue as landlords and employ a farm manager to operate the land in-hand and full time agents are still associated with the management of a number of the larger properties. It would be true to say, however, that the present generation of large landowners generally takes a more active interest in estate management than their forefathers.

A landed estate is no longer solely a luxury item or unit of consumption but a productive economic unit based on a scarce and diminishing resource. The ability of the private owner to adapt estate policies in line with the changing demands of the times has been a key to the survival of many historic properties. But increasing pressure for public access to the countryside and the demands for multiple land-use ultimately raise the question of the appropriateness of private landownership in the present day, an issue over which opinion is divided. On the one side sit the staunch defenders of the fundamental rights of private landowners, large or small, represented for example by the CLA who hold up private ownership as 'a cornerstone of our political system and political liberty'.[11] On the other extreme sit the advocates of land nationalisation.

State ownership of land appeared imminent in the early decades of the twentieth century and continued to be part of the Labour Party manifesto up to 1945. Though not explicitly stated as a party platform since World War II the more extremist left wing frequently attempts to revive the issue within the party caucus. In 1973 the 'Campaign for Nationalising Land' advocated unequivocally that a reinstated Labour Government should settle for nothing less than comprehensive nationalisation and proposed a scheme for immediate transfer of all land to a 99-year lease which, upon expiration of the period, would leave the state in complete freehold possession.[12] Given the prevailing climate of inflation and tax discrimination against private landownership it has been suggested that

> some owner-occupiers and landowners would probably prefer some kind of secure long-term leasehold arrangement with the state - a form of national lease-back - if this removed the prospect of a break-up of their businesses on their retirement or death.[13]

In the immediate future land nationalisation appears unlikely. With regard to the agricultural sector little concern has been evident from those who propose nationalisation over the practicalities of land transfer, its effect on agricultural efficiency or cost of food production. Land nationalisation is a political rather than an economic issue.

Greater public control over land is needed to prevent speculation and exploitation of its scarcity value. A middle-of-the-road case for control of land values as an alternative to the extreme of state ownership was advocated in the nineteenth century by

Henry George in his treatise *Progress and Poverty* and land-value taxation was contained in Lloyd George's ill-fated budget of 1909.[14] More recently the notion of a register of land values has been proposed for the purpose of monitoring land sales.[15] Incremental gains arising from the sale of land would accrue to a public-authority land fund so preventing private profiteering. The Development Land Tax introduced in 1976, in principle aims to curb land speculation by taxing profits from increases in the value of land as an outcome of development or a change in existing use. Liability is applicable at all times whether or not land is sold.[16]

It is widely supported that variety within the structure of landownership is healthy for the economic environment and there is merit, if only from a public cost point of view, in retaining an element of large-scale private landownership within the mix. There is need, however, for policy-makers to clarify the position of the large private landowner in the system. A conclusion reached by the Northfield Committee stated that

> Most of us would ... wish to see the pressures on the private landlord lessened so that the rate of his decline can be steadied... On agricultural grounds we see no reason to wish to hasten the departure of the good private landlord.[17]

Furthermore the Committee also observed that

> It is disturbing that so little is known about the pattern of acquisition, ownership and occupancy of agricultural land and that Governments should have to take decisions, which may have far-reaching effects on agricultural structure on the basis of incomplete or non-existent data.[18]

There is a need for a comprehensive system of registration including identification of land-use and beneficial interests as a base not only for policies that affect the agricultural sector, but for policy and planning decisions affecting all land whether agricultural, residential, industrial or commercial. Only through such means will the actual extent of private landownership be revealed and only then can the impact of government policy on the structure of ownership be accurately measured and evaluated.

Major policies currently affecting landownership and land-use, putting aside for the moment the added complication of heritage and environmental conservation, are seemingly incompatible. The application of capital taxation is fundamentally social and political with an objective to reduce private wealth and speculative gains from land development. As long as private landowners are viewed as investors in rather than managers of land[19] such a fiscal policy is in conflict with others affecting rural land-use, principally agricultural policy, the latter being economic in emphasis and designed to achieve maximum food production under conditions of maximum farm efficiency.[20] Agricultural growth will be increasingly thwarted as private owners of agricultural estates are required to set capital aside to meet the impact of present and future capital taxation; a proposition that for the large owner-occupier can detract from investment in the farm enterprise, and for the agricultural landlord can weaken the ability to maintain fixed capital, with an inevitable long-term deterioration in the estate fabric. Under such a system incentives for private landowners to remain in agriculture as farmers or landlords are reduced, and as the pressures of fiscal policy continue, it is predicted that many private owners will inevitably opt to sell out, by necessity as much as choice, to public, semi-public and institutional buyers.

The imposition of capital taxation is dictating the direction of the land market which may in any case be progressing towards greater public and institutional landownership, present policy merely accelerating an inevitable process. But is large-scale public and institutional ownership of land any better than large-scale private ownership regarding the long-term future of historic landed estates in particular and the English countryside in general? Even from an agricultural viewpoint the relative merits of different tenure and ownership factors - whether owner-occupiers are more productive farmers than tenant farmers, or whether farm businesses in private ownership are more productive than institutional or state owned - pose questions as yet unanswered.[21] For wider concerns embracing the countryside as a whole the issue is even less clear.

The rural landscape with which we are familiar owes much of its creation to the private landowner of past centuries. The present-day arguments put forward for ownership remaining in private hands largely stem from the belief that resident private estate owners have greater concern for the local community and sensitivity towards long-term landscape conservation ideals involving environmental and heritage preservation. 'The good private landlord who lives on the land and whose successor is brought up on it, has a permanency and commitment that no institution can match'.[22] Under present legislation, with the exception of planning controls on farm buildings (see p. 204), little direct pressure can be brought to bear on any landowner, large or small, private or institutional, who through efficiency and profit maximisation motives encouraged by financial incentives from the Ministry of Agriculture, inadvertently or deliberately destroys wildlife habitat or a heritage landscape. Conservation practices are predominantly an individual landowner-ship decision. No doubt among the large-private-estate owners there are those who, moving with the conventional wisdom of the times, are unwilling to compromise or adapt their farm enterprise for conservation considerations while others are absentee landlords or passive investors in land, with little interest in either estate management or wider landscape and heritage-related issues. For large-scale institutional landowners, more especially financial institutions, management policies are geared to income potential. Investment in land to maximise returns *mutatis mutandis* implies little concern for the impact of intensive farming on the landscape, or the continuity of an estate property as an historic link with the past. Such generalisations, as with private landowners, do not hold true in all cases, but with financial institutions the time is considered too soon to evaluate their positions as landowners. The Northfield Committee recognised however that

> Financial institutions generally have recourse to far greater funds for investment in improvements than private landlords and...may, as the years go by be able to contribute increasingly to farm efficiency and may give greater attention to their estates than, say previous absentee landlords.[23]

It was also recently concluded by the CLA that 'There can be little doubt that the regard paid to the social aspects of landownership and to involvement in the rural community will be one of the crucial tests by which institutional ownership is judged by public opinion.[24]

One future direction of historic-estate ownership lies in the transfer of property to a non-profit organisation registered as a charitable trust, well exemplified at present by the National Trust. Within its present framework, however, the National Trust cannot afford to undertake the responsibility of upkeep for all traditional estates should private landowners retire from the field. A further option lies in the formation of private charitable trusts in which an owner relinquishes legal ownership of the property but the estate can be kept together, free from the burdens of capital taxation.[25] The original owner's direct control of the property is lost, but an element of management control can be retained if they and their family are trustees in perpetuity. Such an alternative to the break-up of estate property was foreseen and recommended by the Northfield Committee.[26] For owners of let-land estates a further consideration was put forward for the creation of a special class of company 'the landed estate company', an incorporated body involving a 'partnership between the landowner and the community at large'.[27] Shares in a recognised landed-estate company would be accepted in lieu of CTT and a new public body, a National Land Trust (NLT), would hold such shares and, by means of an agreement, have an element of control in the objectives of estate management.[28]

In the long run ownership of land is not as critical as control of its use. The idea of 'social trusteeship', an acknowledgement that there is an ultimate public right to decide on the priorities of land-use, is assuming greater significance.[29] Greater public control does not necessitate state acquisition of land, but can be implemented within a policy framework that allows scope for individual responsibility. No matter who owns the land, in theory legislation can be enacted to ensure its best use in the public interest, whether by intervention through planning controls or licensing, by contractual requirements attached to grant-aid or via new forms of management agreements. As yet, however, present land-use decisions affecting the major part of the rural environment are made by farmers and landowners and there is little in the way of government intervention. But greater public control of rural land-use is inevitable given the growing and often competing demands for agriculture and amenity space and a wider cognisance of the need for better heritage and environmental conservation measures.[30] In the long-term future of ongoing landed estates it is control of land-use as much as landownership that will determine the survival of heritage and other estate landscape features.

THE FUTURE OF THE LANDED ESTATE

Little concern has been shown by policy makers or planners for the traditional landed estate as a unit. Yet failure to treat the landed estate as an entity has been another factor in its decline, particularly in the loss of associated heritage features. In order to examine some of the more important changes over the past century it has been necessary to dissect the estate to discuss each component, but the individual parts, whether abstract or physical traits, are not independent of one another but together form an integrated economic unit, such that changes affecting one part of an estate can have repercussions on the entire property.

Examination of the 500 sample estates, properties of the former landed elite of England, reveals that less than a quarter remain intact as a unit of ownership comprising over 3,000 acres with the original country house and amenity land as well as supporting farmland, while a further 15 per cent fall within this survival category if 1,000 acres is taken as the minimum size of an estate. Of these ongoing properties over 85 per cent are in private ownership whether held by the original family or a different family from that of c. 1880. Well over half of the traditional landed estates no longer survive as such, though in many cases the country house, amenity land and other physical components remain in the landscape as testimony to the former existence of an extensive landed property.

Before the process of decline eliminates an even greater number there is a need to examine the historic landed estate with regard to its future as part of the English countryside. A case can be made to stop the disintegration of such properties and to recognise that they can play as important a role today as they have done in the past, that they are not an anachronistic form of land organisation but are capable of adaptation to meet present and possible future requirements of twentieth-century society with little loss of their essential historic character. A large historic estate as a unit of land management can forge together elements of productive land-use with landscape and environmental conservation practices as well as providing for public access and recreational enterprises. In effect a large estate can be regarded as a microcosm of the countryside and as such has potential as a demonstration unit embodying integrated aspects of the rural mix.

The agricultural sector presently has priority in policies affecting rural areas, but it is now recognised that agricultural policies need to be co-ordinated within a broad rural development framework that takes into account amenity and recreation interests as well as concerns of landscape, environmental and heritage protection, to safeguard the future of the countryside. Under present competitive uses for rural land it is possible to envisage not greater but even less integration between various ministries and organisations as each strive to maintain their own single land-use interests to reach possibly incompatible goals. Development along such lines could ultimately result in a countryside compartmentalised into single land-use zones, as described by Wibberley; better quality land areas being solely in agricultural use, pockets of land being set aside for conservation purposes, possibly with no public access in order to protect species of flora and fauna, while other less productive land, probably in upland regions, would be reserved for recreation.[31] The operation of a large estate unit can take into account multiple demands on land and can optimise a range of land-uses rather than maximise one to the long-term detriment of others, as can be evidenced by a brief examination of existing and potential estate enterprises.

Heritage Preservation and Tourism
With regard to country houses of outstanding architectural merit or historic interest, it is recognised, as much by their owners as others, that they are fundamentally artefacts created for a system of society that has vanished, but this does not mean that the houses themselves should disappear. Similarly with landscape parks. Country houses, their associated gardens and parks represent a continuity within our society, a cultural and historic link with the past and at least a representative number should be preserved. Preservation is the dominant concern, and at present, especially where public funding has assisted the process, preservation is linked with access to the public and tourism. Thus, a number of listed country houses still serve as the residence of an ongoing estate and are regularly accessible to the public for at least the summer season.

Agriculture and Recreational Land-use
The balance between agriculture and recreational land-use can be apportioned according to a local assessment of the need for recreational space and facilities and the quality of land vis-à-vis agricultural production. To allow for the development of active

and passive recreational pursuits land areas have been set aside on a number of estates either within an existing landscape park and/or on marginal agricultural land, in wooded or forested areas, on reclaimed waste or former quarry sites. It has been observed, for example, that the public who visit historic properties tend to be a different population group from those who seek more active recreation in the countryside; thus, the policy to date on a few estates has been to provide a country park, or its equivalent, in a setting detached from the country house (see p. 194).

Recreational provision need not, however, be specifically place-confined in the sense of occupying a block of estate land. There is potential for passive recreation within highly productive agricultural areas through the medium of well-maintained public footpaths and organised farm and nature trails.

A home farm, as in the past on some of the great estates, can be operated as a demonstration unit for the benefit of the surrounding agricultural community, and farm open days could provide educational opportunities for enhancing the urban dweller's awareness of the countryside. Farm holidays have potential as an additional tourist enterprise and adapted historic buildings can assume a new role in an estate economy that combines agriculture with recreation and tourism. In this light it is possible to envision a revitalised role for some estate villages in which employment opportunities can be generated not only through recreation and tourism[32] but also through the introduction of small businesses and workshops associated with rural handicrafts or other light industry. The outcome would serve the dual purpose of helping to sustain village communities, many of which have been adversely effected by declining employment in farming, and of preserving historic buildings by creating alternative uses for those made redundant by changes in agricultural technology.

Environmental and Landscape Conservation
In theory, environmental and landscape conservation practices can be better planned and implemented on a large operational land unit, more especially one that is spatially cohesive. Greater tolerance of small areas of woodland and more selective preservation of hedgerows could be expected in the land-management plan of a large estate than on a small owner-occupied farm where capital costs are spread over fewer land resources and the pressure to use all available land is potentially greater. The adoption of a publicly supported system of 'management' or 'countryside agreements' would well serve the purpose of maintaining landscape and environment by ensuring some form of compensation where conservation policies or public access lead to a loss of productive farm land.

Integrated Reality
A number of large historic estates that remain in private hands

embody a variety of the enterprises described above, but there is considerable scope for further development of the large estate as a land resource. In the sample population Lord Montague's Estate at Beaulieu (Hants) provides a major example of the multiple land-use potential of an historic estate. Sutherland in his description of post-war development on the estate concluded that 'The example set by the Beaulieu estate in land utilisation is one of the most outstanding in the country.'[133] He noted that not only is the property a centre of tourism and recreation catering to a wide sector of the public, but such enterprises have been set up without detracting from the agricultural component of the estate[34] (see p. 196).

The recently published case of an ecological appraisal undertaken on the 6,000-acre West Dean Estate (Sussex) may provide an example to other large estate owners of the value of such a study as a tool of land management.[35] The study in question was undertaken to advise the estate trustees 'on how farming, forestry, game, horticulture, countryside education and nature conservation could be integrated'.[35] Part of this estate forms the country park known as the Weald and Downland Open Air Museum and the gardens of the country house are open to the public, though not the house itself, which has been adapted for use as an educational facility.

A Heritage Estate
It is widely recognised that without land revenue to support them many country houses have not survived and the long-term future of others lies in the balance. A plea has been made by those with concern for heritage preservation to designate country houses and their amenity land setting as conservation areas or the equivalent to Areas of Outstanding Natural Beauty. Some, it is true, already lie within such designated areas. Taking a more comprehensive view it would be appropriate to extend the idea of a conservation unit to embrace an estate as a whole. That special consideration should be given to estates with heritage value has been implicitly recognised by the CLA when it was written that

> The case for maintaining our national heritage of country houses and parks is a strong one...The extension of this case to embrace supporting funds or *associated land* [my emphasis] as an integral part of heritage assets might attract sympathy from within all parties in Parliament.[37]

In a recent study Butler used a hypothetical case to estimate the minimum area of agricultural land necessary to support a country house in private ownership. An estate of 2,500 acres (3,000 if the garden, park and woodland are included) with around 1,000 acres in hand, was sufficient to generate enough income to maintain the estate fabric including farmhouses, cottages, and other buildings and to support a country house with an annual running cost of around £30,000. Half of the latter figure was covered by opening the house to the public.[38] In terms of economic viability, conceivably, there is a range of estate sizes where the integration of enterprises involving a proportional mix of agriculture, forestry and recreation would be such as to maintain the overall estate fabric and provide sufficient funds for the general upkeep of an historic house and amenity land. Thus, a property designated as a 'heritage estate' could be defined with a minimum area of support land to the extent that the only means of transfer or sale would be as a complete unit. Land owned over and above the designated minimum would be subject to existing policies regarding taxation, would not be protected, and would be freely at the disposal of the owner. An option could be built in allowing additional land to be added to a 'heritage estate' in perpetuity or for a fixed minimum period subject to current taxation on withdrawal.

The survival of many large landed estates to date has been dependent on periodic injections of capital from outside the estate operation; often capital from a private landowner's personal wealth. Irrespective of ownership designated 'heritage estates' should, when necessary, be supported from public funds on the basis that benefits accrue to the public at large. It is possible to devise policies that would assist private or institutional owners of designated 'heritage estates' via taxation allowances and/or grant-aid not only to preserve country houses and associated amenity land but, through the use of 'management' or 'countryside agreements', to maintain landscape and heritage features and to develop, where feasible, the recreational potential of the estate even at a possible marginal loss of productivity and revenue from agriculture. Grants for the renovation and maintenance of historic buildings and amenity land and for the establishment of country parks, and taxation exemptions for outstanding heritage features already provide a number of links in a chain that can be welded together to embrace an entire estate unit.

Landowners who neglect upkeep of heritage features or who are unwilling to comply with conservation measures or suggested codes of land management can be penalised, as a last resort, through the reserve power of compulsory purchase. Present legislation regarding preservation of listed buildings has the proviso whereby if an owner fails to take reasonable steps towards preservation a local authority may be entitled to buy the building compulsorily, or repair it and recover the cost from the owner; though state ownership of large landed estates under such piecemeal and opportunist acquisition would be an expensive proposition for the public purse and ultimately the taxpayer.

If the concerns expressed by private landowners over the loss of heritage due to the break up of traditional estates are to be taken at face value, then they should not be adverse to a policy which designates a landed estate as a protected area and contains measures to ensure its long-term survival. If a private landowner is willing to undertake the responsibilities of estate management within a framework of greater public control of land use that guarantees heritage preservation, environmental conservation measures and public access in return for tax concessions and grant-aid, then why remove ownership from private hands? Purely in terms of historic continuity there is still something to be said for retaining family ties with a property as well as maintaining the property itself. Long-established landed families in such a situation in effect become the public guardians of an historic property. Some in fact already perceive their role in this light. The Earl of March has been quoted with reference to the Goodwood Estate as saying, 'in the long run there might be a few economic benefits for the family, but apart from that I am a steward for the community.'[39]

In a few cases private owners have already taken one step towards the creation of a 'heritage estate' under the auspices of a charitable trust to preserve the country house and grounds with an endowment of land as support (see p. 174). Change of ownership structure in this manner provides an option for a landed family to remain on an ancestral estate. Combining a property held as a charitable trust with greater public land-use control through management agreements would, however, effectively place a family in the position of caretaker. Under such a situation many private owners would possibly choose to opt out and forego their association with a property leaving other institutional owners concerned with heritage preservation and conservation such as the National Trust, or ultimately the state, with total responsibility.

While the idea of a 'heritage estate' has appeal the precise mechanism for recognition, establishment and support has no simple solution and lies within the complexity of present-day issues surrounding planning in the rural environment, a subject beyond the scope of the present study, which has been designed to be descriptive rather than prescriptive. Certainly, on the surface the Countryside Commission would appear to be the appropriate body for co-ordination at the national level, while increased power could be given to local planning authorities to make 'countryside agreements', though the proportion of costs allocated from public funds would be a major issue for Parliament to resolve. Perhaps Regional Countryside Planning Authorities as proposed by Shoard would be better suited than local authorities to oversee 'heritage estates', negotiate agreements that involve the integration of a variety of goals and cut across the jurisdiction of a number of government departments and ministries.[40] Such Regional Authorities may be more appropriate in a spatial sense when dealing with a land unit that potentially spans the boundary of more than one district or local authority.

Finally, in recent years quality-of-life considerations have begun to assume increasing importance in our society relative to economic values that have dominated twentieth-century development to date. Within the gradually changing value system there is room for a range of options to preserve and conserve at least part of what already exists as well as to develop new landscapes and new living environments. There is often a ten- dency to harken back to the 'good old days' and to refer to the rural economy of the past with nostalgia as a harmonious com- munal way of life. While historians are quick to point out the social and economic injustices of earlier centuries, the abject poverty of the landless, the exploitation of agricultural labour and the often squalid living conditions of the rural poor, there was none the less a more cohesive local and community identity than generally exists today. Though the product of an elitist society, the landed estate was, and in a number of cases remains, the core of a community and has proven viable as the hub of local land organisation and administration. Voices are now being raised against the prevailing current of growth, large-scale technology and isolationism of present society, with the sugges- tion that there is a need to re-establish more community-based levels of interaction and organisation.

The tendency in agriculture, as in other sectors, towards greater consideration for mechanisation than for man has led the industry to become energy-intensive and dependent on oil-related technology. Such a dependency in the face of ever diminishing world resources inevitably must change. Part of an option for the future as predicated by Schumacher,[41] for example, can be envisaged within the setting of a 'heritage estate' where the scope for a community based decision-making management policy is not untenable. The operational framework of a 'heritage estate' that generates communal responsibility for the mainten- ance of the environmental and historic fabric and shares resour- ces of machines and labour for agricultural production, presents a somewhat futuristic scenario for a society with a more human scale of values and local scale of social organisation.

At this point in time, however, there is a need to clarify objectives and to weld together existing and new policies to ensure a future for surviving historic estates. There is mount- ing pressure, partly reflected in the increase in membership of amenity and conservation groups, to maintain and preserve much that is held of value in the rural landscape.[42] Even the more staunch defenders of the farming interest, the CLA and the National Farmers Union, are becoming more aware of their members' potential as conservationists.[43] The traditional landed estate is an entity with potential flexibility to accommodate the pressure of demand on land resources in the countryside. The question of ownership is undeniably significant in the short-run future of ongoing estates, but ultimately what is of greatest importance is the land itself, the living environment and the heritage features upon it. The fate of the remaining historic landed estates within the next generation will be an interesting reflection of the priorities and values of late twentieth-century society.

NOTES

1   R.S. Gibbs and A. Harrison, 'Landownership by public and semi-public bodies in Britain' (Univ. of Reading, Dept. of Agric. Econ. and Management, Miscellaneous Study No. 56, 1973).

2   A. Harrison, R.B. Tranter and R.S. Gibbs, 'Landowner-ship by public and semi-public institutions in the UK' (Univ. of Reading, Centre for Agricultural Strategy, Paper no. 3, 1977), p. 9.

3   Ibid., p. 14.

4   The Rt. Hon. Lord Northfield (Chairman), 'Report of the Committee of Inquiry into the Acquisition and Occupancy of Agricultural Land (HMSO, London, 1979), Cmnd. 7599, p. 67 (Hereinafter referred to as the 'Northfield Report').

5   Ibid., p. 70.

6   It was a common addendum to many of the questionnaires completed by private owners of ongoing estates that the property stood little chance of being passed intact to the next generation.

7   Country Landowner's Association (CLA), 'The Future of Landownership: A CLA Discussion Paper' (London, 1976), A. 438, p. 8.

8   'Estates Gazette', Aug. 1921.

9   See note 67, Chapter 6.

10   R. Perrott, 'The Aristocrats' (Weidenfeld and Nicolson, London, 1968), p. 157.

11   CLA, 'The Future of Landownership', Foreword by N.G. Quicke, President, CLA.

12   P. Wormell, 'Anatomy of Agriculture' (G.G. Harrap, London, 1978), p. 121.

13   R.J.C. Munton, Agricultural Land Price Survey in England, 1971-73: some preliminary results, 'Chartered Surveyor: Rural Quarterly', vol. 2, no. 4, (1978), p. 59. Already, some owner-occupiers have sold out to institu-tional buyers and, armed with new capital for their agri-cultural business, have remained attached to the land under various forms of lease-back agreement.

14   H. George, 'Progress and Poverty', 4th edn (Robert Schalkenback, New York, 1931), p. 413. See also p. 110.

15   E.F. Schumacher, 'Think About Land' (The Catholic Housing Aid Society, 1973).

16   Development Land Tax 1976, Eliz. 2, c. 26; a tax on the realisation of the development value of land. Under section 2 it is stated that immediately before any material develop-ment is begun on land all major interests will be deemed to be disposed of for a consideration equal to its market value at that time.

17   'Northfield Report', p. 211.

18   Ibid., p. 109.

19   Suggested by Munton to be the attitude taken by the

government in formulating fiscal policy since the early 1970s. Agricultural Land Price Survey in England, p. 59.

20   See, 'Food from Our Own Resources' (HMSO, London, 1975), Cmnd. 6020; 'Farming and the Nation' (HMSO, London, 1979), Cmnd. 7458.

21   A. Harrison et al., 'Landownership by public and semi-public institutions in the U.K.', p. 5.

22   'Northfield Report', p. 210.

23   Ibid., p. 210.

24   CLA, 'Evidence presented to the Committee of Inquiry into the Acquisition and Occupancy of Agricultural Land' (CLA, London), A. 600, p. 12.

25   A charitable trust is not liable for capital taxation so long as it is created more than one year before death.

26   'Northfield Report', pp. 220-1.

27   Ibid., p. 222.

28   Ibid., p. 222.

29   Lord Henley, Introduction in M. MacEwen (ed.) 'Future Landscapes' (Chatto and Windus, London, 1976), pp. x-xi.

30   For a recent statement on this issue see M. Shoard, 'The Theft of the Countryside' (Temple Smith, London, 1980).

31   G. Wibberley, The Proper Use of Britain's Rural Land, 'The Planner', vol. 60, no. 7 (1974), p. 782.

32   For a discussion of the role of villages in recreation and tourism see, M. Binney and M. Hanna, 'Preservation Pays' (Save Britain's Heritage, London, 1978), pp. 52-70.

33   D. Sutherland, 'The Landowners' (Anthony Blond, London, 1968), p. 101.

34   Ibid., p. 101.

35   M. Heymann and R. Tittensor, Ecological appraisal of an agricultural estate, 'Chartered Surveyor', Jan. (1981), pp. 424-5.

36   Ibid., p. 425.

37   CLA, 'The Future of Landownership', p. 2.

38   J. Butler, 'The Economics of Historic Country Houses' (Policy Studies Institute, London, 1981), No. 591, pp. 72-7.

39   R. Strong, M. Binney and J. Harris, 'The Destruction of the Country House' (Thames and Hudson, London, 1974), p. 171.

40   Shoard, 'The Theft of the Countryside', pp. 218-25.

41   E.F. Schumacher in his book, 'Small is Beautiful', subtitled, 'A study of economics as if people mattered' (Blond and Briggs, London, 1973), advocated a system of intermediate technology based on smaller units of enterprise, communal ownership and regional workplaces utilising local labour and resources.

42   It has been estimated that around three million people in Britain are members of environmental pressure groups. See, P.D. Lowe, J. Clifford, S. Buchanan, The Mass Movement of the Decade, 'Vole', Jan. (1980).

43   CPRE, 'Annual Report, 1979' (CPRE, London, 1980), p. 3.

APPENDIX ONE: GREAT LANDOWNERS AND GREATER GENTRY: PER CENT LAND AREA OWNED AND DENSITY OF SEATS PER COUNTY c. 1880

County	Great landowners		Greater gentry	
	% Area owned	Density of seats[a]	% Area owned	Density of seats
Bedfordshire	25.8 (14)[b]	71 (12)	17.3 (29)	29 (22)
Berkshire	18.7 (29)	143 (29)	21.7 (8)	20 (3)
Buckinghamshire	21.8 (21)	76 (14)	19.8 (19)	23 (8)
Cambridgeshire	11.9 (35)	260 (38)	9.6 (39)	47 (36)
Cheshire	29.7 (7)	55 (6)	22.6 (6)	24 (13)
Cornwall	26.7 (13)	84 (19)	21.7 (9)	39 (25)
Cumberland	19.1 (28)	243 (37)	9.9 (38)	52 (39)
Derbyshire	28.0 (9)	206 (36)	19.9 (17)	25 (14)
Devon	22.1 (19)	108 (22)	14.1 (35)	38 (34)
Dorset	36.7 (4)	57 (9)	20.3 (16)	36 (31)
Durham	30.8 (6)	65 (11)	10.7 (37)	52 (38)
Essex	9.2 (38)	158 (34)	18.2 (25)	27 (18)
Gloucestershire	17.4 (31)	81 (18)	18.4 (24)	24 (11)
Hampshire	21.1 (23)	63 (10)	25.6 (2)	21 (4)
Herefordshire	9.5 (37)	126 (26)	24.4 (4)	27 (17)
Hertfordshire	20.9 (25)	55 (7)	17.8 (26)	24 (12)
Huntingdonshire	19.2 (27)	112 (23)	21.9 (7)	25 (15)
Kent	11.1 (36)	119 (25)	21.2 (12)	23 (6)
Lancashire	21.9 (22)	118 (24)	18.5 (23)	28 (19)
Leicestershire	18.6 (30)	129 (27)	19.8 (18)	31 (27)
Lincolnshire	26.9 (12)	146 (30)	14.5 (34)	52 (37)
Middlesex	3.7 (39)	– (39)[c]	10.7 (36)	36 (30)
Norfolk	19.6 (26)	77 (16)	22.8 (5)	26 (16)
Northamptonshire	27.7 (10)	42 (2)	21.4 (10)	23 (7)
Northumberland	53.7 (1)	52 (3)	14.6 (33)	41 (35)
Nottinghamshire	38.4 (3)	72 (13)	18.7 (22)	30 (23)
Oxfordshire	14.4 (33)	149 (32)	25.2 (3)	20 (2)
Rutland	51.8 (2)	31 (1)	17.6 (28)	23 (9)
Shropshire (Salop)	24.9 (15)	131 (28)	29.2 (1)	17 (1)
Somerset	23.5 (17)	156 (33)	15.1 (32)	36 (32)
Staffordshire	29.0 (8)	53 (5)	21.0 (14)	30 (26)
Suffolk	21.9 (20)	76 (15)	17.7 (27)	37 (33)
Surrey	12.2 (34)	56 (8)	16.1 (30)	28 (21)
Sussex	24.0 (16)	79 (17)	21.1 (13)	24 (10)
Warwickshire	21.0 (24)	90 (21)	19.4 (21)	30 (24)
Westmorland	22.6 (18)	167 (35)	16.0 (31)	34 (29)
Wiltshire	35.6 (5)	52 (4)	19.7 (20)	33 (28)

	Great landowners		Greater gentry	
County	% Area owned	Density of seats[a]	% Area owned	Density of seats
Worcestershire	15.5 (32)	147 (31)	20.3 (15)	22 (5)
Yorkshire[d]	27.6 (11)	88 (20)	21.3 (11)	28 (20)
England	24.2	87	19.0	28

Notes: a. 000s acres per seat. b. All numbers in brackets represent rank in England. c. Middlesex contained no great-landowner estates. d. Demarcation of acreage between the three Yorkshire Ridings was not clear in many cases, hence Yorkshire has not been subdivided.

Source: J. Bateman, *The Great Landowners of Great Britain and Ireland*, 4th edn (1883).

APPENDIX TWO: THE SAMPLE SELECTION

THE TOTAL POPULATION

The 4th edition of J. Bateman, *The Great Landowners of Great Britain and Ireland*, 1883, provided the primary data source for the total large landowner population. All landowners owning a minimum of 3,000 acres in England with a minimum gross annual value of £3,000, were first abstracted from Bateman and listed alphabetically along with their total acreage in England, under the county in which the principal residence or home estate was located (total 1,363). Other than the 3,000 common minimum no other land value was attached to acreage for purposes of classification though it was apparent that the vast majority with over 10,000 acres had above a £10,000 gross annual value. Each county listing was further subdivided into 'great landowners' - ⩾ 10,000 acres - and 'greater gentry' - 3,000 to 9,999 acres - (Table A2.1). Every landowner was then given a county identification number.

Landowners with over 3,000 acres but less than £3,000 gross annual value were excluded, as were those with estates exclusively in Scotland, Ireland and Wales and those with less than 3,000 acres in England even if their total landholdings in Britain exceeded 3,000 acres.

Landowners whose principal residence was outside England but who had over 3,000 acres in England and a major country house were included.

Problems

(1) One major known omission from Bateman was added to the list, namely the estate of J.H. Manners-Sutton at Kelham Hall in Nottinghamshire. In the *1873 Return of Landowners* his name was listed incorrectly as J.H.M. Lutton, which possibly accounts for Bateman's omission.

(2) For the most part the address listed by Bateman was taken to be the principal estate residence in 1880. In a few sample cases this later proved incorrect, but fortunately the major residences were in the same county. For example, Hoghton Tower (Lancs.) was the major seat of the DeHoghton family, not Walton Hall (Lancs.), and Heydon Hall (Norfolk) was the major seat of the Bulwers, not Quebec House (Norfolk).

(3) A number of landowners appear to have had no country house but merely to have owned land. For example Lord Wynford had no country house at Wynford Eagle, the address listed by

TABLE A2.1: Total Population and Sample Number according to County and Landownership Categories

County[a]	Total large landowners	Per cent in England	County sample number	Total great landowners	Sample number	Total greater gentry	Sample number
Bedfordshire	14	1.05	5	4	1	10	4
Berkshire	25	1.87	9	3	1	22	8
Buckinghamshire	26	1.95	10	6	2	20	8
Cambridgeshire	13	0.97	5	2	1	11	4
Cheshire	36	2.69	13	11	4	25	9
Cornwall	34	2.54	13	9	3	25	10
Cumberland	17	1.27	6	3	1	14	5
Derbyshire	28	2.09	10	3	1	25	9
Devon	54	4.04	20b	14	5	40	15b
Dorset	26	1.95	10b	10	4	16	6
Durham	18	1.35	7	8	3	10	4
Essex	41	3.07	15	6	2	35	13
Gloucestershire	40	2.99	15	9	3	31	12
Hampshire	57	4.27	21	14	5	43	16
Herefordshire	23	1.72	9	4	2	19	7
Hertfordshire	23	1.72	9	7	3	16	6
Huntingdonshire	11	0.82	4	2	1	9	3
Kent	50	3.74	19	8	3	42	16
Lancashire	43	3.22	16	9	3	34	13
Leicestershire	21	1.57	8	4	2	17	6
Lincolnshire	42	3.14	16	11	4	31	12
Middlesex	4	0.29	1	–	–	4	1
Norfolk	64	4.79	24	16	6	48	18
Northamptonshire	40	2.99	15	14	5	26	10
Northumberland	52	3.89	19	23	8	29	11

County[a]	Total large landowners	Per cent in England	County sample number	Total great landowners	Sample number	Total greater gentry	Sample number
Nottinghamshire	24	1.80	9	7	3	17	6
Oxfordshire	26	1.95	10	3	1	23	9
Rutland	7	0.52	3	3	1	4	2
Shropshire (Salop)	52	3.89	19	6	2	46	17
Somerset	32	2.40	12	6	2	26	10
Staffordshire	33	2.47	12	12	4	21	8
Suffolk	37	2.77	14	12	5	25	9
Surrey	21	1.57	8	7	3	14	5
Sussex	48	3.59	18	11	4	37	14
Warwickshire	24	1.80	9	6	2	18	7
Westmorland	12	0.90	5[b]	2	1	10	4[b]
Wiltshire	41	3.07	15[b]	16	6	25	9[b]
Worcestershire	23	1.72	9	3	1	20	8
Yorks.East Riding	26	1.95	10	7	3	19	7
Yorks.North Riding	51	3.82	19	11	4	40	15
Yorks.West Riding	77	5.76	29	19	9	58	20
Total	1,336[c]	100	500	331	124	1,005	376

Notes: a. County boundaries prior to the Local Government Act 1972. b. In the actual sample there were 16 landowners from Wiltshire (one extra greater gentry) and 9 landowners from Dorset (one less greater gentry). c. 1,363 less 27 landowners with no known country house; land only.

Source: J. Bateman, *The Great Landowners of Great Britain and Ireland*, 4th edn (1883).

Bateman in the 1880s. Twenty-seven cases were found prior
to sample selection and were removed from the total population
as the property did not constitute a 'landed estate'.
(4) A number of landowners in the total population had land
elsewhere in the British Isles, but only their English acreage
was used for the purpose of classification between 'great landowner' and 'greater gentry'. In the final sample twelve landowners would have been moved to the great-landowner category
if their acreage outside England had been included.

The Sample Selection
A sample size of 500 was decided upon as being a number that
accounted for over a third of the total landowner population,
provided a viable number for analysis in each of the six identified regions (Table A2.2) and was manageable in terms of time
and financial constraints.

The total number of large landowners in each county was
calculated as a proportion of the total population of 1,336
in England, and the proportional figure was applied to the total
sample number to determine the number of landowners required
to be selected from each county.

The county sample number was then proportioned according
to the number of great landowners and greater gentry. (Table
A2.1).

The sample population was selected from each county group
according to identification numbers randomly drawn. A list of
spare numbers was also drawn for each county according to
landowner class.

TABLE A2.2: The Regional Breakdown

Region	Number of large landowners	Per cent in England	Region sample number	Number of great landowners	Sample number	Number of greater gentry	Sample number
1. North	150	11.23	56	47	17	103	39
2. North West	208	15.57	77	49	20	159	57
3. East	193	14.44	73	50	20	143	53
4. Midlands	223	16.69	84	52	19	171	65
5. South East	335	25.08	125	69	25	266	100
6. South West	227	16.99	85	64	23	163	62
Total	1,336	100	500	331	124	1,005	376

The counties contained in each region are:

1. Cumberland, Durham, Northumberland, Westmorland, Yorkshire North Riding.
2. Cheshire, Derbyshire, Lancashire, Nottinghamshire, Yorkshire West Riding.
3. Cambridgeshire, Huntingdonshire, Lincolnshire, Norfolk, Suffolk, Yorkshire East Riding.
4. Herefordshire, Leicestershire, Northamptonshire, Rutland, Shropshire (Salop), Staffordshire, Warwickshire, Worcestershire.
5. Bedfordshire, Berkshire, Buckinghamshire, Essex, Hampshire, Hertfordshire, Kent, Middlesex, Oxfordshire, Surrey, Sussex.
6. Cornwall, Devon, Dorset, Gloucestershire, Somerset, Wiltshire.

APPENDIX THREE: THE SAMPLE POPULATION

It was admittedly the original intent of this study to trace the fate of each home estate of the total population of 1,336 large landowners. Under this aspiration an initial survey was undertaken in 1977 whereby the county lists were circulated in order to obtain the following primary information:

(1) The availability and nature of nineteenth-century and twentieth-century estate records for each property, particularly surveys and valuations, sales catalogues and maps.

(2) The best source of information concerning the present status of the property. This fundamentally implied the best person to contact whether it be the present owner of the country house, a former landowner or member of the family, a local estate agent, a family solicitor, a local historian, or a local study group.

The individuals and organisations who assisted in this preliminary enquiry included all County Record Offices in England, a number of County Planning Offices, Local Secretaries of the CLA, and a number of local historians or landowners with extensive knowledge of a particular county. Many, in fact, completed a survey of basic data for properties in the county, a survey that was later used as additional verification for a number of individual questionnaire responses, but which proved on the whole an inadequate means of collecting fairly detailed information.

Equipped, however, with such knowledge concerning the majority of the 1,336 estates it proved a relatively straightforward task to acquire data for a sample of 500 owners and their estates.

Five hundred were initially selected plus a list of reserves sampled for each county. Postal questionnaires were sent to the relevant contact person or institution. Where a sample estate was known, or thought to have been broken-up and no contact was available, the questionnaire was completed, where possible, by personal research at the relevant local archive office using estate records, when available, but more often obtaining piecemeal data from secondary sources. In many cases though estates had been split-up it often proved possible to obtain information on the property from present-day members of the original landed family.

A number of questionnaires were not returned, others were returned blank or only partially completed, but only a few came back with a note stating refusal to disclose information. In some cases questionnaires were returned because the contact address proved to be incorrect. After a period of three months from the first mailing a variety of strategies were adopted to fill in the gaps. In the case of no response or a refusal from the present landowner, where the property was in the possession of the original landed family, a questionnaire was sent to another sample estate in the same landowner category. If the first questionnaire had been sent to a third party, or former owner, another contact was tried where possible. And if data were unclear a follow-up letter was sent to the original respondent.

In total 642 questionnaires were used to obtain fairly comprehensive data on 500 estates. By no means all 500 questionnaires were initially complete in all sections, but provided a base upon which to build.

Accuracy in some cases was questionable. One can but trust that landowners responded to the best of their knowledge regarding questions with an historic dimension and indeed even questions concerning the present-day state of their property. The greatest margin of error would possibly be on those questionnaires completed by a third party in cases where neither a present owner or former landed-family member could be contacted.

For all 500 sample properties additional data to supplement the questionnaire were obtained by research of secondary sources. That is, information was gathered on such topics as: the dates of construction of the country house, the grading of the house if listed by the National Buildings Record, whether the park was landscaped by one of the more famous landscape gardeners, whether the country house and amenity land is open to the public or listed under the National Gardens Scheme. The consequence of such investigations enabled verification of much of the data obtained from the questionnaire and in some instances filled in previously blank items of information.

APPENDIX FOUR: NON-PRIVATE OWNERSHIP: CLASSIFICATION
OF PUBLIC, SEMI-PUBLIC AND INSTITUTIONAL LANDOWNERS

Major category	Breakdown of landowners found in sample population
1. The Crown	The Crown Estates; The Duchy of Cornwall, The Duchy of Lancaster
2. Central government departments	Ministry of Agriculture, Ministry of Defence, Secretary of State for Social Services, Secretary of State for the Environment, the Home Secretary
3. Local authorities	County, Borough and District Councils, Metropolitan, City and Town Councils
4. Statutory agencies and nationalised industries	Central Electricity Generating Board, National Coal Board, British Railways
5. Educational establishments	Universities, colleges and schools (except those owned under category 3)
6. Conservation authorities	National Trust, County Naturalist's Trust
7. Financial institutions	Insurance companies, banks, pension funds
8. Religious institutions	Church Commissioners, religious communities
9. Miscellaneous and unclassified	Royal National Institute for the Blind, Royal British Legion, Mutual Households Association, Co-operative Wholesale Society, joint stock companies and businesses, identified as public body on questionnaire but not specified

Source: Major categories taken from A. Harrison, R.B. Tranter, and R.S. Gibbs, *Landownership by public and semi-public institutions in the UK* (Centre for Agricultural Strategy, Reading, CAS Paper 3, December, 1977).

INDEX

Only country houses and estates that figure prominently in the text appear in the index. The remainder are listed under the appropriate county entry (pre-1974 counties). The list of 500 sample estates and their owners has been omitted due to space restrictions.

agriculture/agricultural 11, 81, 214, 215, 216; acts 98, 99; depression 50, 74, 98, 137; Great Depression (1873-96) 2, 98, 102, 103, 104, 109, 110, 123; high farming (1840-70) 47; land 14, 122, 143, 157, 213, 220, 222; landscape 75-6; land-use 181, 182, 189-90, 220-5 passim; policy 200-1, 216-17, 220
amenity land 59, 67-70; extent of 70-1, 178-80; preservation 200-6, 223; public access 180, 199-200, 220; use of 122, 180-1, educational 196-7, recreational 192-9, rural land use 189-92, transport and communications 187-9, urban and industrial 181, 184-7; see also Country Parks; deer parks; gardens; parks
ancient monument(s) 134, 167; acts 170, 171, 192
Anson, Thomas (Earl of Lichfield) 78, 79
Appleton, J. 202
Arbury Hall (Warwick.) 141-2
architects 42-8 passim, 52-3, 66, 70, 79, 88, 134, 140-4, 187

Bateman, J. 7, 8, 15, 18, 20, 27, 35, 36, 160
Bath, Marquis of 112, 167; see also Thynne
Bearwood (Berks.) 47, 53, 86, 91
Beaulieu (Hants) 42, 165, 167, 196, 222
Bedford, Duke(s) of 18, 80, 89, 116
Bedfordshire: country houses 41, 46, 48, 134, 139, 164, 166; landowner-ship 125; parkland 181, 199; villages 86
Belton House (Lincs.) 36, 69, 165
Berkshire: country houses 46, 47; estates 34, 35, 87, 112, 123, 199; landowners 22, 25; villages 86, 204
Bewerley Estate (W. Riding) 66, 115

Blaise Hamlet (Glos.) 85, 205
Bretton Park (W. Riding) 44, 194, 195, 197
Bridgeman, Charles 64, 67, 68, 80, 202
British Tourist Authority (BTA) 167, 195
Brocklesby (Yarborough) Estate (Lincs.) 22, 34, 75, 98, 99, 101, 104; buildings on 78, 87, 89, 90, 91; country house 144, 166; park 68; woodland 64, 76
Broome Park (Kent) 43, 164
Broughton (Oxford) 41
Brown, Lancelot 'Capability' 64-70, 80, 85, 141, 181, 186, 188, 189, 190, 195, 202
Brownlow, Earl 34, 36
Bryanston (Dorset) 48, 140, 145, 162
Buckinghamshire: country houses 121, 144, 147, 161, 162; estates 17, 34, 81; landowners 25; parks and gardens 67, 188, 194, 199
Burghley (Northants.) 34, 43, 184, 200
Burlington, Lord 45, 141
Burton Agnes (E. Riding) 42-3, 174
Buscot Park Estate (Berks.) 123

Cadlands (Hants) 141, 186
Cambridgeshire 21, 22, 23, 80
canals 18, 55, 74, 185
Carlton Towers (W. Riding) 48, 103, 137
Carr, John 45, 84
Cassiobury Park (Herts.) 140, 184, 197-8
Central Electricity Generating Board (CEGB) 186, 189, 197, 213
Charities Act 1960 174
Chatsworth Estate (Derby.) 25, 35, 44, 70, 85, 117, 204
Cheshire: country houses 45, 53, 141, 142, 164, 170; estates 86, 124, 125,

187; landowners 22; parks and gardens 67, 194, 196; villages 88
Chillington Estate (Staffs.) 27, 188, 196
Chilston Park (Kent) 188, 206
Church landownership 9, 10, 11, 41-2, 49, 60, 212, 213
Cirencester Park (Glos.) 63, 184, 199
Clandon Park (Surrey) 44, 60
Cole Orton (Leics.) 162
Cooper, J.P. 8, 13, 14
Corn Production Acts 112
Cornwall: country houses 42, 46, 54, 121, 134, 140, 144, 161, 164; estate buildings 204; landowners 25; parks and gardens 69, 196, 199
Council for the Protection of Rural England (CPRE) 189, 204
country house(s): alternative use(s) 127, 136, 137-8, 142, 154-60 *passim*, 161-8, 185, 194-6, 199, 222; building 48-53, 103, 140, 145, 162, materials 53-5; definition 36, 39, 56n1, 181; demolition 127, 133-5, 152, 160, 184, 185, 186, 194, date of 135-9, partial 144, period of origin 139-42, regional location 143-4; leasing 127, 136-7, 138, 156, 157, 159, 161, 174; maintenance 136-7, 146-7, 156, 157, 168-75 *passim*, 222-3; open to the public 142, 156, 157, 164-74 *passim*, 193, 199, 220, 223, *see also* tourism and recreation; preservation 139-42, 145-7, 158, 161, 169-75 *passim*, 220, 222, 223, 224; sales and transfers 120-1, 123, 135-8 *passim*, 144, 152-62 *passim*, 170, 171, 184, *see also* estate break-up and sales; styles 40-8
Country Landowners Association 204, 213, 215, 218, 222, 225
Country Parks 164, 173, 186, 193-5, 197, 198, 199, 221, 222, 223
Countryside Act 1968 164, 191, 193, 198
Countryside Commission 191, 193, 195, 204, 205, 224
Crown landownership 9, 10, 11, 49, 60, 124-5, 138, 212, 213
Cumberland 22, 23, 40, 46, 69, 160

Dance, George 162
deer parks 60-2, 64, 70, 80, 182, 191-2, 195, 197
Denman, D.R. 34, 38, 122-3
Department of the Environment 134, 139, 165, 171, 213
Derby, Earl of 19, 96, 111, 117, 161
Derbyshire: country houses 44, 45, 46, 48, 53, 134, 136, 164; estates 112, 117, 186, 204; landowners 25,

35; parks and gardens 70, 193-4, 196-7, 198; villages 84
Devon: country houses 40, 48, 54, 55, 144, 160, 164, 177n51; estates 121; landowners 22; parks and gardens 69, 188, 196
Devonshire, Duke(s) of 25, 35, 36, 44, 85, 112
Dingley Park (Northants.) 144, 160
Dissolution of the Monasteries 2, 9-10, 16, 24, 41-2, 212
Dobson, John 52
Dorset: country houses 41, 42, 43, 48, 53, 55, 134, 140, 155, 157, 162; estates 34, 103; landowners 21, 22, 25; parks and gardens 69; villages 84
Drakelow Estate (Derby.) 186, 196-7
Dunster Castle (Somerset) 40, 66, 121
Durham 22, 40, 52, 164, 166, 196
Dyrham Park (Glos.) 17, 171

Eaton Estate (Cheshire) 67, 86, 89, 142
Education Act 1870 89, 100
Elvaston Castle (Derby.) 164, 193-4
enclosure(s) 12, 60, 70, 75-80 *passim*, 84, 87, 90, 184
Essex: country houses 43, 54, 139, 141, 142, 160, 163, 171; County Council 203; landowners 21, 22, 25; parks and gardens 60, 69, 185, 194, 196
estate(s): break-up and sales 103-4, 109-16 *passim*, 119-20, 122-8 *passim*, 134, 136, 140, 151, 160, 184, 185, 186, 212-18 *passim*, 223; buildings 86-91, 103, 201, 203, 204; capital 17, 102-3, 110-17 *passim*, 223; company(ies) 38, 112, 120, 126, 218; definitions 33-8, 118, 128n1, 130n51; duty/death duty 110-17 *passim*, 122, 127, 160, 170, 213; gifting 112, 113, 114; management 75-6, 102, 115, 127, 166, 212-25 *passim*; villages 82-90 *passim*, 203, 204, 205, 221, *see also* rural settlement; *see also* heritage estate
Euston (Suffolk) 44, 60, 84
Evelyn, John 60, 61

Finance Acts 112, 114, 147, 170, 174
financial institutions 113-14, 116, 125, 126, 127, 213, 218
Ford Castle (Northld.) 40, 76, 110, 137
Forestry Commission 76, 190, 191, 205, 213

gardens 80, 180, 188, 192, 193, 197;

definition 59; landscape gardening
59, 63-5, 77; maintenance of 192;
open to the public 199-200, 222,
see also tourism and recreation;
preservation of 201, 202, 203, 206;
styles of 62-3, 66-7, 192; *see also*
amenity land; parks
Garendon Park (Leics.) 42, 65, 138
gentry 11, 17, 52, 54, 80, 89, 90,
214; amenity land 67, 69, 70, 179;
definition 7-9; estates and land area
owned 14, 19, 20-8 *passim*, 35-6,
50, 120-2, 127, 151; greater gentry
14, 33, 53, 76; lesser gentry 12, 14,
16, 19; rise of 29n28
Gloucestershire 102; country houses
45, 160, 171; estates 17; landowners 25; parks and gardens 63,
69, 184, 198, 199; villages 85, 205
great landowners 17, 18, 33, 76, 89,
90; amenity land 69, 70, 178, 179;
definition 7-9 *passim*; estates and
land area owned 11, 12, 13-14, 20-8
passim, 35-6, 111, 119-22, 127, 151

Hagley Hall (Worcester.) 66, 117
Hall Barn Park (Bucks.) 144, 188, 189
Hampshire 102; country houses 42, 46,
134, 138, 141, 144, 157, 165; estates
91, 119, 126, 186, 196, 222; landowners 22, 25
Hampton Court (Hereford.) 41, 156
Harborough, Lord 78-9
Harewood, 5th Earl 111; 6th Earl 112;
see also Lascelles
Harewood Estate (W. Riding) 45, 68,
69, 70, 84, 112, 137, 165, 167, 190
Harlaxton Estate (Lincs.) 41, 46, 86,
91, 123, 163
Harrison, Alan 114, 213
Hawkstone (Salop) 65, 66, 104, 137,
202
Herefordshire: country houses 41, 45,
135, 140, 144, 156; landowners 21,
22; parks and gardens 69
heritage: and tourism 167, 220;
country house 55, 172, 174; education 164-5; estate 127-8, 133, 206,
212, 219, 222-5; farm buildings 203;
parkland 187; preservation 3, 146-7,
169, 173-4, 200-1, 216, 217, 220
Hertfordshire: country houses 41, 50,
52, 55, 140, 141, 161; estates 10,
36; landowners 25; parks and gardens 68, 69, 80, 184, 185, 188, 194,
197-8, 204
Historic Buildings Bureau 147
Historic Buildings Council(s) (HBCs)
138, 139, 146, 147, 148n16, 192;
for England (HBCE) 139, 156, 167-
75 *passim*, 203

Historic Houses Association 165, 169
Hoare, Henry, 66, 67
Holkham (Norfolk) 44-5, 54, 68, 70,
71, 75, 76, 86, 90, 166
housing associations 158-9, 160
Hunstanton (Norfolk) 41, 159
Huntingdonshire 22, 34, 40

inheritance 13, 15-18, 36, 37, 38, 122;
and taxation 114, 116; primogeniture, law and custom of 15-16, 19

Jones, Inigo 44, 137

Kedleston Estate (Derby.) 45, 48, 84,
117, 136
Kelham Estate (Nottingham.) 103
Kent 102; country houses 40, 43, 46,
54, 133, 137, 140; estate buildings
88; estates 121, 125, 184, 185;
landowners 21, 22, 25; parks and
gardens 65, 67, 188, 199, 202, 206
Kent, William 43, 45, 63, 64, 67, 68,
202
Kip, Johannes 63, 67, 70
Knight, Sir Richard Payne 45, 65, 74
Knowsley (Lancs.) 60, 71, 161, 196

Lancashire 102; country houses 46,
48, 53, 133, 161, 164, 171; estates
111, 120, 127; parks and gardens
60, 69, 71, 185, 196, 197
landlord-tenant system 33, 98, 99,
101, 114, 213, 214
land magnates 7-9, 11, 21, 27, 35, 48,
76, 111
land market 9, 16, 103-4, 110, 113-
14, 156; influence of London 21;
influence of taxation 217
large landowners 62, 74, 78, 79, 96;
and agriculture 12, 75, 76, 214,
215; definition 7-9; land area owned
13, 20-8 *passim*, 33; *see also* gentry;
great landowners; land magnates
Lascelles, Edwin 45, 69, 84; *see also*
Harewood, Earl of
Leeds Castle (Kent) 40, 137, 172
Leicester, Earl of (Coke of Norfolk)
35, 44, 75, 76, 86, 91
Leicestershire 79; country houses 42,
54, 137, 138, 162; estates 125;
landowners 22; parks and gardens
65, 78; villages 80
Le Nôtre 62, 63
Levens Hall (Westmorland) 40, 63,
136
Leveson-Gowers 18
Lincolnshire: country houses 41, 42,
46, 54, 134, 138, 142, 144, 163,
165, 166; enclosure 22, 75, 87;
estate buildings 78, 87, 89, 91;

estates 21, 34, 36, 98, 123; landowners 10, 35; 'open' and 'closed'
parishes 81, 82-3; parks and
gardens 68, 69; tenants 98, 100;
villages 86; woodland 76
listed buildings 147, 148n18, 156,
161, 172, 173, 203, 205, 220, 223;
graded status 139, 142, 145-6, 159,
160, 164, 167, 171, 173, of gardens
203; listed building consent 134,
139, 164
Lloyd-George, David 110, 216
local authorities: amenity lands 185,
186, 193, 194, 197, 198, 202;
country houses 156, 162, 163, 170,
171-2; grants and loans 160, 191;
heritage preservation 224; landownership 124, 126, 181, 213;
planning 116; tree preservation
204, 205; *see also* listed buildings
Lockinge Estate (Berks.) 87, 112, 204
London 55, 104; country houses 154,
157; estates 48, 116; Green Belt
194, 198; influence of 21, 24, 25-6,
36, 52, 167, 178, 181
Longleat (Wilts.) 10, 42, 63, 68, 167,
168, 196
Loudon, John Claudius 45, 66-7
Luton Hoo (Beds.) 181, 184, 199
Lydiard Park (Wilts.) 171, 172
Lyme Park (Cheshire) 45, 170, 171,
194

management agreements 205, 219-25
passim
marriage(s) 13, 15-18, 24, 36
Middlesex 21, 22, 23, 43, 164
Mingay, G.E. 8, 9, 14
monastic estates *see* Church

Nash, John 85, 90, 140, 141
National Coal Board 125, 142, 162,
213
National Land Fund (National Heritage
Memorial Fund) 147, 170-5 *passim*
National Trust 125, 165, 168, 200, 202,
206, 218, 224; amenity land 180,
182, 188, 191, 192, 193, 199;
country houses 120-1, 151, 153, 154,
157, 169-75 *passim*; property transferred to 112, 116, 123, 124, 196,
205
Nesfield, W.A. 70
New Domesday Survey 7, 15, 18, 19,
20, 118
Norfolk: country houses 41, 42, 43,
54, 55, 137, 140, 144, 157, 159,
166; enclosure 75; estate building
91; estates 103, 116, 125, 127;
landowners 22, 25, 35, 154; parks
and gardens 68, 70, 71

Northamptonshire: country houses
40, 42, 43, 144, 159, 160, 171;
estates 34; parks and gardens 184,
200, 202; villages 81
Northfield Committee 216, 218
Northumberland: country houses 40,
46, 52, 137, 141, 144, 163, 164;
estates 76, 110, 125; landowners
21, 22, 25, 110; parks and gardens
69, 79, 185
Nottinghamshire: country houses 42,
53, 144; estates 10, 103; landowners 21, 22; parks and gardens
70, 190, 194; villages 83
Nuneham Courtenay (Oxford.) 84, 91,
189

Old Warden Park (Beds.) 48, 86, 125
Osmaston Park (Derby.) 186
outbuildings 157, 160, 161, 203
Oxfordshire: country houses 41, 42,
43, 55, 135, 163, 166, 189; estates
35, 125, 127; landowners 22, 25;
'open' and 'closed' villages 81, 83,
84; parks and gardens 189, 205

Palladio 44
parks/parkland 76, 77, 83, 162, 179-
89 *passim*, 199, 202, 222; buildings
in 65-6, 188; definition and early
origin 59-62; landscape park(s) 78,
79, 80, 84, 85, 90, 181, 184, 187-
93 *passim*, 197, 200, 202, 220, 221;
open to the public 166, 184, 185,
197, 198, 199-200, *see also* tourism
and recreation; preservation 199-
206 *passim*; sale/lease of 127, 185,
195
Paxton, Joseph 70, 85
peerage(s) 8, 9, 11, 13, 27, 97
Penshurst Place (Kent) 40, 67, 88,
166
pension funds 116, 127, 213
Perrott, R. 120, 214
Petworth (Sussex) 41, 121, 188, 199
poor laws 81-4, 87, 101
Portman, Viscount 48, 116
Price, Uvedale 65, 88
primogeniture *see* inheritance
private family ownership: definition(s)
130n52, 131n54, 131n66; future of
212-19 *passim*; of amenity lands 178-
92 *passim*, 198, 199, 200, 205; of
country houses 146, 147, 151-62 *passim*, 167-75 *passim*; of Country Parks
193, 195; of estates 118-24, 127, 133,
174, 212, 219, 221, 223, 224; *see also*
gentry; great landowners; land magnates; large landowners
public, semi-public and institutional
ownership: definition 130n53; of

amenity land 181, 182, 189, 192, 198, 199, 206, grants to 191; of country houses 151-7 *passim*, 161, 162, 168, 171-2, 173, maintenance cost 147, 169, 170, 174; of land 20, 23, 112, 114, 115, 123, 124-7, 213, 217, 218, 223, 224; *see also* financial institutions; pension funds

railways 74, 78-9, 166, 186, 187, 193
Reform Bill(s) 101-2
regions of England 77, 81; amenity land 68, 69, 71, 178, 179, 181, 182-3; country houses in 51, 53, 54, 143-4, 154, 157, 162; property distribution 24, 25, 26, 28, 117; *see also* counties by name
Repton, Humphry 64-9 *passim*, 73n26, 77, 80, 85, 202
roads 74, 77, 78, 84, 85, 90, 185, 187-8
Rufford Abbey (Nottingham.) 10, 42, 144, 190, 194
rural settlement(s): church building 86, 88-9, 100; general building activity 86-91, 103; impact of large landowners on 74, 79-84; 'open' and 'closed' villages 81-4, 88-9; school building 86, 88-9, 90, 100; *see also* estate buildings; estate villages
Ruskin, John 45, 78
Rutland 21, 22, 25

Sandford Group 165
Sandgate Estate (Sussex) 103, 186
Scotney (Kent) 40, 46, 65, 121, 199
Scrivelsby Court (Lincs.) 27, 134, 142
Settled Land Act 16, 38, 103
settlements (strict or marriage) 15, 16, 17, 30n52, 38, 181
Sheffield Park (Sussex) 46, 68, 158, 180
Shirley, E.P. 18, 61-2, 70
Shropshire (Salop): country houses 40, 45, 46, 53, 54, 137, 141, 142, 144, 164, 171; estates 103, 104; landowners 10, 22; parks and gardens 65, 66, 78, 192, 202
Shugborough (Staffs.) 78, 79, 170
Sledmere Estate (E. Riding) 75, 78, 84, 88, 90
Smythson, Robert 42
Somerleyton (Suffolk) 46, 85
Somerset: country houses 40, 46, 54, 135, 137, 160, 169, 171; estate buildings 66; estates 103, 112, 115, 121, 124, 187; parks and gardens 68, 196
sport: game laws 98, 99; hunting 21, 60, 61, 77, 97, 99, 104; shooting

21, 99, 104, 136
Staffordshire: country houses 136, 137, 140, 141, 144, 163, 171; estates 18, 103, 115; parks and gardens 78, 79, 188, 196
Stapleford Park (Leics.) 78, 80, 137
Stone, L. 11, 13, 25, 50
Stourhead (Wilts.) 66, 67
Stowe (Bucks.) 81, 161, 162, 199
Stroud, Dorothy 69, 202
Suffolk: country houses 44, 46, 54, 134, 138, 141, 147, 161; estates 99, 123; landowners 25; parks and gardens 60, 70, 192, 200; villages 99, 123
Surrey: country houses 44, 142; estates 103; landowners 22, 23, 25; parks and gardens 60, 62
Sussex: country houses 41, 43, 46, 54, 135, 139, 141, 144, 156, 159, 160, 171; estates 103, 111, 113, 121, 125, 127, 186, 222, 224; landowners 25; parks and gardens 68, 180, 188, 194, 196, 197, 198, 199
Sutton Scarsdale (Derby.) 44, 134
Sykes, Sir Christopher 75, 78, 84; Sir Tatton 35, 88

taxation 12, 113-17 *passim*, 129n22, 146, 147, 168-74 *passim*, 205, 213-18 *passim*, 223; *see also* estate(s) duty
The Grange (Hants) 46, 134
Thicket Priory (E. Riding) 127
Thompson, F.M.L. 7, 11, 12, 13, 100
Thorndon (Essex) 60, 160, 194, 195
Thynne, Sir John 10, 42; *see also* Bath, Marquis of
Toddington Manor (Glos.) 46, 160
Torrington, 5th Viscount (John Byng) 166
tourism and recreation 2, 3, 127; amenity land 166, 167, 181, 182-3, 184, 186, 192-9 *passim*, 204, 205; country houses 139, 162, 164-72 *passim*, 173, 192, 194, 196; estates 220-1, 222, 223
Town and Country Planning Act(s) 139, 145, 146, 172, 173, 198, 204
Trafford, Sir Humphrey de 185
Trafford Park (Lancs.) 133, 185
trusts 38, 125, 197, 213, 218; discretionary 113, 114; private, charitable and educational 125, 162, 163, 172, 174, 175, 194, 196, 206, 218, 222, 224; *see also* National Trust

University(ies) landownership 116, 123, 125, 164, 213

Walter, John 47, 86
Warwickshire: country houses 44,
141-2, 164, 172; estates 103; parks
and gardens 64, 186; villages 80
Weald and Downland Open Air Museum
see West Dean Estate
Webster, George 52
West Dean Estate (Sussex) 46, 54,
103, 125, 194, 195, 196, 222
Westminster, Duke of (Grosvenor)
67, 86, 89, 116, 142
Westmorland 22, 40, 52, 63, 69, 111,
136
Whitaker, J. 62, 70
Wibberley, G. 205, 220
Wiltshire 102; country houses 42, 43,
54, 137, 140, 141, 155, 157, 171-2;
estates 10, 34, 111, 112, 119; landowners 21, 22, 35; parks and
gardens 63, 66, 68, 69, 196
Wimpole Estate (Cambs.) 80
woodland(s) 75, 190-1, 200, 204;
dedication schemes 191, 205; estate
and park woodlands 59, 60, 63, 64,

70, 76-7, 180, 181, 182, 188, 189,
196, 222
Worcestershire 22, 55, 66, 70, 117,
196
Wyatt, James 46, 48, 140, 141
Wyatt, Samuel 86

Yarborough, Lord 35, 76-7, 78, 87,
89, 99, 100, 101, 104
Yorkshire 18, 21, 22, 35, 44, 45, 55;
East Riding: 102, country houses
42, 142, 163, 171, 174, enclosure
75, 87, estate buildings 88, 91,
estates 127, parks and gardens 78,
196, villages 83, 84; North Riding:
country houses 53, 140, 171,
estates 111, 113, landowners 100,
parks and gardens 70, 196, 199;
West Riding: country houses 40, 48,
137, 140, 154, 164, 165, estate
buildings 66, 88, estates 103, 112,
115, 119, 184, parks and gardens
68, 69, 70, 189, 190, 194, 195, 196,
197, villages 84